Depoliticization

EDITED BY
INGERID S. STRAUME
J.F. HUMPHREY

Depoliticization

THE POLITICAL IMAGINARY
OF GLOBAL CAPITALISM

NSU Press

Published in Sweden by NSU Press
Norra Vallgatan 16
SE-211 25 Malmö, SWEDEN
http://www.nsuweb.net

Produced by Söderströms Förlag
Georgsgatan 29A, 2 vån
PO Box 870
FI-00101 Helsingfors, FINLAND
http://www.soderstrom.fi

Printed by Kariston Kirjapaino Oy
Tavastehus, 2011

Distributed by Århus University Press
Langelandsgade 177
8200 Århus N DENMARK
http://www.unipress.dk

ISBN 978-87-87564-21-2

Contents

Acknowledgements

The editors want to thank the Nordic Summer University (NSU) and the NSU Press for providing the funding for this project through all its phases. A great amount of voluntary work is involved in the organization of the Nordic Summer University, for which we are deeply thankful. Ingerid S. Straume would like to thank the Institute for Educational Research at the University of Oslo for funding language corrections. We also thank Sage publishers for granting permission to republish the essay *Capitalism in Context* and the Icelandic E-Journal of Nordic and Mediterranean Studies, *Nordicum-Mediterraneum* for permission to publish a revised version of J. F. Humphrey's essay. Last, but not least, we want to thank all participants in the NSU network *Samfunnskritikk og –analyse under globalkapitalismen* for their enthusiasm and valuable comments on the drafts during various symposia. Most of all, the editors want to thank the authors for their contributions, for their good will, and for their patience.

September 2010
Ingerid S. Straume and J. F. Humphrey

Introduction

Ingerid S. Straume and J. F. Humphrey

In a globalized world, relations between the political sphere and the economy are marked by practical tensions and theoretical contestations. While for many decades the regime of deregulation and non-interference in the market sought to discredit the political sphere altogether, the ongoing economic crisis serves to restore the status of politics and regulations with support from hitherto unexpected sources. In September 2010, for example, the International Monetary Fund (IMF) discusses its "new role" thus on its homepage: "In the wake of the crisis, policymakers around the world are looking for ways to fix the international financial system: how to better regulate banks and other financial institutions, how to more effectively address risk, and how to strengthen economic cooperation." A few years ago, the very idea of 'fixing the financial system' would have made the IMF see red. Under the current conditions, however, where the world hegemony might be changing rapidly, political analysis has certainly earned a position within the economic sphere.

The relations between politics and the economy – discussed since Aristotle and given special attention in the works of Karl Marx – are neither linear nor causal; while it is beyond the scope of politics to simply steer the economy, neither can the former be totally determined by economic interests. To complicate matters, both spheres are invested with cultural and symbolic meaning, making them resistant to efforts towards transparency for the sake of analysis and/or rational administration. In the time period around the 1970s, to hold an interest in political thought usually implied an interest in economic matters, e.g., questions about distribution of economic resources, capital structures, matters of ownership and control, class matters, etc. In the following decades, this changed, until at the end of the 20th century a division had been established between scholars who did economic analyses (economists) and those who did political and social theory with little or no regard for economics. In the same period, accordingly, much of political thought had turned to focus on cultural matters such as identity politics, rights, and religion.[1] In a certain sense, this represented a 'depoliticization' of political and social thought; because when economic matters are left out of political thought, the political sphere loses importance. We will return to this point below.

What do we mean by depoliticization? While many phenomena could be classified under this heading, a common denominator here is a decline in democratic, political creativity.[2] More generally, 'depoliticization' can be seen as a tendency inherent in modernity, accompanying and simultaneously threatening efforts to make social phenomena subject to political-democratic processes, i.e., politicization. Hannah Arendt addressed the problem of depoliticization directly in her seminal text, *The Human Condition* from 1958. Arendt returns to the Greek distinction between *oikos*, i.e., the household (the private sphere) and *polis*, i.e., the city (the public sphere). While these two spheres were clearly distinguished and mutually exclusive in the ancient Greek and Roman worlds, with modernity and the emergence of the nation state they become absorbed more and more by a third sphere that Arendt calls 'society.'[3] In its first appearance, society was "an organization of property-owners who ... demanded protection" from the public sphere in order to accumulate even more wealth.[4] With the rise of the social sphere, Arendt notes a

---

1. See, e.g., Thomas Frank, *What's the Matter with Kansas? How Conservatives Won the Heart of America*, New York, Henry Holt, 2004.
2. Examples of depoliticizing tendencies are bureaucratization, technocracy, oligarchy, *Brave New World* new-speak, propaganda, certain forms of individualization, moralization, etc., etc. The examples are countless, as new forms will always emerge.
3. Hannah Arendt, *The Human Condition*, Chicago/London, University of Chicago Press, [1958] 1989 (*HC*).
4. *HC*, 68.

marked "decline of the family," which "indicates clearly that what actually took place was the absorption of the family unit into corresponding social groups."[5] Similarly, Arendt remarks that 'society' also absorbed the public sphere with the rise of bureaucratic governments, "the most social form of government," – "the rule by nobody" – which "is not necessarily no-rule; it may indeed, under certain circumstances, even turn out to be one of its cruelest and most tyrannical versions." As society takes on the functions of the *oikos* – health, education, and welfare – and the functions of the *polis* through which citizens act to govern the city, society excludes political action. The functions of the private and the public spheres had thus become, according to Arendt, a matter of "housekeeping." Even though Arendt has been duly criticized on her diagnosis of 'the rise of the social'[6] – where she fails to acknowledge the political aspects of social struggles – her acute sense of the depoliticizing tendencies of modern bureaucracy and technocracy is exemplary. When we consider current developments in public administration and the globalized economy, the central task is still to secure a space for politics.

In an article on contemporary depoliticization, the American journalist, Tom Crumpacker, is concerned with the democratic ideal of neoliberalism that places such faith in the free market economic system. To neoliberals, 'democracy' is seen as

> an elected parliament or legislature based on a 'free market 'economy, with limits on government action as it relates to the individual. Government is thought of primarily as the power of coercion, to be restrained. ... Liberal Democracy is the synthesis where the ruling master and the ruled servant live in peace together.[7]

5. *HC*, 40.
6. See Cornelius Castoriadis, "The Greek *Polis* and the Creation of Democracy," id., *The Castoriadis Reader,* translated and edited by David Ames Curtis, Oxford, Blackwell, 1997, 267–89 and Dana R. Villa, *Arendt and Heidegger. The Fate of the Political,* New Jersey, Princeton University Press, 1996.
7. Tom Crumpacker, "The Politics of Depoliticization and the End of History," *State of Nature,* 2, Winter, 2006, 1. http://www.stateofnature.org/politicsDepoliticization. html.

According to Crumpacker, however, there is a contradiction in the neo-liberal notion of democracy. He asks: "What happens when one person's free pursuit of self interest encroaches on another's[?] Where one is of the master class and the other not, which will receive the benefit of governmental coercion? Does the neoliberal idea of democracy promote the freedom of the big fish to eat the little fish?"[8] Crumpacker worries that "the larger, more powerful, more 'developed' the nation, the less democratic it is"; indeed, the "national governments" in the current liberal democracies are "essentially oligarchic and authoritarian rather than democratic."[9] The result of a political system that serves large corporate interests is "corporatism" and "its ultimate form," Crumpacker warns, "is fascism." One thinks of the Tea Party movement in the US that is promoting large corporate interests in the guise of populism and funded by wealthy business people like the radical right-wing libertarian Koch brothers.[10] On the other hand, a political system that truly serves the people is "one where decisions are sought to be made collectively and the primary needs served are peoples' rather than those of capital, property, or status."[11]

In his 1989 collection of essays, entitled *The New Conservatism*, Jürgen Habermas also takes up the general depoliticization of the public sphere in Western societies brought on by economic and administrative developments whose "imperatives" were constraining more and more domains of life, "increasingly transforming relationships into commodities and objects of administration."[12] One aspect of his diagnosis is the "exhaustion" of "utopian energies" capable of procuring political and social *alternatives*, i.e., alternatives to existing social institutions.

8. "Politics of Depoliticization," 1.
9. "Politics of Depoliticization," 2.
10. See, for example, Jane Mayer, "Covert Operations – The Billionaire Brothers Who Are Waging a War against Obama," *The New Yorker* August 30, 2010, http://www.newyorker.com/reporting/2010/08/30/100830fa_fact_mayer?currentPage=1.
11. "Politics of Depoliticization," 3.
12. Jürgen Habermas, "Neoconservative Cultural Criticism in the United States and West Germany," id., *The New Conservatism*, Cambridge, Polity, 1989, 44. See also id., "The New Obscurity: The Crisis of the Welfare State and the Exhaustion of Utopian Energies" in the same volume.

Through the functional division of the state apparatus – a development largely uncontested by political thought – the steering institutions were effectively sheltered from the public sphere with its disagreements and social conflicts, and left to steer in peace; first and foremost by guaranteeing to secure the peace. To Habermas, 'depoliticization' was a more or less intentional development by contemporary neoconservatives who preferred to run public affairs without too much interference from the public, and who put issues of security and economic growth before politics. In his analysis, Habermas indicates that there are certain groups in society whose interests are served by the depoliticization of public affairs, and consequently, others who would generally benefit from politicization. Such assumptions are also a guiding principle in this collection. Moreover, even though many important events have taken place since Habermas wrote, tendencies toward depoliticization have not diminished; indeed, new forms have even appeared. No doubt the clearest examples are to be found in the workings of the economy, where the system produces 'by-products,' i.e., 'externalities,' that negatively affect the environment, life conditions, mental and physical health, political stability, etc. These 'by-products' appear very different depending on whether they are viewed from a conservative, i.e., system-affirmative, free market point of view, or whether they are seen from a more critical or radical viewpoint. When problems in the economic realm impinge on economic and social justice, the conservative tends to point to individual responsibility and morality. For instance, at the onset of the current global economic crisis, neoconservative analysts in the USA were quick to point a finger at the 'low morals' on Wall Street, and especially the 'greed' of agents, indicating that 'bad seeds' had corrupted an otherwise neutral, innocent system. This finger-pointing serves to deflect attention from the systemic and political structures. From a system-affirmative viewpoint, the crisis was attributed either to morality, or simply as a series of events, mishaps, and byproducts.[13] Radical commentators, on the other hand,

---

13. Another example of moralization is the interpretation of the near-collapse of the Greek economy.

have attempted to *politicize* the economic crisis by identifying systemic problems and proposing structural changes.[14]

Most of the laws and regulations passed immediately after the onset of the crisis were alleviative, aimed to stabilize the economic system in place.[15] To prevent a collapse in the international financial system, many Western governments raised loans and guarantees worth several thousand billion US dollars. The governments of most of these countries were legally able to nationalize bankrupt financial institutions, but they chose not to do so. The value of – and public losses suffered from – these guarantees are hard to estimate. In the USA, approximately 100 billion of the 700 billion in so-called TARP-funding is considered as lost money. The International Monetary Fund (IMF) estimates that the fiscal costs of the crisis to the G-20 countries averaged 2.8% of the GDP, with unrecovered costs of 4–6% in the most affected countries. Furthermore, as an effect of the crisis government debts in these countries are estimated to rise by almost 40 percentage points from 2008 to 2015.[16] Additionally, the austerity policies meant to correct the crisis at the national level could very well lead to a deepening of the global economic crisis. In his 2010 book, *Freefall*, Joseph Stiglitz estimates the "global budgetary and real costs" of the crisis in "trillions of dollars."[17]

Now, suffering the greatest global recession since the 1930's, conservatives and radicals have both reached the conclusion that the financial sector has attained a size that has become problematic in relation to the economy of production. Even the IMF – whose rationale since its foundation has been to abolish regulations on capital and investments – has now spoken out in favor of economic regulations. A heated global

---

14. See, for example, Joseph Stiglitz, *Freefall: America, Free Markets, and the Sinking of the World Economy*, New York/London, Norton, 2010. Of course, just *how* radical Stiglitz really is could be discussed, but his proposals for deep, systemic changes are radical in the strictest sense of the term.

15. We owe many thanks to Petter Håndlykken for his assistance with the economic-political examples in these sections.

16. International Monetary Fund, *A Fair and Substantial Contribution by the Financial Sector*. Final Report for the G-20, IMF, June 2010, executive summary.

17. *Freefall*, 8.

debate about taxation and regulation of the financial sector has emerged, raising the prospects of reducing the relative size of the financial sector. Many nations have also advocated greater transparency and increased control over financial transactions nationally and internationally, in order to prevent further crises and increase political control of the financial sector. Among these measures are taxes on banks, on stock exchanges, and on financial transactions, and of course the abolishment of tax havens.

An important question concerning taxation and regulation that hovers in the background of the discussion above is the question of *who should bear the burden* of the crisis and its consequences. This problem becomes acute when public monies are used to bail out large financial corporations, and 'austerity measures' are implemented at the national level. If for analytical purposes we invoke the traditional poles of workers and capital – or labor and management – most of the burdens have so far been placed at the former. Even though the IMF, the G-20 and national authorities[18] have made efforts to place a greater responsibility on the latter, critics of free market capitalism are accused of fanning the flames of class warfare.[19] A more fair distribution of the burdens could, for instance, be achieved by taxation of the financial sector that brought on the crisis in the first place. Many large trade unions and trade unions' organizations such as the Trade Union Advisory Committee (TUAC) to the Organization for Economic Co-operation and Development (OECD) actively promote such taxes. Again, to politicize the crisis would mean to discuss the distribution of these burdens, while to depoliticize it means, in reality, to let the most powerful agents – the investment banks and speculators – have their cake and eat it, too. While speculators do not run any (personal) risk – relating as it were only to the gains and opportunities of new markets – politicians cannot allow institutions to fall to pieces. Politicization is therefore also about holding each other – larger portions of the society – responsible.

Although often overlapping, three 'areas' of depoliticization may be distinguished. First, there is the context in which the *public agenda* is

18. For example in the USA, Germany, and France.
19. See, for example, John Buell, "The New Republican Populism — Humanistic Economics – Column," *Humanist* (May–June 1996).

established, in which the themes for public consideration is determined; second, there is the *'juridification'* of the political sphere, whereby certain themes are removed from political discussions and (instead) subjected to juridical processes; and third, the symbolic or *imaginary* dimension, which includes political theory, representations, psychological investment, emotions, and belief in politics. All the essays contained in this volume deal with one or more of these dimensions. Even though these areas of depoliticization often appear in combination with one another, a brief outline of each, with some examples, will be instructive.

1) Today's global capitalism is dominated by large, multinational corporations and an enormous concentration of capital in the hands of a very small elite, combined with a gargantuan financial sector (the value of global financial assets is thirty times the size of the global gross development product, GDP).[20] Due to the lack of global regulations and through pressure on national authorities – via large campaign contributions in local and national elections (USA), juridical loopholes, fluctuating corporate structures, poorly regulated 'transit states,' etc. – corporate agents have to a large extent been able to influence and manipulate the conditions under which they operate. These players have justified their oligarchic positions through ultra-libertarian ideology and market fundamentalism, where 'freedom' is merely a nicer word for oligopoly. When corporations and investors operate beyond the reach of political bodies and institutions, important decisions that influence and shape the conditions of the lives and work of ordinary people are exempt from popular-democratic scrutiny. Moreover, through these structures, public income is reduced while tremendous fortunes circulate, adding to

---

20. In 1980, the value of the financial sector *equaled* the world's GDP, that is, the total production. From 1990 to 2006, the number of countries where financial assets *exceed* the value of their gross national product more than doubled, and before the current crisis erupted, the value of financial assets in the United States had reached 450% of GDP ("Mapping global capital markets," *McKinsey Report*, October 2008). In the European Union, it stood at 356% of GDP (Saskia Sassen, *Too Big to Save: The End of Financial Capitalism.* Published by Open Democracy at http://www.arnolfini.org. uk/downloads/misc/sassen-EndofFinancialCapitalism-0904.pdf).

the already enormous disparity in wealth and income. Additionally, the movement of capital through poorly regulated regions also facilitates the devastating destruction of the natural and social environment, as we see today, for example, in the Niger delta.

2) Another limitation on the political sphere is the vastly growing body of juridical-bureaucratic structures that influence, manipulate, and limit national political bodies, such as the IMF, OECD, EU, the many international agreements, and various levels of national and international court systems. Though the laws and regulations emerge from political processes, juridification is, in a certain sense, politics frozen, and works like a double-edged sword: where rights are institutionalized, politics become superfluous. Again, the best examples are in the economy. When large corporations appeal to juridical bodies in order to serve their interests, even politicians' hands are tied. Juridification takes a sinister turn when court decisions make laws that were made to address certain needs and problems bear on totally different areas of the social fabric. In the US, there is notably the controversy over the notion of 'corporate personhood.'[21] Proponents of this notion argue that people should not 'lose their human rights' just because they have joined collectively in corporations, and therefore, corporations too have 'human rights.' Accordingly, The European Court of Human Rights is now being used to deal with the *business rights* for juridical companies.[22] The Chair expands its capacity as law-making authority by expanding – some would say, abusing – the notion of human rights. A gross example is the US producer of Budweiser beer, Anheuser-Busch, who appealed a Portuguese Supreme court decision to the European Court of Human Rights in order to outlaw the production of the original Czech Budweiser beer. Anheuser-Busch argued that the 2001 decision in favor of the Czech producer "violated its rights to the

---

21. Confer the 1886 US Supreme Court decision that applied the Fourteenth Amendment of the US Constitution to corporations, defining them as 'legal persons' having similar rights as 'natural persons,' and the 1978 *First National Bank v. Bellotti* ruling that extended first amendment rights to corporations.
22. CBS interactive business network, October 17, 2005, http://findarticles.com/p/articles/mi_m3469/is_42_56/ai_n15792971/

'peaceful enjoyment' of the trademark," and that the Portuguese ruling infringed upon Article 1 of the European Convention on Human Rights, which guarantees individuals and companies protection of property." The case was lost on technical ground, but not on account of the principle.

3) The third area of depoliticization concerns the belief in politics, i.e., the imaginary dimension. Politicization is very much a question of power, knowledge, access, and control – but it is also about having faith in the capabilities of politics. Behind and running through all depoliticizing tendencies is a general lack of investment in political ideas, political affairs, and political processes – the lack of belief that the existing institutions can really be changed.[23] From this perspective, it could be argued that the greatest threat to politicization is not the lack of power, knowledge, or means, but *indifference.* That politics is ignored out of indifference is certainly true for some parts of the world, while in other parts – also within affluent societies such as the USA – an even greater threat to democratic politics is probably the *general fear* that permeates these regions. This general fear inhibits trust in ordinary people's capacity for political creation, thus paving the way for authoritarian measures.

To theorists such as Jürgen Habermas, Cornelius Castoriadis, Claude Lefort, Chantal Mouffe, and a few others, politicization is the heart of democracy. Through public deliberation and collective will formation, the society in question concerns itself with substantial political decisions, social and political critique, and the justification of political power (political legitimacy). The politically active public sphere is, among other things, the very condition for society's collective reflections upon its use of power, its laws, its education, principles of fairness and responsibility, and many other things. *Depoliticization* then represents a decline in activity in all of these matters. When political activity recedes, so does the scope of political visions, limiting alternatives and ideas for sociocultural creation. Depoliticization is therefore a disinvestment in the political as such, a loss of political significance, and a loss of political stories and myths. Indeed, as a political thinker Hannah Arendt was

23. Confer the works of Slavoj Žižek, Fredrick Jameson, and especially Cornelius Castoriadis whose work appears in several texts in this volume.

extremely concerned that politics could disappear altogether from the human realm, the *vita activa*. She feared the tendencies of the 1950s such as technocratic management and the developments of the welfare state – interpreted as signs that 'labor' and 'work' had taken the place of politics – both of which have in fact advanced enormously since the publication of *The Human Condition*. What is at stake with depoliticization is nothing less than the end of the possibility of leading a political life, which, to Arendt and Castoriadis, is an autonomous life, a life of freedom. Even though there is no return to the direct democracy of ancient Greece, the editors of this book still see democracy as a worthwhile project that needs attention and care, both in theory and in practice.

In light of this background, an interdisciplinary group of scholars from the Nordic countries met in a series of symposia from 2003 to 2006 to discuss the conditions for social criticism in connection with the conditions of contemporary global capitalism. One of their aims was to reconnect economic theory and political thought by focusing on political themes, economic theories, and capitalism. This collection of essays, which now includes contributions from three continents, has thus emerged from this cooperation. The essays approach their themes from various angles; some theoretical, some practical. An underlying idea is that contemporary global capitalism is fed by and thrives on, depoliticization. Even though this collection provides no definitive diagnoses, the themes explored all point in the direction of increased political and social agency, i.e., politicization. The collection consists of two parts: one focusing mainly on capitalism and economic theory, the other on political thought.

The Essays

In her opening article, "The Political Imaginary of Global Capitalism," Ingerid S. Straume poses the question of why global capitalism is so resilient to political change. Concentrating on the larger perspective, the article elucidates the 'depoliticizing imaginary' that connects contemporary global capitalism, economic theory, and political thought. While 'capitalism' is bolstered by the attractive illusions of individual independence, control, and in the long run, prosperity for all, neoclassical theory evokes the impression that economic insights require a certain theoretical (computational) expertise. Since contemporary political thought seems unable to puncture these illusions, Straume argues that the current economic system is held in place through a collective detachment from the political sphere, whose result is often personal suffering.

In "Capitalism in Context: Sources, Trajectories, and Alternatives," Johann P. Arnason pursues the analysis of capitalism, and its expansive, adaptive, and self-transformative capacities which also enables capitalism to coexist with – and to co-opt – *critique*. Arnason warns us against seeing capitalism as a unified, self-contained economic system; rather, we should look to the cultural and context in which the *economic logic* has been given primacy. Through time and across regions, varying contextual and civilizational patterns have given rise to varieties of capitalism. While Arnason pins down 'the spirit of capitalism' in the notions of 'abstract power' and the 'promise of wealth to all,' he also sees tensions between capitalism's different components. Through a combination of sources, Arnason outlines a framework for a comparative approach to varieties of capitalism within a historical and civilizational perspective.

In "Castoriadis, Veblen, and the 'Power Theory of Capital'," D. T. Cochrane also emphasizes contextualization when he examines the concept of *capital* by developing a critique of the 'labor theory of value' found in both Marxist economics and neoclassical theory. Contrary to the assumptions made by both of these very different traditions, he argues that neither 'labor' nor 'production' are vital elements in understanding capital; both are erected upon the concepts of utility and abstract labor, i.e., the 'postulation of transcendent and unobservable entities.' Nor are the categories of 'exploitation' or 'productivity' sufficiently suited to analyze and understand the capitalist economy. Acknowledging that capital accumulation involves the exercise of *control and power within social institutions*, Cochrane argues that the central drive within capitalism is the drive to expand ownership claims and increase the earnings of existing claims. From the premise that capital and capitalization is 'the valuation of control itself,' i.e., the organizing logic of the social order, a perspective is opened for empirical analyses where, e.g., the behavior of capitalist enterprises can be interpreted within complex relations consisting of 'purely economic' dealings as well as other social events. When attention is directed towards power coalitions in the economy, markets can thus be analyzed as 'empirical representations of control.'

The importance of analyzing global capitalism in terms of power and control becomes evident in Anders Lundkvist's "From Market Economy to Capitalistic Planned Economy." This text is based on the study of developments in transnational corporate structures in the 1990s. During this period, the relative share of transnational corporations in the global trade and production rose enormously. According to Lundkvist, the main problem with the global economy today is not 'free trade,' but corporate power. Mapping out various structures of corporate cooperation, such as strategic alliances and oligopolies that increase the concentration of economic power, Lundkvist shows how transnational corporations have become large enough to avoid competition, which, after all, is the enemy of capital concentration. The current organization of world trade, he argues, is not market capitalism, but an oligarchic system which could be called 'capitalistic planned economy.' From a certain perspective, a freer market would mean diminishing the dominance of these agents, but the 'real choice,' according to Lundkvist, is between democratic *or* capitalistic control.

21

To round off the papers on economy, in "The Transcendental Power of Money" J. F. Humphrey discusses the theoretical foundations of the most severe crises of the capitalist economic system since the Great Depression of 1929. To understand the transition from money as a medium of exchange to money as a commodity, Humphrey undertakes a detailed analysis of Marx's discussion of the sphere of production. Although it would seem that products are produced to satisfy specific needs, once money becomes the end or aim of production, use value is supplanted by exchange value. According to the logic of capitalism, production is concerned with acquisition of money, i.e., capital. Without consumption, capitalist economy is sluggish; hence, economic crises, unemployment, and recessions are inevitable. As the acquisition of capital becomes the end of production, large financial institutions emerge that are willing to make extremely risky investments; and since these institutions are essential to the economic and political stability of nation states within which they operate, they have become immune to risk, 'too big to fail.' Even though taxpayers' livelihood may depend upon this economic system, they have little if anything to say regarding the solutions to these economic problems. Thus the roots of the crisis are deeply political.

A major problem for contemporary scholars is how to theorize political action in terms of *agency*. In the main stream of political theory, political liberalism, this question is not as pressing since the political agency of liberalism is confined to the institutions of representative democracy, set within the state apparatus.[24] Popular agency is thus limited to 'participation,' such as the lobbying of interest groups, and 'citizenship' seen as a capacity of the electorate. If, however, we find that political agency is not sufficiently conceptualized in these terms, the theoretical alternatives are quite limited. Kåre Blinkenberg's and Mogens Chrom Jacobsen's articles take up the question of agency in the context of two of the most widely read current poststructuralist thinkers, Jacques Rancière and Michel Foucault.

---

24. See, e.g., Axel Honneth, "Das Gewebe der Gerechtigkeit," id., *Das Ich im Wir*, Frankfurt, Suhrkamp, 2010.

In "Jacques Rancière and the Question of Political Subjectivization," Kåre Blinkenberg points out the strong connections between democracy, politicization, and political agents acting from *outside* of the established institutional apparatus. Political subjectivity, for Rancière, is not something that is donated or granted – like formal citizenship – but something that groups of people do *against* the general consensus of the existing social order, when powerless (formerly non-existing) groups demand a share of the power and thereby posit themselves as legitimate agents ('equals'). With Rancière's original distinction between politics (*la politique*) and 'the police' *(la police)*, Blinkenberg is able to highlight the depoliticizing aspects of dominant political thought, and theorize the ineradicable possibility of political action.

In "Foucault, Relativism, and Political Action," Mogens Chrom Jacobsen examines the relation between Foucault's theoretical work and his political praxis. For Jacobsen, the question is: Can Foucault's thought inform his notion of political agency?[25] Even though Foucault was personally involved in political struggles – and has inspired many theoretical and empirical analyses that have had political effects – Jacobsen finds that his philosophy ultimately fails to provide the foundations that can motivate, in the sense of justifying, political action. Through a careful investigation of Foucault's two 'methods'– as a descriptive empiricist who calls himself a 'positivist,' and as an 'interventionist' who poses alternative descriptions of the world – Jacobsen points out how both of these approaches undermine the idea that political action is worth its while; indeed, Foucault's methods fail to elucidate the 'why' of political creativity.

The impotency of contemporary political thought reflects the real life experience of political powerlessness. One of the clearest manifestations of a general depoliticization can be seen in the language and discourse current in the public sector of many Western institutions, such as universities and schools. The lack of a political vocabulary to describe

---

25. In fact, Rancière develops his notion of subjectivization in discussion with, and in contrast to, Foucault's.

one's activities in a politically meaningful way is striking, as the language of computability – echoing the significations of power and control – is taking over more and more areas of the life-world. In the article "'Learning' and Signification in Neoliberal Governance," Ingerid S. Straume provides a set of examples of depoliticizing policy processes from the educational sector, where the notion of 'learning' is connected to the capitalist imaginary of 'computability.' The predominant notion of 'learning' serves to rationalize the discourse of education, leaving out other aspects of the sphere of education such as the meaning of education itself, in other words: politics.

Håvard Friis Nilsen takes the economic and political analysis into the analysis of culture and the arts. In "Deterioration of Trust: The Political Warning in Kubrick's "Eyes Wide Shut," Nilsen explores the thematic of director Stanley Kubrick's last film, *Eyes Wide Shut*. Contrary to its critics, who saw little of general interest in this film, Nilsen discloses the deeper political and psychological layers of the film, and the short story published and set in Vienna in 1920s which the film is built upon. In a time of looming economic crisis, Nilsen argues – characterizing the time of the short story as well as Kubrick's film – the deterioration of trust within the general social fabric serves to activate undercurrents of an authoritarian character.

While the authors of the papers presented in this volume come from different perspectives, and different disciplines, they are united in their general concern with depoliticization and the threat that it poses to democracy and democratic processes. It is our hope that this volume will contribute to a public space in which a transnational dialogue may take place concerning our common fate, our common future, and the kind of world that we will leave to the next generation.

PART I
ECONOMY

The Political Imaginary of Global Capitalism

Ingerid S. Straume

Why are there no serious alternatives to the capitalist economic system today?[1] Since capitalism[2] as an economic system produces many un-desirable 'externalities' that should – *rationally* speaking – undermine its claim to dominance, its 'sheer success' is hardly a sufficient explanation. The lack of alternatives to capitalism seems to be a problem belonging not to the economic, but to the *political sphere* – for even though many Westerners are intensely critical of their societies' central institutions today, few serious efforts are being made to create new ones. To account for the tremendous resilience of capitalism, therefore, one should look to its 'political imaginary,' rather than its 'rational outcomes.' This imaginary, I shall argue, represents a general *depoliticization*, where the *social imaginary significations*[3] of contemporary global capitalism are up-

---

1. Many thanks to Chris Saunders, Asgeir Olden, Stephen Dobson and Bent Sofus Tranøy for useful comments and support at various stages.
2. The term 'capitalism' is used in accordance with Cornelius Castoriadis to denote the "ongoing transformation of the process of production in order to increase output while reducing costs." ("The 'Rationality' of Capitalism," id. *Figures of the Thinkable*, translated by Helen Arnold, Stanford CA, Stanford University press 2007, 53. Hereafter, *FT*).
3. Castoriadis's concept 'social imaginary significations' refers to the dimension of instituted meaning that infuses and holds every society together. The social imaginary significations of a society are embodied its institutions (in the broadest sense of the term). The notion is influenced by Max Weber's analyses of social institutions, but has more profound implications.

held by a collective detachment from the political sphere. To highlight these significations and the meaning they embody, lines will be drawn and arguments constructed across different fields of inquiry such as political philosophy, economic theory, and cultural sociology. These broad, sweeping analyses necessarily lead to the loss of details and nuances. As a case in point, to argue that depoliticization represents a crisis in Western societies' capability to create and reform themselves politically, I will consider the sphere of conscious social self-reproduction, *education*.[4] Let us begin, however, with a closer look at the significations and workings of capitalism itself.

Promises of Global Capitalism

Do you want to do something for your country? Then shop!

George Walker Bush, President of the United States of America, 2001

In the last few months of 2001, the economic infrastructure of the United States of America was driven to the brink of a total breakdown, as the recent terrorist attack on the World Trade Centre and Pentagon brought on a dramatic decline in shopping. The then Mayor of New York, Rudi Giuliani, and the President of the United States, George W. Bush, both addressed the people with a plea to save their country – by shopping as usual. Then again, in October 2008, when the global financial crisis was brought on by the collapse of the US credit market, a similar concern arose in Western countries whose economies are fuelled by consumption. The greatest threat, one that would render all policy measures pointless, was stagnated consumption, which would mean stalled growth. In Norway, the Minister of Finance – a representative of the Norwegian Socialist Left Party – gave the following advice to citizens on how to respond to the threatening crisis: Act as usual, and above all, keep shopping! This message was delivered on national television with the smiling socialist minister carrying shopping bags.

The financial crisis *could* have been a golden opportunity to create

---

4. See more in Ingerid S. Straume, "'Learning' and Signification in Neoliberal Governance," in this volume.

new economic institutions, systems, and practices. Indeed, it would have seemed logical to attempt to replace global capitalism with a more stable system. The problems connected to capitalist development, like financial crises, mass unemployment, concentration of capital, resource depletion, and various environmental problems, are well known, even though scholars argue whether these problems are internal or external to the capitalist system. Neoclassical economic theory, the theory currently taught in institutions of higher education, typically considers many factors irrelevant and external to its model of 'the economy.' One attempt to account for – and neutralize – externalities is the policy of *environmental decoupling*, meaning to 'decouple' economic growth from environmental pressure, so that growth can take place without costs to the environment. The concept is aligned with the principles of the Brundtland Report,[5] where policy makers attempt to meet the demands of environmental activists *without compromising economic growth*. Environmental decoupling, primarily through technological innovation and recycling, is said to create a win–win situation for the environment *and* the general economy, while present environmental problems are alleviated.[6] An example of such *technological* innovation is the growing industry for carbon capture and storage (CSS) connected to fossil fuel power plants; while a *financial* innovation is the emissions trading system (the 'carbon market') of the Kyoto protocol. In any of these cases – like in the Brundtland Report – the premise of growth and expected revenue is kept intact. Carbon capture and emissions trading are merely new mechanisms in the same system; the system itself is not questioned. Since the capitalist economy depends on growth, even slower growth rates – which, of course, still represent growth – would be detrimental to many capitalist institutions, such as commercial and financial banks. To prevent capitalist investors from the continued exploitation of resources, therefore, an infinitely expanding regime of regulations would most certainly be needed.

5. The World Commission on Environment and Development, *Our Common Future*, United Nations, 1987.
6. See also the OECD's *Environment Programme for the 21st Century*, from 2001, where indicators for decoupling are set forth.

Whereas resource depletion is, at least technically, connected to perpetual growth, a problem like unemployment is even more inherent to the economic system. For what is 'unemployment' really? Certainly not lack of 'work.' In straight physical terms, unemployment has as little to do with lack of work as poverty with lack of food: there can be unemployment even while there is work to be done, and there can be poverty and hunger even when there is food enough to feed everyone; indeed, this is a reality. This indicates that unemployment, poverty, etc. are more or less essential *factors* of the capitalist system. Still – and this is the great paradox that keeps capitalism alive in the collective imaginary – the *promise* of capitalism is to abolish all such problems – in the long run. Through the Fata Morgana of perpetual growth and unlimited expansion, capitalism holds a promise of surplus, overabundance, in which we all can take part, when our turn eventually comes. In this respect, capitalism is a beautiful dream.

Meanwhile, the inherent problems of capitalism abound. For instance, as several economists have pointed out, capitalist economies tend to enter a state of crisis at more or less regular intervals. Building on the economic theory of Joseph Schumpeter, a central factor of which is *innovation*, Carlota Perez and Christopher Freeman have demonstrated that the crises tend to come in cycles of about 50–60 years, through shifting "techno-economic paradigms" in which new innovations give rise to variations in the relationship between finance capital and production capital.[7] New technical innovations typically lead to expansion and development in several spheres of society, accompanied by excitement in the financial sector and increasing interest in investing. The financial sector responds to technical innovation by inventing new *financial* products. Perez's and Freeman's historical examples are connected to the cotton industry,

---

7. Perez and Freeman have developed these points together and individually, e.g. in *The Economic Legacy of Joseph Schumpeter*, edited by Horst Hanusch, Edward Elgar, London, 1998. Also, see Freeman (below) and Perez, "Technological Revolutions, Paradigm Shifts and Socio-institutional Change" in *Globalization, Economic Development and Inequality: An Alternative Perspective*, edited by Erik Reinert, Cheltenham, Edward Elgar, 2004.

steam engines, steel and electrification, oil and automobiles, and micro-electronics.[8] At a certain point, however, the potential of each new technology to stimulate knowledge and secondary innovation is exhausted. The innovative phase then culminates in an economic crisis – creating in turn a foundation for new innovation and growth. These cycles will continue as long there is innovation in the productive sector, according to Perez.[9] Since the relationship between production capital and financial capital is inherently unstable – dynamic at best – the instability cannot be totally absorbed by the political system; although it could be better regulated if these trends were taken into account.

Another, classical, problem with capitalism is the unwanted effects of interest and compound interest, such as capital accumulation and lack of circulation (non-growth). Within, and parallel to the capitalist system, several attempts have been made to overcome capital accumulation, such as taxing or devaluating capital that is not circulated (demurrage).[10] But if these and other weaknesses are well known to economists and policy makers alike, a determined effort to replace global (interest bearing) capitalism is not very likely; nor is there reason to expect policy makers to pursue other major economic transformations in the foreseeable future. An illuminating example is the handling of the recent financial crisis. Even if most analysts would agree that the origins and causes of the crisis are to be found within the financial sector, all the affected governments reacted by shoring up the existing financial institutions in an effort to save export rates in an ever tightening global market. Governments, whether left, center, or right, met the crisis with measures intended

---

8. Christopher Freeman, "Income Inequalities in Changing Techno-Economic Paradigms," in Reinert, *Globalization*.
9. Carlota Perez, *Technological Revolutions and Financial Capital: The Dynamics of Bubbles and Golden Ages. Cheltenham*, Edward Elgar, 2002.
10. Consider, for example, Silvio Gesell's alternative economic system of 'stamped money.' Theorists with practical alternatives, like Gesell (1862–1939), are hardly taken seriously by today's economists, nor taught in economics departments. John Maynard Keynes, however, spoke favorably of Gesell in his major work, *The General Theory of Employment, Interest and Money* from 1936.

to soften the fall; while keeping the basic economic institutions, from which the crisis flowed in the first place, intact. For critics of capitalism and proponents of alternative economy the crisis represented a golden opportunity – but somehow, the *Zeitgeist* prevented a thorough critique of the system, making Fredrick Jameson's (alleged) words true: "It is now easier to imagine the end of the world, than the end of capitalism."[11]

But the question remains: What is it – even in the face of failures and obvious problems – that makes capitalism so resilient? What is it about capitalism that makes alternative economic systems seem so *unrealistic*? The answer cannot be traced to a lack of alternatives – the Internet abounds with practical suggestions, alternative systems, and examples – but, rather, that the very idea of replacing capitalism appears as utterly naïve. Even to voice the idea of radically changing the economic world order makes one stand out as overly idealistic, idiosyncratic, and possibly mad; even though the idea *itself* is perfectly logical. In other words, the resistance to systemic change in economic policy is stronger than can be accounted for by facts.

One fact that makes capitalism so robust is, of course, its extension. Replacing capitalism implies profound changes that will surely evoke some psychological resistance. But sheer size is hardly enough to explain why the notion of challenging capitalism appears almost absurd. In my view, the explanation can be found in the very strong *significations* embodied in capitalism's imaginary, such as the notions of free choice, individual agency, perpetual growth, and – in the long run – prosperity for all. It is first and foremost *these significations* that render capitalism superior to all of its alternatives. This claim will be developed in the next section.

---

11. Contrary to what is often claimed, Jameson is not the father of the quote; in the essay "Future City", *New Left Review*, no. *21* (May–June 2003), Jameson writes: "Someone once said that it is easier to imagine the end of the world than to imagine the end of capitalism. We can now revise that and witness the attempt to imagine capitalism by way of imagining the end of the world."

Independence – Control

> There never has been and there never will be a purely 'functional' society. Social imaginary significations organize the proper world of each society under consideration and furnish a 'meaning' to this world.[12]

According to Castoriadis, it is essentially the social imaginary significations that differentiate one social-historical form – *a society* – from another. Significations are not merely cognitive, but consist of representation(s), affect, and drive/will/intention.[13] They are 'embodied' in society's institutions, and as such, provide the bearings for social conduct, norms, sense and non-sense, etc. Among the most distinctive significations in contemporary Western societies are *freedom* and *rationality*. These significations are central to capitalism, in science, and in political liberalism – classical and modern.[14] Accordingly, there exists a connection between these spheres – historical more than logical – which grew especially strong during the Cold War, as capitalist expansion and political liberalism was consolidated into theory by such influential thinkers as Isaiah Berlin, Raymond Aron, and Karl Popper.[15] From their political-ideological works in the theory of science and political philosophy emerged a powerful, integrated notion of 'capitalist liberalism' as *the only sane and moral world order*. This idea, although rarely spelled out, was echoed again and again in political and economic theory; and historical events seemed to make it true. Even the term 'democracy' was for a long time seen as a property of the Western liberal-capitalist regimes, where capitalism's institutions were treated as necessary conditions for a

---

12. Cornelius Castoriadis, "Psychoanalysis and Philosophy," id., *The Castoriadis Reader,* edited and translated by David Ames Curtis, Oxford, Blackwell, 1997, 358. Hereafter, *CR.*
13. *CR,* 353.
14. As elaborated by Peter Wagner, *Modernity as Interpretation and Experience,* Cambridge, Polity, 2008.
15. See Jan-Werner Müller's paper, "Fear and Freedom: On Cold War Liberalism," http://www.princeton.edu/~jmueller/ColdWarLiberalism-JWMueller-2006.pdf.

viable democracy.[16] Within the ideology of 'Cold War liberalism,'[17] and its continued impulses within neoliberalism, the historical *facts* of the Second World War, the Cold War, and the crumbling of the Eastern Communist regimes became instruments to strengthen the position of capitalism. In the last decades of the 20th century, history, notably totalitarianism, was taken as proof of the desirability – indeed, necessity – of a polity based on market capitalism and a relatively weak, regulatory state. As a consequence, it became increasingly more difficult to articulate alternative theories to political liberalism.[18]

In his sociological-historical analysis of modernity in Europe and the USA, Peter Wagner claims that in the US version – due to a lack of common political-moral justification – 'modernity' became "theoretically extreme" in terms of "individualism and instrumentalism." This alleged poverty of political thought brought forth what Wagner calls a "rationalistic-individualistic interpretation of modernity" that gave rise to the dominant form of capitalism as we know it today.[19] The close association of individual-based, political liberalism with capitalism is supported by an extremely simple political and social ontology. Its theoretical elements – setting the stage for socio-political considerations – consist of individuals in relationship to things: *'man vis-à-vis objects'*. These objects can be anything from physical objects to elements in a model world; such as 'goods,' 'interests,' and 'the global market.' In this scenario, the relevant theoretical subject-type is the *agent*; a prototype that did not exist prior to social science. It is also possible to identify

16. The World Bank and the International Monetary Fund were, especially during the 1980s and 90s, involved in *structural adjustment programs* whose impact on domestic policy in developing countries in many ways represented a continuation of Cold War politics against 'socialism.'

17. Müller, "Fear and Freedom."

18. For a long time, left-leaning political theorists and radical democrats were routinely accused of (at least theoretically, or secretly) supporting totalitarianism, even genocide – from Gulag to Cambodia. In light of the recent, failed "crusade" for freedom and democracy in Iraq and Afghanistan, these inferences have lost much of their force.

19. *Modernity*, 113–14.

an ideal relationship between the agent and things, characterized by freedom – or control – wherein the agent-subject should be *independent*, not dependent. Insofar as 'man' is able to choose between, control and manipulate objects, he is seen to be *free*. This ideal takes an explicit form in political liberalism, and is implicit in economic liberalism and science. The essence of freedom, then, means to be in control of, or unaffected by, one's environment. Such freedom is attainable through rational means: By patiently developing his technoscience, 'man' could become master of nature. Hence, through the notion of a free market the economic sphere could become a model of freedom, rather than a sphere of dependence, as Hegel thought.[20]

The striving for mastery of the world of objects (i.e., *agency*) is characteristic of that tendency in the natural and social sciences that Charles Taylor labels 'naturalism.'[21] Naturalism, like free market ideology, is really about the agent:

> [B]ehind and supporting the impetus to naturalism […], viz. the understandable prestige of the natural science model, stands an attachment to a certain picture of the agent. This picture is deeply attractive to moderns, both flattering and inspiring. It shows us as capable of achieving a kind of disengagement from our world by objectifying it.[22]

According to Taylor, this objectification of the world builds on a much deeper, metaphysical notion, viz. the *myth of the disengaged self*, which holds a certain status of freedom, dignity and power.[23] Because of its desirability, the impetus to naturalism is strong even in disciplines where the natural science model and 'the spectator's theory of knowledge' (Dewey) are less than adequate. The myth of the disengaged self also has a societal aspect:

20. Georg W. F. Hegel, *Elements of the Philosophy of Right* [1817].
21. Charles Taylor, *Philosophical Papers, Volume I. Human Agency and Language*, Cambridge, Cambridge University Press, 1985. Herafter, *PP1*.
22. *PP1*, 4.
23. *PP1*, 6.

The ideal of disengagement defines a certain – typically modern – notion of freedom, as the ability to act on one's own, without outside interference or subordination to outside authority. It defines its own peculiar notion of human dignity, closely connected to freedom. And these in turn are linked to ideals of efficacy, power, unperturbability, which for all their links with earlier ideals are original with modern culture.[24]

The pleasure acquired from viewing oneself as free, disengaged, and dignified, Taylor claims, makes these – distinctly modern – theories resilient to critique. They offer flattering, yet unrealistic ideas of the nature and conditions of the human being, especially in terms of agency. Theories that conceive of individuals as able to construct their own meaning, choose their own values, etc. are, of course, much more enjoyable as interpretative repertoires than sociologically orientated theories that place emphasis on structural power and collective meaning making, not to mention false consciousness and repression.

Taylor sees disengagement as a distinctly modern ideal. Nevertheless, as Johann Pàll Arnason, Peter Wagner, and others have argued, modernity is not one, but many.[25] This becomes clear when modernity is theorized in terms of significations that lend themselves to multiple formations and interpretations. Inspired by Cornelius Castoriadis, Arnason's and Wagner's analyses of modernity are orientated around the 'double signification' of *autonomy* and *rational mastery*. Running deep through modern societies, these 'core significations' constitute these societies' notions of power, critique, thinking, meaning making, socialization, etc. Autonomy and rational mastery are mutually irreducible to, and in persistent tension with, each other. They are embodied in institutions at various levels, including the economy, politics, and in *epistemes* such as science. In Castoriadis's analysis, the prime embodiment of "the project

---

24. *PP1*, 5.
25. See Johann Pàll Arnason, "The Imaginary Constitution of Modernity" in *Autonomie et autotransformation de la société. La philosophie militante de Cornelius Castoriadis*, edited by Giovanni Busino, Genéve, Librarie Droz, 1989; and Wagner, *Modernity*.

of autonomy" is *democracy*, whereas the embodiment of the "unlimited expansion of rational mastery" is *capitalism*.[26] This means that capitalism, as the embodiment of a core signification, cannot simply be 'seen through' and 'discarded' without threatening the very foundations of Western modernity. To Castoriadis, all the central, modern institutions are orientated around the expansion of such rational (or "pseudo-rational") mastery:

> The presentation of science and of technique as neutral means or as instruments pure and simple is not a mere 'illusion': it is an integral part of the contemporary institution of society – that is, it partakes of the dominant social imaginary of our age. This dominant social imaginary can be encapsulated in one sentence: The central aim of social life is the unlimited expansion of rational mastery.[27]

According to this scenario, capitalism is much more than an economic system; it is also a social regime, and as such, an embodiment of social imaginary significations that orient societies in a very deep sense. The limitless expansion of rational mastery concerns mastery of matter, but also of the mind, e.g., through socialization. In Castoriadis's words:

> [T]he tendency toward 'rationality' reorganizing and reconstructing all spheres of social life – production, administration, education, culture, etc. – transforms the whole institution of society and penetrates ever further into all activities.[28]

Against this background, the main reason for capitalism's success should be sought in its powerful representations of freedom and independence, although it perhaps could better be characterized as *expansion* and *control*, following the aforementioned discussions by Castoriadis and Wagner. And as previously mentioned, one reason why capitalism is seen as

26. "From Ecology to Autonomy," *CR*, 239–52.
27. *CR*, 240.
28. *CR*, 240.

the only *realistic* economic system today is partly because of its alleged 'rationality,' and partly because it is so hard to believe that anyone could actually replace it. Put differently, so much psychological energy and *faith* is invested in capitalism that it just seems 'natural.' However, in its early days, capitalism did not appear natural at all, as it gradually took the place of other economic practices and perspectives. It is time to take a closer look at economic theory and its history.

Economic Theory and the Loss of History

The leading economic theory at institutions of higher education throughout the West today is neoclassical theory (or microeconomics). By providing a theoretical stage for notions such as the (ideally independent) agent, control, and expanding rational mastery,[29] neoclassical theory provides theoretical support for market capitalism. Its present dominance in higher education parallels a decline of economic history in the curricula; as economist Erik Reinert argues, the theory holds hegemony, in spite of its apparent weaknesses, by *denying historicity*.[30] Neoclassical theory is basically model-based, with little or no need for history, practical insights, or contextual modifications. Instead of context and history, neoclassical theory rests on *metaphors, models,* and *mathematics*. I will address each of these aspects in the following.

The widespread dependence on *metaphors* is a rather obvious weakness, shared by several economic theories.[31] Metaphors can be imported from various domains of life, such as the living organism, sports, or in the case of neoclassical theory, physics. In early neoclassical theory, metaphors were taken from thermodynamics and the behavior of gases under pressure, as

29. In his later texts, Castoriadis would say "pseudo-rational pseudo-mastery."
30. Erik Reinert, *Spontant kaos. Økonomi i en ulvetid,* Oslo, Res Publica, 2009 (*SR*); Reinert, *How Rich Countries Got Rich ... and Why Poor Countries Stay Poor,* London, Constable, 2007 (*HR*); see also Cornelius Castoriadis, "The 'Rationality' of Capitalism", *FT,* 47–70.
31. See, e.g., the works of Deirdre McCloskey. See also Berit Von der Lippe, "Metaforer i økonomisk språkbruk," in *Retorikk, samfunn og samtid,* edited by Odd Nordhaug and Hans-Ivar Christiansen, Oslo, Forlag 1, 2007.

shown in expressions such as over-heated economy, inflation/deflation, pressure, liquidity and more specifically, market entropy. Underlying these well-established expressions is the mother of all neoclassical metaphors: *equilibrium*, i.e., the fundamental principle of thermodynamics. From the central, organizing metaphor of equilibrium a giant *equation* is projected, of economic variables rising and falling, producing pressure and heat, all of which conform to internal economic 'laws.' Even though the notion of equilibrium itself is unfounded in empirical economy, the set of metaphors is well suited to the ideology of the 'perfect market.' Equilibrium is also necessary to found models based on mathematical equations. Castoriadis notes that:

> The obsession with balance has two roots, both ideological. Positions of equilibrium are chosen because they are the only ones in which precise, univocal solutions are possible: systems of simultaneous equations provide a disguise of scientific exactness. Second, equilibriums are almost always presented as equivalent to situations of 'optimization' ('cleared' markets, fully employed factors, consumers achieving maximum satisfaction, and so forth).[32]

The metaphor of equilibrium highlights the contingency of mathematical models, which is discussed below. But first, a few words on the historical background for the present situation.

Along with the formation of the modern nation-states in Europe during the seventeenth century, political economy developed as one of the central *savoirs* for 'handling people and things,' as Foucault would put it.[33] The separation between economic theory and political philosophy, however, is more recent. In the eighteenth century, when the classical English liberalists John Stuart Mill and Adam Smith were discussing the distribution of wealth and the allocation of political rights, economic

---

32. *FT*, 61.
33. Michel Foucault, "Governmentality," in *The Foucault Effect*, edited by Graham Burchell, Colin Gordon, and Peter Miller, Chicago, University of Chicago Press, 1991.

theory and political philosophy went hand in hand. Economic theories were still drawing on historical experience, and aligned with contextual factors concerning production and the market. In other words, economic activity was seen as different in different parts of the world, and not subject to standardization. Economic liberalism, the school of thought founded by Adam Smith, was instrumental in doing away with these insights; by concentrating on the exchange function of the economy, where both trade and production were theorized as 'labor,' Smith's theory eliminated the context of the production.[34]

David Ricardo took this reductionism a step further in his classical 1817 work on trade, labor, and value in which he expounded his theory of 'comparative advantage.'[35] Trade (or exchange) will benefit all parties, he proposed, even if one of them (e.g., a resource-rich country or a highly-skilled artisan) is more productive in every possible area than the trading counterpart (e.g., a resource-poor country or an unskilled laborer), as long as each party concentrates on the activities in which it has a *relative* productivity advantage. The theory argues against every kind of protection of domestic trade and industry, as countries are advised to specialize at whatever developmental stage they happen to find themselves – regardless of how they got there. So while a highly industrialized nation, like Great Britain, should specialize in advanced industry, a nation with very little technology should specialize in delivering raw materials. The theory disregards the historical fact that all industrialized nations built their industrial technology and infrastructure with the aid of trade restrictions, customs barriers, etc.[36] When poor nations whose economies were based on raw materials and agriculture were denied the possibility to develop their own industry and infrastructure, they were forced to compete with industrialized nations whose infrastructure was built up during a period of strict protectionism. Under the postulate of 'comparative advantage' and 'free market,' poor

---

34. Reinert, *SK, HR.*
35. David Ricardo, *On the Principles of Political Economy and Taxation* (1817).
36. The theory was very beneficial to the colonial powers, justifying England's industrial superiority, and Ricardo himself was able to build a substantial fortune.

countries can only "specialize in poverty," says Reinert.[37]

Ricardo, and Smith before him, created abstract economic theories that ignored context and history. Today, such 'model theories' of the economy are almost universally accepted by university departments.[38] The models of neoclassical theory build on the notion of *input and output*, where all factors are seen as computable, and therefore, in principle, comparable. As already indicated, this presupposition is clearly false – though this statement is not particularly controversial: anyone studying economics learns that theoretical models of the economy do not 'work,' i.e., they cannot really help us predict the future. Even so, it is hard to see any other reasons for the widespread use of mathematics in neoclassical economic theory than a striving for exactness in prediction.[39] The depiction of the economy as a model creates at least two illusions: First, that economic reality can only be properly understood by experts, and second, that economic reality is *rational*, that is, understandable and computable in principle, provided adequate information is available on all relevant factors.[40]

The connection between the physics metaphors, the model-image, and the dependence on mathematics now becomes obvious, as the image of economy as a model whose natural/optimal state is equilibrium facilitates – and from a methodological viewpoint, necessitates – mathematical computability. If such computability is unachievable, however, the model-image itself would be inappropriate. The first question needing investigation, then, is whether the different economic factors are really comparable and arithmetically calculable. For instance, are labor and production amenable to arithmetic computation? Castoriadis and Reinert are unanimously dismissive, claiming that the 'arithmetic factors' of economic theories are

---

37. Erik Reinert, *HR*.

38. *HR*.

39. See for instance Don Ross, *Economic Theory and Cognitive Science: Microexplanation*, Cambridge, MIT Press, 2005 (*ETCS*).

40. Cf. Max Weber, The *Protestant Ethic and the Spiral of Capitalism*, London, Unwin University Books, 1968. Castoriadis (*FT*) explains why such a total 'rationalization' can never be achieved.

arbitrary, often practically indistinguishable, and heterogeneous. Using numerous examples, Castoriadis discredits the theoretical postulates of separability and separate imputation. Here is an example concerning the computation of economic results:

> The imputation of an economic result to any one firm is purely conventional and arbitrary: it follows boundaries set by law (private property), conventions, and habits. It is no less arbitrary to ascribe a productive result to any one factor of production, be it 'capital' or labor'. Capital (in the sense of the means of production produced) and labor contribute to the productive result without any possibility of sorting out their respective contributions [...][41]

In recent years, the guiding metaphors of economic theory have shifted from thermodynamics to systems theories, whose models and metaphors involve artificial intelligence (AI), simulation models, cognitive science, evolutionary theory, and behavioral science.[42] Keeping the principle of *computation* intact, contemporary economic theories are concerned with the *optimization* of something or other.[43] The theorists concentrate on systems – models of computation – whose goal is prediction. Philip Mirowski, a historian of economy, calls this a theory tradition closed in on itself – the "Grand Theory of Everything," where all is computed.[44] As Don Ross points out, following Mirowski, the simulation approach does indeed produce results, but with diminishing returns: "simulation makes things happen, but it becomes unclear how to characterize what is happening or why."[45] AI-simulation, for example, seeks to find the basis for behavioral patterns in the internal dynamics of modular parts of the simulated system itself. Whether the phenomenon under exploration is

41. Castoriadis, *FT*, 57.
42. Philip Mirowski, *Machine Dreams: Economics Becomes a Cyborg Science.* Cambridge University Press, 2002 (*MD*).
43. Ross, *ETCS*.
44. Ross, *ETCS*, 11–12, Mirowski, *MD*, 533–34.
45. *ETCS*, 11.

an individual's internal organization (rational agency), or dissolution of the self into 'rational systems theory,' the theoretical building blocks are still computation and algorithmic mathematical modeling.[46]

These brief considerations of neoclassical theory and its fundamental assumptions should give an indication of why the status of the capitalist economic system can remain almost unchallenged by leading economic theorists. The ideological power of theory is central: When (theoretical) *form* is given priority over (practical) *relevance*, an illusion is created that the economy can be understood by obtaining insight into *theories* – eliciting the notion of *control via calculation* (i.e., rational mastery). The central notion of computability is still closely related to Ricardo's principles of abstract production and context-free goods. But the use of mathematical operations presupposes a homogeneity and factor stability over time that simply does not exist in a real market, nor in a national economy; requirements that become acute when it comes to the use of complex mathematical operations like the differential calculus and functions.[47] But, as Amartya Sen has pointed out, most economists prefer to be exactly wrong, than to be approximately right.[48]

Thinking Inside the Matrix

Let us try to imagine an economic theory whose principle is de-growth, lessened consumption, production, transportation, and which, above all, is based on leaving all earth's remaining minerals in the ground – forever. In the light of the current economic doctrine, such ideas are plainly absurd. In light of resource ecology and planetary sustainability, it is perfectly logical. As this thought experiment shows, it is very hard, if not impossible, to think wholly 'outside capitalism.' The significations of capitalism – instrumentalism, consumerism, rational control, computation, etc. – are deeply rooted in the social world, and therefore in the socialized psyche of all individuals in capitalist societies. To think under global

---

46. *ETCS,* 11.
47. Castoriadis, *FT,* 61.
48. Erik Reinert, *Global Økonomi, hvordan de rike ble rike og hvorfor fattige blir fattigere,* Oslo, Spartacus, 2004, 23.

capitalism, then, means to think 'inside the matrix' where these ideas and significations are embodied. This does not mean that in modern societies everything is subject to rational control, far from it; but, as seen by Max Weber, the idea that *if we wished*, we *could learn* how to control all things.[49] Increasing intellectualization and rationalization, therefore, does not signify "an increased and greater generalized knowledge of the conditions under which one lives" – in this respect, Weber considered the savage to be at least as knowledgeable – but rather:

> ... the knowledge or belief that if one but wished one could learn it at any time. Hence, it means that principally there are no mysterious incalculable forces that come into play, but rather that one can, in principle, master all things by calculation. This means that the world is disenchanted. One need no longer have recourse to magical means in order to master or implore the spirits, as did the savage, for whom such mysterious powers existed. Technical means and calculations perform the service.[50]

Inside the capitalist matrix, learning how things work is thought to be achievable in principle, e.g., by means of modern science and/or calculation. It should therefore be possible to understand, and through this, control, all objects – if not in practice then at least in theory. For those who are in the position to make the necessary effort mastery and control is within reach – if not in the short run, then certainly in the long run. Rational investigation – which Castoriadis calls 'positing and assembling' – makes control possible. By contrast, the world before rationalization was seen to be ruled by, or ridden with, forces that were mystical and inexplicable to man. Hence, 'man' was easily humbled and scared.[51] To be in control, then, means to be free of concerns caused by insecurity,

---

49. The *"Entzauberung der Welt,"* see Max Weber, "Science as a Vocation," id, *Essays in Sociology,* translated and edited by H.H. Gerth and C. Wright Mills, New York, Oxford University Press, 1946,129–56 http://www.leonardbeeghley.com/docs/SYG%206125/Weber,%Science%20as20a%%20Vocation.pdf (*ScV*).
50. *ScV*.
51. *ScV*.

humility, and mystery. In short, rationalization is the systematic denial of human mortality – and also the elimination of *politics*, in the special sense of the term cast by philosopher Hannah Arendt. At this point, we encounter one of the many intersections between the dominant capitalist imaginary and the imaginary significations of *politics*, where the latter is threatened by the former.[52] In the remaining part of this article, I will concentrate on this tendency towards depoliticization.

One of the few thinkers to thoroughly analyze and conceptualize depoliticization is Hannah Arendt.[53] In her analysis, the totalitarian regimes that gave birth to Gulag and Holocaust were characterized by, and effectuated through, the destruction of politics, as individuals were pitted against each other in an atomized totality where everybody monitored everyone else, thus, destroying what Arendt calls *our common world*.[54] The emotional climate of totalitarianism was – and is – tempered by fear and distrust, indecision and unpredictability. Today, it could be argued that politics – and 'thinking' in Arendt's emphatic sense – are once again in a precarious state, as individuals are lined up against each other as competitors and consumers, where fear is a driving force: "shop, or else ... ", and the logic of competition is extended to more and more domains in life.

Still, when consumption is concerned, it is likely that most people consume with a certain ambivalence, since most of us know that consumption – the consumption *by some* – will be the ruin of us all in the long run. I will elaborate the psychological implications of this claim in the final section of my essay, drawing a diagnosis of a society in crisis – a crisis of political creation – using *education* as a heuristic.

---

52. The depoliticizing effects – if not the theoretical principles themselves – are paralleled by those of Habermas' colonization thesis, where the 'life world,' whose organizing principle is communicative rationality is threatened by the 'system,' driven by instrumental rationality. Jürgen Habermas, *Theorie des kommunikativen Handelns*, two volumes, Frankfurt am Main, Suhrkamp, 1981.
53. Hannah Arendt, *The Human Condition*, Chicago, University of Chicago press 1989 [1958] (*HC*); Hannah Arendt, *The Origins of Totalitarianism*. New York, Shocken 2004 [1951] (*OT*).
54. *OT*.

Political Creation in Crisis

The *free, rational agent* of political liberalism and market capitalism has been thoroughly criticized for its reductionism, abstractness, anomy, and more[55] – and in practical reality, this figure is far from rational. Cornelius Castoriadis claims that 'man,' under global capitalism, is rather the opposite: "Man is [...] like a child who finds himself in a house with chocolate walls, and who sets out to eat them without understanding that the rest of the house is soon going to fall on his head."[56]

Somewhere in the collective imaginary, there is probably a fairly acute sense of the *true* state of the construction: No person raised and educated in a modern democracy can be totally ignorant of the planet's limited resources, nor of the interdependence between resource levels, policies of growth, industrial production, and the inflated level of consumption in capitalist societies. The problem is not so much to imagine the disasters ahead, but rather to believe in the possibility of change, as I have argued in the opening sections of this essay. To further the analysis, I now turn to my case in point, education.

The following is based on the premise that political creation draws on the capacity to visualize that society could have been different, since society, with its norms, values, and institutions, is a social creation. To account for this premise, Cornelius Castoriadis distinguishes between what he calls the 'instituting' and the 'instituted' society. The *instituting* society is society's capacity for self-creation; it is society's capacity to create itself as a certain social 'form.' The *instituted* society is the creat*ed*, i.e., the product of the instituting society, consisting of laws, norms, and institutions in which significations are embodied.

> Society is self-creation. 'That which' creates society and history is the instituting society, as opposed to the instituted society. The instituting society is the social imaginary in the radical sense. The self-institution of society is the creation of a human world: of 'things,' 'reality,' language,

---

55. Zygmunt Bauman, Cornelius Castoriadis, Alisdair MacIntyre, Charles Taylor, Arne Johan Vetlesen and many others.
56. *FT*, 145.

norms, values, ways of life and death, objects for which we live and objects for which we die – and of course, first and foremost, the creation of the human individual in which the institution of society is massively embedded.[57]

In order to change the existing institutions (the instituted) and create new social imaginary significations, it is necessary to realize that things could be otherwise. If this insight is not properly instituted, however, society will see itself as a product of forces outside its own control. The instituting society remains unacknowledged, and the instituted society is not conceived as created by society itself. For instance, capitalism could be conceived as a law-like force to which the social world is subject – one that can only be followed and cannot be questioned in any profound sense.

In the sociological tradition from Max Weber, this 'deep questioning' – i.e., political-philosophical questioning – is seen as a defining characteristic of the project of modernity itself. In modernity, the existing (traditional) social values are no longer seen as valid *per definition*, something which has deep implications for conscious social reproduction, and therefore, education. At least since Marx, Nietzsche, and Freud, the critique of culture and civilization is constitutive of the project of modernity, and a premise of theories and practices of education. A striking example is the 'critical education,' taught in Nordic schools in the 1970s and 80s as a deliberate counter influence to mass culture.[58] In the following, I will argue that this self-critique has now started to turn back on itself, where critique threatens to turn into cultural self-contempt. This becomes quite clear if we analyze the typical relationship between parents and children in contemporary global capitalism in light of the previously developed sections of this paper.

Together with the rise of 'critical consciousness' in Western societies, at least since '1968,' many parents have found themselves in a social and

---

57. Cornelius Castoriadis, *Philosophy, Politics, Autonomy*, translated and edited by David Ames Curtis, New York Oxford, Oxford University press, 1991, 84.

58. Cf, e.g., the Norwegian book title *The School as Counter-Culture* (Alfred O. Telhaug, *Skolen som motkultur*, Oslo, Cappelen, 1987).

natural setting that they sometimes find undesirable, even disturbing and harmful. For example, the natural surroundings and countryside, which until today have been very important in the socialization of Norwegian children,[59] are no longer representations of pure or clean nature. Things in the countryside, in woods, and water, are now potentially harmful in an 'unnatural' way. This transformation happened in just a few years. The shocking implication is, of course, that human beings are the agents of this destruction – humanity is undermining its own existence. From this fact comes the notion of *humanity as inherently harmful*. And while we cognitively and technically appear to have the capacity, we still *seem* unable to stop the destruction of the natural environment. The situation is inherently 'pathological.' Now, if and when these ideas enter the field of education via literature, educational programs, etc. the pathology is affirmed and consolidated.

In the Nordic countries, for example, children's literature has tended for some time to thematize *adulthood*, and especially the shortcomings of adults in political and environmental matters. Books and TV-programs illustrate how 'silly' grown-ups are: always in a hurry and through their grown-up-actions ruining the environment. The authors often try to form an alliance with the children against 'the grown-ups.'[60] But since the world of grown-ups is the only resource for the child in the process of becoming an adult self, the subject-position offered to the child in this literature is very problematic. Systematically denigrating adults and adult behavior is detrimental to the child's opportunities for identification, as there are no other ideals available. The child is forced to identify with ambivalence or nothing at all.

My main point is that the conflict between adults and children portrayed by this literature points to a deeper conflict, between the culture and the individual – or rather, within the culture itself – where the central imaginary significations that organize Western societies, no longer offer sufficient meaning for its members. And since capitalism's significations

59. My comments are based on experiences from living in Norway.
60. These observations are based on literature studies from Norway, especially from the 1990s.

– such as rational mastery, consumerism, and instrumentalism – still provide the compass points for our practical orientation as a collective, the situation is deeply 'schizophrenic.' It represents a form of alienation, a *split* within society's self-image, where the relationship between the instituting and the instituted society is distorted. As Slavoj Žižek has pointed out, we detest it, and we don't believe in it, but we still perform and live it.[61] The split runs deep, arising within modern society itself, and there is no (rational) escape. This was tragically demonstrated by the Norwegian socialist minister of finance, who probably felt obliged to pose for the photographer holding shopping bags.

Still, the adult world is the only available template onto which the child's aspiration to grow up can be projected. If this *world* is discredited, the child is left without the cultural resources necessary to build a self. This is the problem that Hannah Arendt addressed in her controversial essay *The Crisis in Education*, claiming that: "Anyone who refuses to have joint responsibility for the world should not have children and must not be allowed to take part in educating them."[62] In Arendt's view, adults have a duty to hand over an 'intact world' to the next generation – even when they (the adults) wish to change this world, and wish it were otherwise. Practices of education that ignore, or are unable to follow this principle, are in a state of crisis.

Now, while the crisis I have described here is a socio-cultural one, its manifestations – as always – affect people individually and in relation to one another. For instance, children in capitalist societies express in their wishes and actions the demands of a consumer culture – a culture of which many parents are critical. In other words, the consumption-oriented, seemingly selfish attitudes of the young are, to a large extent, attitudes derived from and reflective of the consumer culture at large – *played out as conflicts in the home*. Hence, the parent or educator is forced to wrestle with problems far beyond the sphere of the personal and educational, such as consumerism, instrumentalism, reification, and cynicism. The

61. Slavoj Žižek has elaborated these points in many of his works.
62. Hannah Arendt, *Between Past and Future. Eight Exercises in Political Thought*, New York, Penguin, 1977 [1961], 189.

scene is set for individuals to resist their own culture; a fight they can never 'win.' Ambivalence and collective self-contempt takes the stage.

Depoliticization, as we have seen, rests on the inability of existing institutions to provide sufficiently robust *meaning* to act as resources for addressing the political problems of the society in question. Put differently: when a society is not able to justify its own significations, it is alienated from itself and its own creative capacity. Under these circumstances, social reproduction becomes very problematic. The instituting society has given birth to a monster – here, the institution of capitalism – and is paralyzed by it. The deepest effect of depoliticization, therefore, is society's abdication of its own creative capacity, which, as I have argued, also implies cultural and personal suffering.

Capitalism in Context: Sources, Trajectories, and Alternatives[1]

Johann P. Arnason

Capitalism is, as Max Weber famously put it, 'the most fateful force of our modern life.' More precisely, his view was that when capitalism – after a long history of more limited development – acquired its distinctively modern form, it became by the same token the most irresistibly disruptive and transformative among the forces involved in the making of a new world. Karl Marx took a similar view of capital as a uniquely dynamic force, even if his expectations as to its ultimate destiny differed markedly from Weber's. And although Emile Durkheim's conceptual framework did not allow for explicit theorizing of capital or capitalism, a keen awareness of capitalist trends and their impact on social life is evident at a turning point in his work. His analysis of the pathological forms of the division of labor can be read as a comprehensive critique of unregulated capitalism; the social problems encountered in this context did more than anything else to prompt a revision of his original approach. It is therefore misleading to divide the classics into theorists of capitalism and theorists of industrial society. At least in the three most important cases (and similar considerations would apply to others), a broadly comparable grasp of capitalism as an epoch-making force takes different theoretical forms, and none of the alternative models assumes an autonomous or dominant

---

1. This article has formerly been printed in *Thesis Eleven* 66 (2001), 99–125. Reprinted with permission from Sage Publications.

logic of industrialism (Durkheim had to retract his early moves towards the latter position).

The high visibility of capitalism can easily lead to conflation with modernity as a whole. Extreme versions of that view are not uncommon on the level of middlebrow ideologies; the prime contemporary example is the cult of global deregulation as the revealed essence of modernity. Advocates of a 'modernizing left' have found this drift of the *Zeitgeist* hard to resist. But when it comes to more genuine theorizing, the most interesting over-interpretations of capitalism do not simply equate it with modernity; rather, they present capitalism as the single most formative component or main driving force of a modernity which is defined in broader terms and expected to reach full maturity in a non-capitalist domain or a post-capitalist phase. Marx's theory of capitalist development and its coming self-destructive turn exemplifies the critical version of this approach. A new society with an anti-capitalist orientation is envisaged as a result of capitalism's internal logic, and the progressive absorption or subordination of all non-capitalist sides of existing modernity will in the long run pave the way for a transition to post-capitalist conditions of economic life. Admittedly, Marx never came up with a sustainable formulation of this thesis, but his intention was clear (the most streamlined statements are to be found in the *Communist Manifesto*). If we compare the classical view with the most influential contemporary offshoot of the Marxist tradition, Immanuel Wallerstein's world system theory, the main difference is obvious: Wallerstein goes beyond Marx in relying on the logic of capitalism as a universal key to the workings of the modern world, but he is much less convinced that the capitalist system has had an overall progressive impact on the human condition, and more willing to admit that the outcome of its expected self-destruction remains uncertain. His most succinct survey of the modern epoch[2] makes capitalism virtually synonymous with modern civilization, but lays a very un-Marxian emphasis on its dark sides.

But among contemporary theorists of capitalism, the over-identi-

---

2. Immanuel Wallerstein, *Historical Capitalism, with Capitalist Civilization*, London, Verso, 1995. Hereafter, *HC*.

fication with modernity is more often linked to pro-capitalist views. Jean Baechler, whose two-volume treatise is probably the most sustained defense of capitalism ever produced by a sociologist, rests his case on an overall vision of modernity as a world-historical mutation. In this context, democracy plays the most decisive role. Baechler's claims to this effect are partly based on general assumptions about the primacy of politics and the importance of political order for economic life: "without peace and justice, prosperity is impossible."[3] But there are more specific reasons to insist on the importance of democracy. As a political regime, it amounts to the institutional recognition of human nature as "that of a free, rational, goal-oriented and fallible species."[4] Capitalism is simply the application of this anthropological principle to the economic sphere, and therefore the most adequate and effective form of economic life (some of the particular mechanisms singled out in Baechler's account are discussed later). And since there is no superior principle, a post-capitalist economy is, strictly speaking, a contradiction in terms. But if capitalism is thus an offspring of democracy, rather than the other way around, its unique dynamism overshadows the primary force. The growth and expansion of the capitalist economy were crucial to the spread of modernity beyond its original historical setting. Baechler distinguishes three phases of this process. At first (roughly from the 16th to the mid-18th century), early expressions of trends commonly described as modern do not represent more than an aspect of a much older Western civilization. From the mid-18th to the early 20th century, a rapidly maturing modernity transformed the whole of Western civilization. Finally, the end of the 20th century has seen a definitive global triumph of modernity, most decisively aided by the globalization of a now unchallenged capitalist economy. From this point of view, the shorter 20th century (1914–1991) appears as a 'great parenthesis.' The conspicuous merits of capitalism as a main (albeit not prime) mover of the modernizing process should not be mistaken for ultimate ends. This consideration brings us back to non-economic domains

---

3. Jean Baechler, *Le capitalisme*, vols 1–2. Paris, Gallimard 1995, vol. 2, 418. Hereafter, *LC1, LC2*.
4. *LC2*, 427.

and criteria: capitalism is not only dependent on political premises, but also subordinate to broader civilizational horizons. An economic regime, even the most effective one, belongs to the realm of means, and even the most strategic means to multiple ends – such as the economic and political organization of society – must be distinguished from the genuine ends that lend meaning to life. Familiar examples of the latter can be found in the religious, moral, aesthetic and cognitive domains. For Baechler, the triumph of modernity does not entail any specific configuration of ends: "modernity is not a civilization, but a matrix of virtual civilizations."[5] It represents, in other words, a new framework for the development and cultivation of human diversity, comparable to the breakthrough achieved – on a more limited scale – when historical civilizations began to take shape in the aftermath of the Neolithic revolution. Baechler admits that this is a highly speculative hypothesis, and seems to have become more conscious of its risks in the course of writing. At the beginning of the book,[6] he admits that it will take a few centuries to verify, but at the end,[7] he speaks of a few millennia. In any case, the anthropological implications are clear: the triumph of modernity under the auspices of capitalism makes "humanity itself the actor of human history," and "for the first time, human history has become one."[8] Here the argument becomes more than a little reminiscent of classical Marxism. Obviously, Baechler's 'species being' is not identical with the Marxian one, but it is in the same philosophical category and has a similar historical mission.

Baechler's theoretical perspective is anything but congenial to the present writer; it may, however, be possible to learn some indirect lessons from his work. The underlying affinities with Marx can serve to remind us of a point that will prove important when the discussion moves on to more specific issues. Incompatible interpretations of capitalism are not necessarily unrelated on the level of imaginary premises; the pro-capitalist and the anti-capitalist imagination have more important

---

5. *LC2*, 430.
6. *LC1*, 12.
7. *LC2*, 425.
8. *LC2*, 421–22.

contents in common than the ideological and political conflicts of recent history would suggest. So far, I have dealt with different – and in part antagonistic – ways to theorize an oversized image of capitalism. There have, of course, been attempts to integrate more balanced views into multidimensional theories of modernity (for our purposes, it does not matter whether the theorists in question spoke of capitalism, private enterprise or a market economy). But such approaches are often open to twofold criticism. On the one hand, the dynamics of capitalism are filtered through a rationalizing model which minimizes their revolutionary impact and their discontinuous history; on the other hand, the overall framework imposed on the core patterns of modernity tends to reflect assumptions which draw on perceived or imputed patterns of a capitalist economy. The Parsonian version of modernization theory is a prime example. Parsons sees the economic subsystem of modern societies (based on private enterprise) as an integral and functional part of the 'main pattern,' but at the same time, the features central to his vision of modernity in general – adaptive upgrading and cybernetic control through functional subsystems – bear a strong resemblance to a program for sustainable capitalism: the activism of private enterprise was to be tempered by rational management and enabling state intervention. Since Habermas' revised version of critical theory relies on a modified variant of the Parsonian model, similar problems arise – albeit in more nuanced terms – within its frame of reference. The capitalist economy now appears as a more problematic and potentially disruptive aspect of modernity, but its pathological traits are still only overdoses of the rational ones. Other variations on the same theme – a mutually reductionistic association of capitalism and modernity – have emerged within the broad spectrum of modernization theories. In short, the question of capitalism and its place within the constellation of modernity has proved difficult to pose in adequate terms, let alone to solve in a convincing way.

Defining Capitalism
A brief look at basic concepts will help to clear the ground for a more focused discussion of the problems bequeathed to us by classical and

post-classical theory. But if we follow the lead of the classics in thinking of capitalism as a complex and long-term historical phenomenon whose dynamic is still unfolding with unpredictable effects, definitions of the streamlined kind favored by economists do not seem very useful. It does not throw much light on the workings of historical capitalism to describe it as an economic system based on the free formation of prices and the free ownership of the means of production.[9] The only definitions relevant in the present context are those which open up lines of historical inquiry and remain adaptable to the results of further work in that field. Even within the limits of such approaches, there is room for conflicting interpretations. The above comments on Baechler and Wallerstein should be enough to suggest that a confrontation of their views might prove instructive. I will therefore use a debate between them to pinpoint the main themes of the following reflections.[10] The debate begins with 'a simple question: "what is capitalism?"[11] Baechler proposes a definition in terms of four interconnected features. Capitalism is, to begin with, an economy where all factors of production are subject to specified property rights. Let us note in passing that this does not amount to an equation of capitalism with narrowly understood private property; the emphasis is on the delimitation of property rights, but Baechler's thesis seems compatible with Luhmann's claim that all property is in a basic sense private property, in as much as it separates ownership from non-ownership. Second, capitalism presupposes the allocation of scarce resources through markets, i.e., through the direct or indirect encounters of producers and consumers. The third aspect has to do with the dominant type of economic action: capitalism is an economy of entrepreneurs who take initiatives, make decisions and calculate risks. Finally, the fourth characteristic is

9. Michel Albert, *Capitalism vs. Capitalism*, New York, Four Walls Eight Windows, 1993. It should be added that the concrete analyses contained in this book are more insightful than its stated premises would suggest.
10. Jean Baechler and Immanuel Wallerstein, "L'avenir du capitalism," *Comment peut-on être anti-capitaliste? Revue du M.A.U.S.S* 9 (1, 1997), 13–35. This text is the record of a public encounter that took place in 1996. Hereafter, *AdC*.
11. *AdC*, 14.

– for Baechler – the most important one: capitalism is not simply an economy, but also a 'civilizational condition' *(état de civilisation)*[12] which puts its stamp on cultures and customs. The economic institutions at work (summed up in the first three points) operate within a context which entails the primacy of economic values and an inbuilt tendency to subordinate social activities to the goal of unending economic growth. Capitalism is, as Baechler also notes, synonymous with what Aristotle called the 'chrematistic' mode of life, i.e., the pursuit of wealth for its own sake and the elevation of economic success to an ultimate human end. Wallerstein's response links up with Baechler's fourth point: the orientation towards growth ad infinitum, more precisely the permanent accumulation of capital, is the most important and the only invariant feature of capitalism as an economic system. This unprecedented shift from finite to infinite goals of economic life – and the concomitant drive to impose economic norms on all domains of social life – is the main determinant of all other aspects. Baechler's three institutional components are crucial parts of the capitalist complex, but never alone in the field. Markets cannot guide or coordinate everything, private property rights cannot extend to everything, and (most importantly) "the game is not always open to entrepreneurs."[13] All three factors function in changing combinations with other forces, and the primacy of accumulation can be enforced in ways that relegate them all to more marginal roles, so that the conventional notions of capitalism are no longer applicable. As Wallerstein sees it, the command economies of self-styled socialist states represent the culmination of a more general trend to replace markets, proprietors and entrepreneurs with state-controlled strategies of development, without questioning the imperatives of accumulation. In short, historical capitalism should be analyzed in terms of changing institutional mixtures, rather than paradigmatic models.

Baechler objects that we can recognize the fundamental and irreplaceable role of markets (as well as the other institutions associated with them) without denying that practice always falls short of pure

---

12. *AdC*, 14.
13. *AdC*, 15.

logic. Here he clearly misses Wallerstein's point: it is not a matter of empirical imperfections, but of other specific factors interfering with three supposedly defining features and sometimes gaining strength at their expense. He has more pertinent things to say on the fourth point. The primacy of accumulation is, strictly speaking, only one aspect of a more complex phenomenon. The civilizational core of capitalism is the ethos of 'ever more,' and this also translates into permanent technological progress and the development of new human abilities. But as Wallerstein argues in response (and in line with Baechler's own formulation of the problem), capitalism imposes the prospect of infinite growth and accumulation on more problematic and unpredictable patterns of change. If we synthesize the arguments of both sides, they seem – in this regard – to be converging on a view close to Marx's conception of capitalist goals: the dynamics and results of human development are subsumed under the form of abstract wealth (neither Baechler nor Wallerstein quote Marx in this particular connection, although they agree elsewhere on his seminal contribution to our understanding of capitalism).

At this point, the debate changes track and shifts to historical questions that are less relevant to our present purposes. But the arguments summarized above can serve as pointers to the most central problems of sociological analysis. The views held by the two theorists are instructive in direct and indirect ways: not only on the level of explicit agreement or disagreement, but also with regard to the questions conspicuously neglected or minimized on both sides. There is no dispute about the inbuilt commitment to unlimited growth. Whether the preferred term is accumulation or chrematistics (Baechler's use of the latter word is meant to remind us of Aristotle's pioneering insights), this internal and unending dynamic appears as the most distinctive trait of capitalism, and the workings of core economic institutions must be analyzed in that context, rather than in terms of general economic functions. But as we have seen, closer examination of the trends at work leads to disagreements, and neither side finds it easy to spell out the relationship between the logic of capital and the forces that it releases. At the same time, a shared blind spot invites criticism of both positions: Baechler and Wallerstein are (especially if we take other writings into account) sensitive to the civilizational aspect of capitalism, but disinclined to pursue the more specific question of cultural sources and premises. To put it another way, the notion of a 'spirit of capitalism,' traditionally associated with the very dynamism that they stress above all else, is not important to their respective lines of reasoning. In both cases, the decisive impetus to the capitalist takeoff is supposed to have come from transformations of power structures, rather than any cultural innovations, but the two authors disagree sharply on the specifics of this background. For Baechler, democracy – roughly defined as a contractual relationship between rulers and ruled, and in that sense much older than its revolutionary versions – is the progenitor of capitalism, whereas Wallerstein argues that the modern capitalist system was created by a beleaguered ruling class (the feudal aristocracy of late medieval Europe) in search of new foundations for its social power. Similar considerations apply to the debate on capitalist institutions (Baechler's three driving forces are best understood as institutional factors, although he does not explicitly define them as such). The question of constancy and variety in their relationship to the civilizational dynamics of growth is broached but not posed in adequate terms. Baechler posits a close and invariant connection between the two sides: the synergy of markets, proprietors and entrepreneurs translates into a limitless pursuit of wealth. Wallerstein does not contest the crucial role of the three factors in the successive breakthroughs of historical capitalism (and it goes without saying that they are even more central to its self-image than to its workings); his dissent is limited to the point that they always depend on inputs from less distinctive and less ideologically charged institutions, and may in critical cases be replaced with a different set of means to the same end. The question of historical variations to the structure and interaction of the three key institutions is not raised. And the absence of this problematic becomes even more striking if we note a curious point of convergence between the two approaches. Neither Baechler nor Wallerstein wants to include wage-labor in a general definition of capitalism, but this tacit downgrading of a classical theme (important for both Marx and Weber, albeit in different ways) reflects two very divergent visions of the modern world. Baechler omits wage labor from his list because he sets out to construct a history where capital is much more a central actor than labor, whereas Wallerstein wants to do justice to the experience of societies and populations that fell victim to capitalist expansion, but were not fully assimilated to capitalist forms of organization.

Finally, the question of economic rationality – as an attribute or a legitimizing code of capitalism – is implicit in the controversy between Baechler and Wallerstein, even if it does not come to the fore, and their incompatible answers to it are clearly formulated in other writings. As Castoriadis argues, capitalism was the first social regime to produce an ideology that justified the existing order as an embodiment of rationality;[14] to speak of a social regime may suggest an over-interpretation of the kind criticized above, but if we take the broader context of modernity into account, the capitalist claim to intrinsic and evident rationality appears as a distinctive variation on a more widely shared theme. At the same time, the rationality of capitalism has been an essentially contested notion, and neither the defenders nor the critics agree among themselves. Revised models of economic rationality, more complex than the elementary constructs of neoclassical orthodoxy, have been proposed as better keys to the institutions of capitalism and more adequate accounts of its systemic logic.[15] As for the critics, two main lines of argument can be distinguished. On the one hand, the rationality of capitalism may be accepted as real but partial, and critical analysis can then go on to show

14. Cornelius Castoriadis, "The 'rationality' of capitalism," id., *Figures of the Thinkable*, translated by Helen Arnold, Stanford CA, Stanford University Press, 2007, (*FT*).
15. For example, the paradigm of "transaction cost economics" (Oliver E. Williamson, The *Economic Institutions of Capitalism*, New York, The Free Press, 1985) claims to have found a better way of defending the rationality of capitalist institutions against those who want to explain them in terms of class interest or monopoly power. Transaction costs are "the costs of running the economic system," and economizing on them is the primary rationale of institutions.

that the unbalanced progress of incomplete reason leads to contradictory results. A more comprehensive rationalizing project will, on this view, either abolish capitalism, or at least – in the reformist version – impose the necessary correctives and counterweights. Marx's critique of capitalism was based on half-articulated premises in this vein: within the Marxian tradition, the current known as critical theory has made them most explicit. The other line of criticism leads to a more radical rejection of capitalist claims to and models of rationality: they appear as imaginary constructs, superimposed on a more overtly imaginary stratum (the phantasms of absolute wealth and ever-expanding mastery). This is the view developed – at least up to a point – by Castoriadis after his break with Marxism in the mid-1960s. If we consider Baechler's and Wallerstein's respective positions in light of this background, they seem to represent the very ends of the spectrum. As Baechler sees it, economic rationality and capitalist development are synonymous: if the ultimate test of rationality in the economic sphere is the ability to balance needs and resources, the capitalist economy may be described as the permanent optimization of solutions to this problem. The combination of markets, proprietors and entrepreneurs maximizes the incentives to efficient matching and ongoing exploration of needs and resources. Capitalism is thus a system that allows the economic sphere "to pursue its own rationality to extremes,"[16] and once it has taken shape, a viable alternative is strictly unthinkable. If this results – as we have seen – in an obsessive pursuit of wealth for its own sake that is only the obverse of unhampered economic rationality (analogous symptoms would accompany every type of rationality if it is given free rein). Economic growth as an end in itself is in the long run the most effective way to maximize economic means to other ends, and Baechler seems to rely on some kind of 'cunning of reason' to re-establish the proper order of human values and goals. The closest thing to a concrete scenario for this reorientation is a vision of technical progress culminating in a complete takeover of production by science, thus shifting the main focus of human activities to other fields.[17]

16. *LC1*, 91.
17. *LC2*, 160ff.

Once again, the affinities with Marx (more precisely, the *Grundrisse*) are astonishingly clear. It is ironic that Wallerstein's view on this problem is much farther removed from Marxian perspectives. As he sees it, capitalist rationality is only an ideological mask, an integral part of the universalist model of civilization that the builders and beneficiaries of the world system use to transfigure their power. More specifically, rationality is an ostensible attribute of the scientific culture which "became the fraternal code of the world's accumulators of capital."[18] It is neither (as Marx thought) embodied in a civilizing dynamic at the level of cognitive and technological progress, nor (as Castoriadis would have it) an operative illusion essential to the core institutions and overall coherence of a whole social regime. Here the two sides to the discussion seem to move so far apart that no meaningful exchange is possible.

In Search of a Spirit

I have used the debate between Baechler and Wallerstein to identify themes and problems that go beyond the arguments of both sides. The following reflections focus more directly on these background issues, and it seems appropriate to begin with the question of the 'spirit of capitalism.' This notion stands for a whole set of ideas, variously developed by those who have tried to make sense of modern economic life. A closer examination of the commitment to unending economic growth suggests that a cultural source is needed to inspire and sustain it: the dynamic of accumulation, properly understood, requires an input of meaning in the threefold sense of orientation, justification and motivation (even Marx had a glimpse of this aspect when he contrasted the infinite goals of capitalist production with the self-limiting ones characteristic of pre-capitalist societies). The problem cannot be defused by subsumption under the general rule that all economies and societies depend on cultural premises. Rather, the case of modern capitalism stands out because of specific and paradoxical features which make the point both more obvious and more puzzling than in other contexts. The important work by Luc Boltanski

---

18. *HC*, 84.

and Eve Chiapello[19] begins with comments on this problematic. As the two authors note, capitalism is in some respects an "absurd system";[20] this applies to the protagonists of accumulation, whose strategic goals are disconnected from the satisfaction of needs, as well as to the workforce who has lost control over the conditions and results of its activity. A vehicle of identification and involvement – a spirit, in the complex sense outlined above – must bridge the gap between a finite life-world and a process geared to infinite expansion. But beside the incongruous situations of social actors, described by Boltanski and Chiapello, the spirit of capitalism has to cope with inbuilt ambiguities of the goal-orientations as such. If cultural premises play a role in capitalist dynamics, it is a peculiarly self-disguising or self-suppressing one: not only are the cultural inputs overshadowed by a heightened autonomy of the economic sphere, but the economic value-orientations themselves are expressed in a symbol of abstract wealth. Capitalist development is inconceivable without a comprehensive monetarization of economic and social life. On the other hand, the accumulation of capital presupposes scientific and technological progress, and is thus dependent on a pursuit of rational mastery in domains governed by their own logic. The institutionalization of research and innovation is an essential part of the broader cultural context of capitalism, but the spirit of capitalism combines the capacity to draw on such lateral sources with the compulsion to treat them as means to the end of self-legitimating growth. In short, the reasons why capitalism needs a spirit have to do with problems of mobilization for counterintuitive and contestable purposes. But different definitions of the problems lead to different interpretations of the spirit.

Before going on to consider some seminal statements on this subject, it may be useful to outline a framework for classification and comparison. The Hegelian distinction between absolute, objective and subjective spirit can – with appropriate modifications – be used to map the field of forces involved in the making of a spirit of capitalism. In

19. Luc Boltanski and Eve Chiapello, *Le nouvel esprit du capitalisme*, Paris, Gallimard, 1999. Hereafter, *NEC*.
20. *NEC*, 41.

the present context, the domain of the absolute spirit encompasses not only religious and philosophical world views, but also doctrines of a secular and self-styled scientific type. The objective spirit is embodied in institutions, and particular attention must be paid to "the spirit that lives in the economy and creates its forms,"[21] i.e., the immanent meanings of economic structures and activities. Finally, the category of the subjective spirit relates to questions about the motivations and value-orientations of authors who initiate or maintain trends of capitalist development. This preliminary sketch of the problematic throws some light on classical and contemporary debates. The most familiar and influential analysis of the spirit of capitalism – the 'Weber thesis,' first formulated in *The Protestant Ethic* and inconclusively reworked in later writings – was not only focused on a shortcut between the absolute and the subjective spirit, but was also based on unduly restricted views of the two dimensions that it wanted to connect.

The absolute spirit was represented by a religious culture – more specifically, a religious doctrine – which imposed or necessitated (Weber's account of the interconnection wavered between logical and psychological points of view) a particularly work- and-achievement-oriented way of life; the paragons of the subjective spirit were capitalist pioneers in acute conflict with a traditionalist environment. As a result of Weber's emphasis on direct links between these two factors, the institutional components – core economic institutions as well as the broader complex in which they are embedded – are left out of the picture. But as the argument unfolds, the objective spirit returns in a somewhat degraded guise. The mechanisms of the mature capitalist economy, so constraining that they can supposedly operate without a sustaining ethos or belief, are obviously a case of 'petrified spirit' in the sense which Weber later applied to modern bureaucracy, and a petrified spirit is still a spirit of sorts. It is, of course, not being suggested that this was Weber's last word on the subject. In later writings, he examined institutional forms and

---

21. Otto Hintze, "Der moderne Kapitalismus als historisches Individuum. Ein kritischer Bericht über Sombarts Werk," in *Sombarts Moderner Kapitalismus. Materialien zur Kritik und Rezeption*, edited by Bernhard von Brocke, München, DTV, 1987, 328.

preconditions of modern capitalism from various angles, and the brief analysis of the economic sphere as one of the 'world orders' in multiple mutual conflict can be read in terms of an objective spirit of capitalism (in that sense, it is part of an unfinished theory of modern socio-cultural differentiation). But the insights gained in the course of this work were never synthesized, and reconstructions of Weber's economic sociology are less advanced than those which focus on his sociology of religion and politics.[22] In the absence of a systematic and acknowledged reformulation of its thesis, the *Protestant Ethic* has had a disproportionate impact on later discussions.[23]

Werner Sombart's massive treatise on modern capitalism, much less discussed than Weber's work (although Sombart made no secret of his ambition to be alone with Marx in a league that left Weber far behind), may be seen as an attempt to bring the objective spirit back in. At first sight, Sombart's references to the 'human type' that shapes modern capitalism might suggest a focus on the subjective side. But the main thrust of the argument has to do with institutionalized orientations, and more particularly with those embodied in the capitalist enterprise. Sombart describes the latter as an "objective monster" (*sachliches Ungeheuer*), endowed with a driving force and an unvarying goal-orientation that enable it to make history on a grand scale.[24] Uniformity and continuity on this level are, as he notes, compatible with a vast range of motives – from the will to power to feelings of duty and loyalty to a larger community.

---

22. The most systematic overview is Richard Swedberg, *Max Weber and the Idea of Economic Sociology,* Princeton, Princeton University Press, 1998. For an attempt to systematize the results of Weber's later reflections on capitalism, see Randall Collins "Weber's last theory of Capitalism," id. *Weberian Sociological Theory*, Cambridge, Cambridge University Press, 1986. But to speak of "Weber's last theory of capitalism" is to suggest a more closed model than Weber ever developed, and Collins's account of it is based on a text (the *General Economic History*) which must be regarded as a somewhat less authentic source than the main works.

23. Simmel's *Philosophy of Money* can, of course, be seen – among other things – as a pioneering analysis of the objective spirit of monetary institutions. But Simmel's reluctance to theorize capitalism as such limits the scope of his analyses.

24. Werner Sombart, *Der moderne Kapitalismus,* Vol I–III, München, DTV, v. III, pt.1, 36.

When he goes on to stress the role of the entrepreneur as an economic leader *(Wirtschaftsführer)*, the phenomenon in question is therefore best understood as an institutional complement to the enterprise, rather than in psychological terms. As for the spirit that animates both the enterprise and the entrepreneur, Sombart stresses its composite and double-edged character: it combines "the drive towards infinity ... , the limitlessness of aims," with "cool rational deliberation."[25]

There can be no complete fusion or final union of the two trends, but their joint dynamic has made modern capitalism an exceptional episode in human history. There is no denying that Sombart broke new ground with this account of the spirit of capitalism, but he analyzed it from an angle that soon came to seem obsolete and mixed his insights with assumptions of a less defensible kind. The idea of an infinite dynamic was strangely out of tune with the claim that the trajectory of 'high capitalism' had come to an end in 1919, and that developments after World War I prefigured the replacement of capitalism by a more normative and political order; Sombart's temporary sympathies for National Socialism – which he saw as a promise of a viable post-capitalist order – did no credit to his work. In retrospect, however, his interpretation of capitalism stands out as one of the landmarks in a long-running debate.

This brief summary of classical sources should give some idea of the background to Boltanski and Chiapello's reformulation of the problem. A closer examination of their argument should begin with the explicit moves beyond Weber. The first step is a redefinition of the spirit of capitalism in more abstract terms: contrary to Weber's emphasis on the substantive content of a particular ethos, the focus shifts to a form – a cultural logic capable of dignifying and justifying the dynamic of accumulation – which can be filled with different contents in the course of capitalist development and in response to changing ways of accumulating profit.[26] From this point of view, two durable but dissimilar patterns – both subject to variations in local and historical contexts – exemplify the cultural ambiguity of capitalism. The bourgeois-entrepreneurial spirit,

25. *Der moderne Kapitalismus*, 25.
26. *NEC*, 47.

dominant in the late 19th – and early 20th – century world (Sombart is quoted as a portraitist of its most heroic version) gave way to the managerial one, often associated with 'organization man', which reached full maturity during the middle decades of the 20th century. The question to which Boltanski and Chiapello devote much of their work concerns the third spirit of capitalism: to what extent is the current cult of mobility, flexibility and de-centered networks indicative of changes in the cultural frame of accumulation?

But there is another side to the critique of Weber. The spirit of capitalism is not only reinterpreted with a view to understanding its mutations; it also acquires a legitimizing role and a public dimension that did not figure in Weber's discussion. Here Boltanski and Chiapello draw on Albert Hirschman's well-known analysis of 'political arguments for capitalism' in early modern Europe, but they formalize and generalize Hirschman's thesis in much the same way as the Weberian one. The articulation and stabilization of motivating visions would not be possible without public justification, and this condition can only be satisfied through reference to 'common worlds' or 'orders of worth' which provide the criteria of validity.[27] Several such worlds can be distinguished, without any claim to close the list; references to the civic world, the market world and the industrial world are of particular importance in modern times, but as Boltanski and Chiapello go on to argue, contemporary trends point to a world of projects' emerging as a legitimizing framework *sui generis*. In one way or another, the contexts of justification also impose constraints and correctives on the dynamic of accumulation: they temper the pure logic of capitalism with broadly understood norms of social justice.

This link to conceptions of justice entails a third modification of the Weberian view. The spirit and the critique of capitalism now appear as closely interconnected and mutually receptive. Critical responses to capitalism have accompanied its progress from the very beginning; the more moderate ones among them can draw on pre-established frameworks of legitimization, in as much as practices are bound to lag

---

27. Luc Boltanski and Laurent Thevenot "The Sociology of Critical Capacity," *European Journal of Social Theory* 2(3), 359–78.

behind principles, but a more radical opposition to capitalism as an economic and social regime has also been a salient part of modern thought and culture. Despite its subjective distance from the existing order, the radical critique can affect capitalist development in a number of ways. It may find expression in strategies and programs of historical actors, and thus give rise to more far-reaching constraints than those which follow directly from the spirit of capitalism; its perceived challenge to the foundations of capitalism can prompt institutional and organizational shifts with the aim of disarming it; but elements of radical critique can also be incorporated into the self-reproducing structures of capitalism and used to upgrade their performance.

These ambiguous relations between the capitalist order and its adversaries will be easier to understand if we reconsider the idea of critique. Distinctions between types and themes of critical discourse are central to Boltanski and Chiapello's argument, and changing patterns of interaction between the spirit, the practice and the critique of capitalism play a key role in their account of recent changes. Four main reasons or motives for rejecting capitalism have been invoked by critics during the last two centuries. The capitalist economy appears as a "source of *disenchantment* and *inauthenticity*" in regard to various aspects or whole forms of life; as a "source of *oppression*, inasmuch as it is opposed to the liberty, autonomy and creativity of human beings"; as a "source of *misery* among the workers and of *inequalities* far greater than anything known in the past"; and, finally, as a "source of *opportunism* and *egoism*," and thus destructive of social solidarity.[28] When it comes to the articulation and combination of these themes, two different models of critique dominate the field: an *aesthetic* one, primarily based on a synthesis of the first two themes (Baudelaire is mentioned as one of its founding fathers), and a *social* one, focused on the latter two.

Boltanski and Chiapello then go on to argue that the reinvigorated capitalism of the late 20th century owes much of its strength and confidence to a massive absorption of the aesthetic critique. The details of that claim are beyond the scope of this article. Our main concern

28. *NEC*, 82.

is the more basic question of the spirit of capitalism and its multiple embodiments. Boltanski and Chiapello pose this problem in a way that seems to perpetuate some of the difficulties noted above. To clarify this point, it should first be noted that the spirit of capitalism is explicitly identified with ideology in a broad sense, much closer to Louis Dumont than to Karl Marx: an ideology is a "set of shared beliefs, inscribed in institutions, involved in actions and thus anchored in reality."[29] Here the institutional dimension seems to be taken into account. But the next step raises new doubts. A general and relatively stable background ideology, based on utilitarian premises and backed up by the scientific pretensions of economics, is distinguished from the more variable operative ideologies that serve to motivate key economic actors, especially the managerial cadres.[30] At this point, the institutional level is sidelined; to use the Hegelian model again, a combination of the absolute and the subjective spirit obscures the role of the objective spirit. This does not mean that Boltanski and Chiapello make no use of institutional analysis.

On the contrary, extensive discussions of changes to industrial relations and of the "deconstruction of the world of labour"[31] throw new light on the institutional transformations of contemporary capitalism. But the links between these concrete analyses and the interpretation of the spirit of capitalism leave something to be desired. The conceptual framework is, in other words, not adequately tailored to the task of synthesizing cultural and institutional perspectives. A further indication of this can be seen in the reference to a triangular interaction among "capitalism, the spirit of capitalism, and critique";[32] the logic of this statement is to posit an institutional core of capitalism as analytically separable from its cultural and countercultural contexts. In consequence, the book makes no attempt to link the question of the spirit of capitalism to that of variety in institutional contexts and trajectories.

It thus fails to confront the most challenging issue in the current debate

29. *NEC*, 35.
30. *NEC*, 47–54.
31. *NEC*, 291–344.
32. *NEC*, 73.

on capitalism: to what extent can different cultural legacies and potentials still translate into significantly different patterns and possibilities of capitalist development?

Capitalism and Autonomy

As the above discussion should show, both the idea of and the controversy about the spirit of capitalism are alive and well: not only the constitutive meaning, but also the social and historical contexts of the modern capitalist ethos can still be analyzed from new angles. Given this background (and with regard to persisting difficulties in locating the spirit), it may prove useful to revisit a very distinctive but not widely debated approach to the problems at issue. Boltanski and Chiapello make only one reference to the work of Cornelius Castoriadis;[33] they quote his analysis of capitalism as a self-contradictory form of social organization, striving to mobilize and at the same time to demobilize the wage-earners, and seem to equate it with their own view of the paradoxes inherent in harnessing social actors to capitalist accumulation. This point is, however, only one aspect of a broader problematic. Castoriadis's break with the Marxist conception of history led him to reinterpret modern capitalism with a stronger emphasis on its cultural sources, and to single out – as mentioned above – the imaginary signification of ever-expanding rational mastery as the core meaning embodied in capitalist institutions. Although he did not explicitly link up with earlier work on the spirit of capitalism, his thesis is best understood as a new twist to that tradition, and its main focus is on the domain of the objective spirit (since the perceived need to rethink institutions had been central to Castoriadis's whole critique of Marxism, this was the most obvious direction to take). For this line of argument to be plausible, a prior fusion of Marxian and Weberian insights was required. Before taking the decisive step beyond historical materialism, Castoriadis had come to see modern capitalism as characterized by a bureaucratizing dynamic whose inbuilt conflicts were in the long run more important than the contradictions stressed by

---

33. *NEC*, 678, n. 54.

traditional Marxism. Similarly, his analysis of the modern counterweight to capitalism – the vision of autonomy – reflected a political response to the new conditions created by advancing bureaucratization. The goals previously pursued in the name of socialism were to be redefined in the spirit of a radical democracy whose principles clashed most directly with those of bureaucratic domination, but could be invoked to condemn an unthinking pursuit of mastery as well as the resultant subordination of individual and collective action to the imperatives of endless growth. A self-limiting conception of human development had become essential to a sustainable anti-capitalist project.

It has been objected (with good reasons) that the stark contrast between capitalism and autonomy does not do justice to the complex interconnections and transformations of modern social structures.[34] The interpretation of modernity in terms of an open, radical and unequivocal central conflict can perhaps be seen as a legacy from Castoriadis's activist phase, left unquestioned despite the shift to a more fundamental criticism of 'inherited ways of thinking' but in need of revision if the potential of his later work is to be fully realized. Critical reflections must, however, begin with Castoriadis's own indications of a more nuanced view; here we must concentrate on the question of capitalism and only deal with autonomy to the extent that its changing meanings affect the patterns or visions of capitalist development. A late essay on the 'rationality' of capitalism, written in 1996 and included in a posthumously published collection,[35] would seem to be the most promising starting point for further discussion.

The phantasm of unlimited rational mastery still appears as the core of the spirit of capitalism; but both its force and its novelty are easier to grasp if we also understand it as a transformation of older and deeper foundations. Aspirations to omnipotence, prior to all social projects, are inherent in the 'singular psyche.' At the social level, they translate

---

34. See especially Peter Wagner, "Modernity, capitalism and critique," *Thesis Eleven* 66 (2001), 1–31.

35. English translation: Cornelius Castoriadis, "The 'Rationality' of Capitalism," id., *FT*, 47–70.

into a push for mastery, and in pre-capitalist societies, conquest is the most conspicuous outlet. The capitalist vision of mastery differs from pre-modern ones in several significant ways. More specifically, it involves changes of meaning and direction in external as well as internal contexts. On the one hand, a permanent effort to extend and intensify social control over nature – accompanied by phantasms of complete domination – generates a transformative dynamic unknown to earlier societies. On the other hand, an in-depth drive to enhance the efficiency of human action takes the particular form of maximizing output and minimizing costs; a process of economic rationalization, tied to imaginary horizons but none the less operative for that, is thus set in motion and sustained throughout successive historical phases. Both the extensive and the intensive pursuit of mastery give rise to mobilizing strategies that draw other fields of social life into the orbit of accumulation.

The spirit of capitalism, interpreted as a specific mixture of imagination, power and rationality, develops in close conjunction with parallel trends in other domains. Most obviously, it interacts with and depends on the dynamics of technological innovation, which in turn becomes progressively more intertwined with the growth of scientific knowledge. The process that culminates in contemporary 'technoscience' is both an enabling condition and an internal imperative of capitalist development. Its enduring momentum reflects the permanent drive for rational mastery, but the successive waves of inventive change shape the course of economic history: they add an element of discontinuity and uncertainty to the dynamic of accumulation. Although Castoriadis did not develop his ideas in this context, they are relevant to it. As recent work on the history of modern technology has shown, major transformations of the productive and organizational apparatus are inseparable from interpretive constructs which can grow into mobilizing myths, and it seems appropriate to treat them as crystallizations of the capitalist magma. Imaginary patterns of all-round reorientation are thus superimposed on the more basic vision of rational mastery.

Another accompanying and sustaining process is the construction of the modern state. During the early modern period, the efforts of competing states to build more effective fiscal, administrative and military machines provided both models and incentives for capitalist development. As in the case of economic change, it must be added that the state-centered quest for mastery finds expression in the rise and fall of successive myths. If there was a 'myth of absolutism,'[36] it was not the last of its kind; the most recent invention on offer may be the myth of the 'virtual state'[37] equipped with the skills and mindful of the restraints needed to function as a facilitator for global capital. But state building also entails the formation of more durable cultural frameworks. As Castoriadis notes, the countries that pioneered modern transformations in economic and political fields were also the first nation-states. The demarcation and regulation of a national space is an integral part of the new social imaginary. Finally, the whole process hinges on an "anthropological transformation,"[38] a restructuring of human approaches and attitudes to the world; for Castoriadis, the hegemony of *homo oeconomicus* – and, in more general terms, the paradigm of *homo computans* — is the most massive and visible aspect of this reorientation, but an anthropological interpretation of modernity would also have to deal with complementary developments in other directions.

On the other hand, the modern capitalist project and its historical companions came to the fore in an environment marked by social conflict, and more precisely by conflicts of the radical kind which led to explicit "questioning of the established order."[39] The argument summarized here does not go beyond a brief allusion to this other side of the modern constellation, but Castoriadis had analyzed it at length in earlier writings. As he saw it, the modern counterweight to capitalism was the vision of autonomy; in a broad sense, this involved growing capacities for self-questioning and demands for self-determination in various domains of

36. Nicholas Henshall, *The Myth of Absolutism: Change and Continuity in Early European Monarchy*, London, Longman, 1992.
37. Richard Rosecrance, *The Rise of the Virtual State*, New York, Basic Books, 1999.
38. *FT*, 55.
39. *FT*, 55.

social life, but the most challenging version of autonomy is a project of radical and comprehensive democracy that would invalidate the logic of capitalism. In that sense, the idea of autonomy is incompatible with the unquestioning pursuit of wealth and power, as well as with the inequalities and divisions that result from capitalist development; it entails a revival of political and cultural values against the primacy of economic ones; and it presupposes an ethos of self-limitation that is fundamentally at odds with the spirit of capitalism. As noted above, the stark dichotomy of capitalism and autonomy is out of tune with the more complex and nuanced image of modernity that is adumbrated in Castoriadis's later writings. The underlying problem has to do with unfinished and unequally developed shifts in theoretical perspectives: when Castoriadis tried to legitimize radical democracy – seen as an anti-capitalist and post-socialist option – by deducing it from one of the alternative logics of modernity, he was striving to maintain the essentials of a political project in spite of a philosophical mutation which could not but affect all basic concepts and premises.

The idea of an alternative modernity, long overshadowed by a stronger rival but prefigured from the High Middle Ages onwards and still perceived as a possible future, is a new variation – albeit a markedly self-limiting one – on the theme of transparent meaning in history, and Castoriadis was at the same time rethinking the 'question of the social-historical' in ways that problematized all determinations of meaning. The implications of the latter turn will become clearer if we reconsider the vision of autonomy in its capacity as an imaginary signification, rather than a self-defining project. From this point of view, it appears as a disputed field of rival interpretations.

If the signification of autonomy is inherently ambiguous, it becomes by the same token more difficult to distinguish from the other component of the modern imaginary: the phantasm of rational mastery in unending progress, supposedly central to the workings of capitalism. Castoriadis admits that this boundary is blurred when he refers to the "mutual contamination and interpenetration" of the two significations, but he never discusses the specific figures of autonomy that take shape within a capitalist framework. The whole debate on the spirit of capitalism, not least the new line of argument developed by Boltanski and Chiapello, suggests that such partial fusions of the two imaginary sources are the rule rather than the exception. Both entrepreneurial and managerial models of action, up to and including their recent variants, may be seen as stylizing and mobilizing images of autonomy. Claims to extend the scope of autonomy for broader social strata can be based on genuine advance of individual freedom, brought about by the monetarization of economic life.[40] Invocations of the consumer's freedom to choose represent another side of the same process. In short, capitalist development involves the construction and diffusion of self-interpretations which are at least in part anchored to the signification of autonomy; although they are at best selective projections of capitalist practices, their institutional and ideological impact is evident in a variety of ways. A plausible critique of capitalism can therefore only focus on one-sided or leveling definitions of individual autonomy and obstacles to translation into collective projects.

But if the multiple meanings of autonomy are less separable from the 'total social phenomenon' of capitalism than Castoriadis would have it, the very core of the capitalist imaginary is also more complex. The accumulation of abstract wealth – and the pursuit of the phantasm of absolute wealth – is closely linked but not reducible to the vision of rational mastery. Castoriadis notes this point in passing,[41] but argues that 'unlimited acquisition,' or 'chrematistics' in the Aristotelian sense, acquires a new meaning in the capitalist universe: it is now predicated on development, expansion, and a permanent transformation of the productive forces. However, it must be added that the new constellation does not only place the pursuit of wealth for its own sake on a new basis; rather, the very meaning of wealth is transformed. When money

40. This is a key theme in Georg Simmel's *Philosophie des Geldes*, Berlin 1900/1907. In English, *The Philosophy of Money*, third enlarged edition, London/New York, Routledge, 2004.
41. Cornelius Castoriadis, *Political and Social Writings*, vol. 3, translated and edited by David Ames Curtis, Minneapolis, University of Minnesota Press, 1993, 180.

functions as capital, it opens up horizons that can be taken to promise an unlimited satisfaction of needs, but also an unlimited appropriation of natural resources and human capacities. Self-perpetuating accumulation transforms the phantasm of unlimited acquisition into an operative mechanism, while at the same time enhancing its imaginary reach. This part of the capitalist pattern should be given its due as a distinct and fundamental historical force. The new form of wealth also represents a specific modality of power: a potential command over an expanding spectrum of activities and abilities.[42] The dynamic of abstract economic power manifests itself in the combinations of commercial, financial, and productive uses, which – as Braudel has shown convincingly – have been characteristic of capitalism from pre-modern times. Moreover, the association with state power – subject to historical variations but often of crucial importance – is conducive to a more sweeping vision of abstract power, parallel to abstract wealth.

This analysis of the capitalist imaginary may throw some light on its self-contesting potential. It is a commonplace that the historical twists and turns of capitalism have been accompanied by anti-capitalist currents; Baechler even suggests that anti-capitalism has, historically speaking, been the "most important expression of capitalism ... because it can have political consequences which go beyond the economic context."[43] His interpretation of anti-capitalist trends, however, makes them look more like regressive reactions than expressions. The idea of a constitutive but at the same time trans-institutional imaginary is a better key to the complex interplay of capitalism and its antagonists, and to the double-edged logic that aligns anti-capitalist projects with 'capitalist countercultures.'[44] The capitalist vision of wealth is ambiguous enough to be reinterpreted as a promise of complete fulfillment of human needs, and thus as a rationale

42. This meaning of money as *Vermögen* in Simmel's sense is discussed extensively in Christoph Deutschmann's writings; see especially *Die Verheissung des absoluten Reichtums: Zur religiösen Natur des Kapitalismus*, Frankfurt/Main, Campus Verlag, 2001.
43. *LC2*, 268.
44. Zygmunt Bauman has used this term to describe the Marxist tradition.

for replacing capitalism with an economic order more capable of keeping the promise; this was the line Marx was taking when he spoke of Communism as a way to release the springs of cooperative wealth. When the ostensibly anti-capitalist regimes that claimed to be on the path to affluence lost their credibility, they proved particularly vulnerable to comparison with the preexisting and more resilient version of the project. As for the progress and prospect of rational mastery, the underlying logic can be articulated in more abstract terms and turned against the perceived inability of capitalism to match its own standards. The lack of rational control over social life, notwithstanding an ongoing rational conquest of nature, became a key issue for major currents of the socialist tradition and – at a later stage – a reason for invidious comparison with 'real socialism.' The self-image of the Soviet model centered on its claim to have achieved rational mastery over the essentials of social organization; in practice, it served to legitimize a command economy that could abolish capitalist institutions but was from the outset firmly tied to the capitalist imaginary.

Unity and Diversity

As we have seen, Castoriadis's ideas open up new horizons for the debate on the spirit of capitalism. A critical reconstruction of his arguments is easily compatible with a historical typology of successive 'spirits': they can, among other things, be seen as changing configurations of autonomy, mastery and chrematistics. More importantly, Castoriadis's approach allows us to link the question of historical change to that of internal tensions between different components of the spirit of capitalism. The mutually irreducible imaginary significations and the correspondingly distinctive contexts of rationalization can give rise to varying trajectories and uneven dynamics of development. Another differentiating factor is the interaction with other forces (such as the modern state) which draw on the same cultural and anthropological sources. Finally, the imaginary horizons of capitalist development also constitute an interpretive framework for ideologies and movements which set out to develop anti-capitalist alternatives. In that sense, the spirit of capitalism is not only capable of learning from critique, but also of imposing premises that undermine or vitiate critical intentions. It now remains to be seen whether this redefinition of an elusive but indispensable concept can be related to more specific issues. In particular, our reflections on the spirit of capitalism might have some bearing on the widely debated and seemingly more down-to-earth question of the varieties of capitalism. But to get the latter problem into perspective, two very different approaches to it must be distinguished; we can then go on to consider some less familiar lines of reasoning that would help to bridge the gap between them and bring the debate into contact with broader theoretical horizons.

In classical sociological theory, the question of types, varieties or models of capitalism was raised most explicitly by Max Weber. But two separate outlines of this problematic, both linked to other themes in the last phase of his work, show how uneven and fragmentary the whole discussion still was. On the one hand, the introduction to his collected essays on the sociology of religion distinguishes capitalism – in the sense of a regular and more or less regularized pursuit of gain – from the omnipresent acquisitive impulse, and then goes on to define modern capitalism in terms of a more thoroughgoing rationalization, most evident in industrial organization attuned to a regular market. A noteworthy aspect of this typology is the limited reference to monetary wealth as such. Weber mentions it as an object of the acquisitive impulse and includes the "adaptation of economic action to a comparison of money income with money expenses"[45] in the general definition of capitalism, but when he sets the modern version of capitalism apart from traditional ones, he does not discuss the all-round and in-depth monetarization of social life. On the other hand, the analysis of basic concepts in the first part of *Economy and Society* lists six types of capitalism as a pattern of economic action. They range from the financing of political or military action for the purpose of monetary gain to the pursuit of profit through purely economic activity, and from investment in industrial production

45. Max Weber, The *Protestant Ethic and the Spirit of Capitalism*, London, Unwin University Books 1968, 19.

to speculation in the financial sphere. No comparable attempt is made to follow the structural ramifications of each type, but as the most detailed analysis of this argument has shown,[46] some implicit connections between the micro-dimension and the institutional one can be traced.

In particular, the two types that Weber singles out as most rational and most characteristic of the modern West – industrial and financial capitalism – are linked to a correspondingly distinctive set of institutions. At this point, the conceptual scheme converges with the historical perspective of the introduction to his collected essays, quoted above. Weber's initial interpretation of the spirit of capitalism can then be read as a reconstruction of the cultural sources that fuelled the rise of rational capitalism from a subaltern to a dominant position.

The other approach – now the main line of theorizing about varieties of capitalism – is more directly concerned with contemporary than historical variations and with geo-economic realities rather than general typologies of economic action or outlook; but the analyses in this vein could occasionally draw on Weberian distinctions to describe the orientations of economic elites or regimes.[47] The starting point, however, tends to be a comparison of different settings for the operation of similar but not self-contained structures. Although core institutions of capitalism are by definition based on some invariant ground rules, their dynamic interconnections and their relations to the social context vary in significant ways. A strong tendency to view this problematic from a functionalist angle is reflected in the widespread use of terms like 'governance' or 'coordination' to denote the patterns of overall integration. Those who argue for a stronger emphasis on inbuilt tensions and divisions can draw on Marxian ideas without reverting to Marxist scenarios of crisis and collapse; in particular, the regulationist school has preserved the insight

---

46. Richard Swedberg, *Max Weber's Sociology of Capitalisms*, Working Paper Series, Work–Organization–Economy, no. 65, Stockholm University, Department of Sociology, 1999 (*MWSC*).

47. See for example Marco Orrù, "The Institutionalist Analysis of Capitalist Economies," in *The Economic Organization of East Asian Capitalism*, edited by Nicole Woolsey-Biggart and Gary G. Hamilton, Thousand Oaks, Sage, 1997.

that the combination of market structures with the power structure of the capital-labor nexus is a source of structural problems as well as social conflicts, and that the stabilizing frameworks imposed on this constellation depend on a broader context of social forces and institutional formations. A key part of the Marxian paradigm can thus be put to analytical and comparative uses of a kind incompatible with Marxist orthodoxy. On the other hand, critics of a supposedly structuralist bias in comparative studies advocate an 'actor-centered' approach, with particular reference to the firm as a principal but not sole strategic actor.[48]

The more systematic studies of divergent capitalisms tend to focus on complex institutional patterns, rather than organizational or strategic models. Institutionalist analyses inevitably lead to a stronger emphasis on historical backgrounds and path-dependent developments. The typologies that grow out of such comparisons begin with national versions of capitalism (the nation-state is still the most obvious frame of reference for analyses of macroeconomic alternatives). But they usually go on to aggregate national cases into more comprehensive categories. The results may be formulated in terms of contrasting general principles, such as those of liberal capitalism or trust based capitalism,[49] or regional configurations such as the Anglo-American, Nordic, 'Rhineland' and East Asian types. A less developed but particularly promising variant of this approach is the attempt to relate patterns of capitalist development to civilizational contexts.[50] Civilizational theory is, however, at best a paradigm in the making, and this is one of its least explored fields of application. To avoid the short-circuitings that characterize some of the work on this subject, a few open questions and possible misunderstandings should be noted.

---

48. Peter Hall and David Soskice, *Varieties of Capitalism*, Oxford, Oxford University Press, 2001.

49. David Coates, *Models of Capitalism: Growth and Stagnation in the Modern Era*, Cambridge, Polity Press, 2000.

50. E.g. Shmuel N. Eisenstadt, *Japanese Civilization*, Chicago, Chicago University Press, 1996, 54–64 and Gary G. Hamilton, "Civilizations and the Organization of Economies" in *The Handbook of Economic Sociology*, edited by Neil J. Smelser and Richard Swedberg, Princeton, Princeton University Press, 1994.

First and foremost, the civilizational perspective must not be equated with the claim that basic cultural patterns or premises translate directly into economic structures. Such arguments have often proved open to telling criticism. But from the civilizational point of view, there is no a priori reason to assume that a direct and one-sided impact of culture on the economic sphere is more important than the indirect role that culture can play in releasing the more or less autonomous dynamic of political and economic forces. The most insightful civilizational analyses have dealt with complex interactions of the latter kind; it seems impossible to conceive of civilizational theory without a strong emphasis on cultural orientations, but the relative weight of their direct and indirect effects may vary from case to case.

A second point is closely connected to this question. Civilizational influences on capitalism should, more precisely, be analyzed in relation to capitalist development, and this poses the more general problem of civilizing processes. Research in that field – most notably the work of Norbert Elias and his disciples – has thrown light on links between economic transformations and other long-term processes, especially those of state formation, but the whole problematic has yet to be fully integrated into the agenda of a pluralistic civilizational theory. The third issue has to do with the specific input of civilizational factors: they may give rise to variations in the structure of key capitalist institutions as such, or be more relevant to their mode of 'embeddedness' in social contexts and their interconnections with state structures.

The details of these effects vary not only from case to case, but also from one phase to another within the same civilizational framework: for example, the civilizational imprint on core components of Japanese capitalism seems particularly pronounced, but it is also clear that the institutions in question reflect a reactivation of indigenous patterns after a more imitative phase. Finally, the combined effects of intra-civilizational dynamics and inter-civilizational encounters vary across the spectrum of social life, and their respective roles in capitalist development have yet to be clarified.

To conclude this discussion, I will turn to a major landmark in the debate on capitalism, widely recognized as such but still very inadequately understood in theoretical terms. Fernand Braudel's historical analysis of capitalism, market economy, and material civilization[51] touches upon a vast range of interpretive issues; the main question to be discussed here is whether it can help to clarify the connection between the spirit of capitalism (with due emphasis on the assumption of unity or at least narrative continuity inherent in that notion) and the plurality of historical capitalisms.

This problematic is not a high priority for those who draw on Braudel to develop neo-Marxist models of modern or premodern world economies (e.g. Immanuel Wallerstein and Andre Gunder Frank), but Weberian connections may bring it into clearer focus. "What characterizes Weber's history of capitalism is, first of all, that he saw capitalism as being several thousand years old and, secondly, that it had existed in many different forms".[52] This long-term perspective did not prevent Weber from underlining the new meanings that capitalism acquired in the modern context, as well as its unique impact on the modern transformation *in toto*. Braudel's approach is perhaps best understood as a radicalization of Weber's macro-historical view, and this move beyond the classical horizon may also throw new light on the modern trajectories of capitalism (Weber's stress on the unique and irresistible dynamic of western capitalism made him less interested in diversity at that level).

Braudel gives a more insightful twist to the multi-millennial genealogy when he argues that "a potential capitalism emerges at the beginning of macrohistory and develops and perpetuates itself for centuries".[53] The macro-history *(grande histoire)* in question is the process that begins with the rise of civilization in the singular and its variants in the plural;

51. Fernand Braudel, *Civilisation matérielle, économie et capitalisme*, vols 1–3. Paris, Armand Colin 1979. Hereafter *CM1, CM2,* and *CM3*.
52. Richard Swedberg, *Max Weber and the Idea of Economic Sociology*, Princeton, Princeton University Press, 1998, 9.
53. *CM3*, 532 (translated by the author, as are all further quotations from this source).

capitalism is, from this point of view, a possibility opened up and always to some degree realized by the self-diversifying dynamic of civilizing processes. Both its embeddedness and its distinctive potential are thus emphasized more strongly than in Weber's work. The plurality of capitalisms is also reinterpreted in a more specific vein. A certain ability to combine and alternate activities in different domains – commerce, finance, manufacture, agriculture and transport – is characteristic of the capitalist sector well before the industrial revolution. The notion of separate forms of capital or capitalism, succeeding or coexisting with each other, is therefore misleading: even if the social context imposes strict limits on in-depth development, multiple and mutually reinforcing modes are a defining feature of capitalism as such. This reflexive side to the plurality of capitalisms is one of Braudel's main themes: "it is the fact of having the means to create a strategy and the means to change it that makes capitalism superior".[54] Although he is reluctant to speak of a spirit of capitalism (he tends to equate this notion with a mentality fully embodied in representative individuals, and hence to doubt its relevance), the emphasis on inbuilt reflexivity suggests a way to redefine it with primary reference to the objective spirit, and Braudel admits as much when he cautions against the misunderstanding that capitalism is all material or all social).[55]

If an institutionalized spirit is at work in the recurrent metamorphoses that maintain capitalism as a going concern, its logic and long-term implications emerge most clearly in the domain that functions as the prime outlet for capitalism throughout its pre-modern history. For Braudel, "capitalism is at home in the sphere of circulation,"[56] and most of all in long-distance trade. The latter field provides the most rewarding opportunities for profit making and the most suitable environment for capitalist attitudes to economic life. Moreover, it exemplifies the ambiguous relationship between capitalism and competition. Capitalism is rooted in and remains dependent on a broader market economy, but

54. *CM2*, 353.
55. *CM2*, 355.
56. *CM2*, 329.

it "keeps circumventing the market".[57] Its most distinctive forms are linked to a "sophisticated and domineering type of exchange,"[58] i.e., to the monopolizing efforts that often involve more or less symbiotic relationships to states. In this capacity, the capitalist mechanisms of long-distance trade play a key role in the constitution of large economic units or 'economic worlds', as Braudel calls them (this seems to me a better translation of 'économie-monde' than the commonly used 'world economy', which lends itself to literal misunderstanding). Such formations can be defined from different angles in different contexts. Braudel's classic study of the early modern Mediterranean treated it as an economic world, but from a more long-term point of view, the ascendancy of a European economic world from the High Middle Ages onwards was the most decisive development of its kind, and the only one to culminate in a world economy in the strict sense.

But the capitalist tendency to transcend the more limited networks of routine exchange does not come to an end at the boundaries of economic worlds; the dynamic of the search for extra profits brings separate worlds into contact with each other and paves the way for further integration. Both the formation of economic worlds (which sometimes cross civilizational boundaries) and the more limited contacts between them can lead to inter-civilizational encounters and initiate learning processes. A prominent example is the transmission of economic ideas and devices (mainly related to the organization of commerce) from the Islamic to the western Christian world. Although the borrowed items were adapted to new contexts, sometimes so thoroughly that their origins are hard to trace, Braudel[59] sums up the evidence of inter-civilizational exchange in a very convincing way. Islamic influences seem to have been of major importance for capitalist trends in the western European economy at a crucial moment: the most innovative borrowings took place in Renaissance Italy, especially in Florence from the 13th century onwards. For Braudel,

57. Fernand Braudel, *Afterthoughts on Material Civilization and Capitalism*, Baltimore and London, Johns Hopkins University Press, 1977, 111.
58. *Afterthoughts*, 62.
59. *CM2*, 495–99.

the Renaissance was a 'preface to modernity', and he quotes Hintze's account of the controversy between Sombart and Weber as a debate on the respective parts of Renaissance and reformation in the prehistory of modern capitalism. Braudel's own view is unequivocal: "in this matter, Sombart is right."[60] The inventive, versatile and expansive character of the economic ethos that found its most memorable expressions in Florence is beyond doubt, and Braudel has no doubt about describing this episode as a case of capitalist mentality in action. At the same time, he concedes that Weber's analysis of capitalism may have been a misdirected version of arguments that would carry more conviction if applied to a broader socio-cultural context. The Protestant ethic was not as directly involved in capitalist development as Weber would have it, but a case can be made for an indirect impact. Protestantism was instrumental in dissolving the traditional unity of sacred and secular power; it inspired changes that made the whole tenor of social life more compatible with capitalist principles; and last but not least, it gave a more pronounced civilizational identity to the northwestern periphery of Europe and put an end to its quasi-colonial status vis-a-vis the regions of 'old Latinity'.[61] If we take the logic of Braudel's comments on these points beyond his explicit formulations, it can be argued that they point to the need for a more multilayered conception of the spirit of capitalism.

Braudel's analyses of pre-modern economic history do not go beyond the beginnings of the industrial revolution, but his reflections on that subject suggest ways of applying his framework to more recent phases, with particular reference to the problem of varieties of capitalism. The social impact of the 'industrial revolution' was, as he sees it, more revolutionary than the technological innovations: on the latter level, the late 18th - and early 19th -century transformation appears as one of several landmarks in a long and still unfinished process, whereas the relationship between capitalism and its social context changes in an unprecedented and irreversible way. A capitalist sector hitherto functioning as a "closed,

---

60. *CM2*, 515.
61. *CM2*, 507.

even encysted system"[62] breaks through traditional barriers and imposes itself on an ever-expanding social arena. But the process is double-edged. As Braudel notes, the worst misunderstanding of capitalism is to see it as a self-contained economic system, and to forget that its very drive to assert the primacy of an economic logic remains dependent on social structures, political forces and cultural frameworks.[63] The ascendancy of capitalism is therefore accompanied by ongoing adjustment to the contexts in which it is embedded, and the varying patterns of interaction between the two trends give rise to more or less durable and distinctive varieties of capitalism. The twin dynamics of subsumption (in the Marxian sense of subordination to the imperatives of capital) and contextualization provide the most basic frame of reference for comparative studies; by contrast, the varying ways of systemic coordination take shape at a more derivative level. It follows from Braudel's analysis of capitalist elements in long-distance trade that changing combinations of local and trans-local – or national and transnational – networks have been characteristic of all stages of capitalist development. But his emphasis on the fundamental ambiguity of key capitalist institutions could also be taken as a starting point for comparative inquiry. His work deals most extensively with the tensions between market infrastructures and monopolizing strategies. By the same token, however, property rights represent (notwithstanding their quasi-fetishistic status in mainstream economic thought) an ambiguous form of economic power. On the one hand, the quest for monopoly is also a search for additional sources of power; on the other, managerial control is both an indispensable complement and a potential rival. As for the entrepreneur, Braudel criticizes Schumpeter for treating him as a *deus ex machina* and insists on the importance of the "movement as a whole."[64] In more specific terms, the activities of the entrepreneur presuppose not only the institutional framework of the enterprise, but also the broader social field that he strives to mobilize.

To conclude, the question of the spirit of capitalism should be briefly

---

62. *CM2*, 216, translated by the author.
63. *CM3*, 540.
64. *AMCC*, 63.

reconsidered from the expanded Braudelian perspective that I have tried to outline. An expansive and self-transformative capacity, evident in the construction and transgression of economic worlds as well as in the movement between domains of economic life, has been a defining characteristic of capitalism from early beginnings onwards and may be seen as the pre-existing receptacle for the new cultural orientations variously theorized by Weber, Sombart and Castoriadis. New visions of growth, mastery and wealth represent a break with traditional patterns of contained capitalism, but at the same time, they draw on the older layers of the capitalist imaginary and can develop them in different directions. The need for comparative approaches to this problematic is obvious, and so is the relevance of broader civilizational perspectives.

Castoriadis, Veblen, and the 'Power Theory of Capital'

D. T. Cochrane

In Raymond Carver's short story "What We Talk About When We Talk About Love," a group of adults sit around a table, drinking gin and telling stories of love. It is apparent that none of them can adequately express what love really is.[1] One woman describes the abuse she experienced at the hands of her ex-husband. She insists that his actions, although terrible, were, in their own way, a manifestation of love. Her current husband insists that this cannot be so for love would never provoke someone to violence. Ultimately they agree to disagree. Despite the importance of love in their lives and their assertions that they feel love and loved, they could not provide an exact meaning for the word; a precise understanding of what 'love' signifies – either in form or content – escapes everyone at the table.

Like the characters in Carver's story who have difficulty in knowing how to talk about love, academics experience similar difficulties when speaking of 'capital.' Economists, political scientists, even literary theorists, freely employ the concept, yet few can say what the word 'capital' truly signifies. Either unaware of or unconcerned by the serious problems with both the Marxist labor theory of value (LToV) and the neoclassical utility

1. Thanks to the participants of the 2008 *Great Lakes Political Economy Conference* who provided feedback on this paper. Special thanks to Jonathan Nitzan, Jeff Monaghan, Etienne Turpin and Shelley Boulton.

theory of value, they continue to discuss 'capital' as if it were conceptually unproblematic. By the end of Carver's story, the characters have come to accept the fact that they need not agree on what they talk about when they talk about love: they know it when they feel it. Similarly, academics may have an intuitive grasp of capital that they are unable to articulate adequately: they know it when they 'see' it. However, while we may live perfectly well with fuzzy conceptions of our emotions and the emotions of others, theoretical concepts cannot rest upon intuition; they must be clear and distinct. Otherwise, they risk becoming a catch-all, ascribed to almost anything, explaining almost nothing. If capital is one of the most important institutions of our current political economic system, then it demands as precise a meaning as we can give it. If concepts are meant to help us understand the institutions that order our lives, then we must constantly work to make our theoretical significations resemble, as closely as possible, the real world counterparts to which they refer.

The prevailing, and largely unacknowledged, uncertainty around *capital* puts a question mark behind many proclamations regarding the ideology, theory, and praxis of the *capitalist* system. The 'I know it when I see it'-approach results in a confusing hodgepodge of material and social entities being described as 'capital': money is capital, investment is capital, machinery is capital, workers are capital, political largesse is capital … Eventually, capital is everything and everywhere, and the concept is rendered meaningless. A clearer understanding of 'what we talk about when we talk about capital' is a priority if we wish to distinguish useful theoretical positions from misguided pretenders. Such an understanding aims at a working definition that encapsulates the actual political-economic conditions of business and the on-going efforts of accumulation.

Currently, Jonathan Nitzan and Shimshon Bichler are among the few contemporary theorists calling attention to the hollowness of the dominant theories of capital and the only theorists offering a radically new realist perspective.[2] The neoclassical and Marxist theories conceive of ca-

2. See Jonathan Nitzan and Shimshon Bichler, *Capital as Power: A Study of Order and Creorder, Ripe Series in Global Political Economy,* London, Routledge, 2009, for their most complete treatment of the topic to date. All of their previous works are

pital as a 'bottom-up' construction, in which nominal values are the mere appearance of an underlying realm of 'the real,' based on utility and labor, respectively. Nitzan and Bichler reject this interpretation that accords nominal quantities no independent ontological status. They properly regard the nominal as the real and as such, interpret capital as a 'top-down' assessment by market participants that quantifies the power of capitalists.

Although the Marxist and neoclassical theories of value are radically different, they can both be characterized as 'dual quantity' theories on the basis of their shared postulation of the existence of unobservable, *but quantifiable*, entities that they claim constitute the reality of economic production and accumulation. For neoclassicists, these are the 'utils' that constitute utility, while for Marxists these are units of 'socially necessary, abstract labor.' What both theories attempt to do is explain the ongoing, observable, but merely *nominal*, processes of capitalism in terms of these *real* counterparts. The shared use of this 'dual quantity' analysis is revealed when both Marxists and mainstream economists refer to 'asset bubbles,' a concept that describes a departure of nominal values from their underlying real counterparts. Nitzan and Bichler, on the other hand, deny the existence of this underlying realm and assert that capital represents the quantified power of capitalists, imposed on the rest of society. Developed out of empirical research on what they call "The Weapondollar Petrodollar Coalition,"[3] their theory relies heavily on the quantitative examination of patterns of accumulation.

While the early 20th century political economist Thorstein Veblen had a formative theoretical influence on Nitzan and Bichler's work, they have employed the ideas of the contemporary Graeco-French philosopher-

available online at *The Bichler & Nitzan Archives* (http://bnarchives.net).

3. For more on this concept and a description of how the accumulatory needs of oil and arms companies factor into conflict in the Middle East, see Jonathan Nitzan and Shimshon Bichler, "Bringing Capital Accumulation Back In: The Weapondollar–Petrodollar Coalition – Military Contractors, Oil Companies and Middle East 'Energy' Conflicts," *Review of International Political Economy* 2, no. 3 (1995) and Jonathan Nitzan and Shimshon Bichler, *The Global Political Economy of Israel*, London, UK, Pluto Press, 2002, Ch. 5 (hereafter, *GPEI*).

activist Cornelius Castoriadis to develop and philosophically justify their theories. In this article I will examine the bond that can be discerned between Castoriadis and Veblen on the question of how value relates to capital, and explore the role they play in Nitzan and Bichler's conception of capital. This understanding of capital is, on the surface, the same as that used by business concerns: capitalization. However, while the concept of capital as understood by businesspeople refers to a formal instrument – a means for doing business – Nitzan and Bichler comprehend capital and capitalization in a more significant and meaningful way. In this essay, then, I intend to demonstrate that a critical examination of Castoriadis' and Veblen's views will lead us to a succinct definition of capital as *quantified, vendible ownership claims over groupings of tangible and intangible assets that are expected to generate streams of earnings.* Understood as such, Nitzan and Bichler's work then demonstrates that we must recognize capital accumulation as the process that involves an exercise of control within social institutions so as to expand ownership claims and increase the expected earnings of existing claims. Although labor and production are vital elements of this process, they are neither singular, nor even central. Rather, the complex 'magma' of social interaction gets translated through capitalization, which then informs the actions of owners as they strive to increase their control.[4]

Cornelius Castoriadis began his theoretical and political life as a young Trotskyist in Greece. He would eventually break with Trotskyism and Marxism, although he remained highly critical of the capitalist status quo. In France, he was one of the founders of the radical group, *Socialisme ou Barbarie* (*SouB*), which included among its members Claude Lefort, Jean-François Lyotard, and Guy Debord. The membership of *SouB* was never large, but its journal was influential, particularly the writings of Castoriadis, who had to publish under pseudonyms because he was not a French citizen and faced deportation with no means of judicial recourse.

---

4. In *Capital as Power*, Nitzan and Bichler devote three chapters (9–11) on the meaning of capitalization as both a formula of pricing and a mechanism of order. Hereafter, *CP*.

One of the visible figures of May '68, Daniel Cohn-Bendit, wrote that the ideas he and his brother Gabriel present in *Obsolete Communism: The Left-Wing Alternative* "are those of P. Chaulieu,"[5] which was one of Castoriadis's pseudonyms. Castoriadis's major theoretical critique is against all forms of determinism. His reflections on human society and history reveal human beings with a propensity to imagine heretofore unseen notions, ideas, concepts, and things. Such creativity and the contingencies it provokes are, he claims, inseparable parts of Being, and undermine any effort to pronounce external laws of social and historical motion. In Marx, Castoriadis finds both determinism and an affirmation of humanity's responsibility for its own history. He objects, however, to Marx's economic analysis, with its 'discovery' of the laws of historical motion. Rejecting all notions of teleological progress, Castoriadis notes that our constant creation and transformation of social institutions is an on-going project thoroughly contained within the social-historical – the *nomos* – and therefore, is capable of taking on innumerable forms with contents that cannot be known in advance.

An iconoclastic thinker who never held a full professorship, Thorstein Veblen was nonetheless able to find an outlet for his work, because he earned the praise and approval of F. W. Taussig, editor of the prestigious *Quarterly Journal of Economics*. He shares his understanding of social and institutional change with Castoriadis's open-ended conception of history. Decidedly more of a functionalist than Castoriadis, Veblen believes that institutions are transformed in response to the constantly changing needs of a society's population, but the institutional changes can never quite keep up with the social changes and therefore 'what is, is wrong.' This means that there is no *telos*, no endpoint, no goal toward which a society is moving; there is no clear progressive track along which history moves, although there is progress. Castoriadis and Veblen also share the belief that it is the heteronomous force of powerful elites who dominate society by working to maintain the status quo and their vested interests, and

---

5. Gabriel Cohn-Bendit and Daniel Cohn-Bendit, *Obsolete Communism: The Left-Wing Alternative*, trans. Arnold Pomerans, London, Penguin, 1968, 133.

who push for any change as is necessary to achieve these desired ends.[6] Despite the fact that Veblen and Castoriadis were non-Marxist critics of capitalism, both writing at times when such ideas were marginalized, Nitzan and Bichler's theory of capital appears to be the only work that bridges the thought of these two radicals. They make particular use of Castoriadis' essay "Value, Equality, Justice, Politics,"[7] which carefully analyzes and critiques the LToV. Castoriadis suggests that value, rather than being a trans-historical essence, as theorized by Marx, is better understood by Aristotle as immanent to the particular society in which valuation occurs, but he does not explain how this theory of value might translate into a theory of capital.[8] Nitzan and Bichler's theory, however, specifically addresses this problem and demonstrates that Veblen's work provides the necessary account of how such a theory of value might be transformed into a theory of capital.[9] They go on to highlight how this

---

6. A central concept for Castoriadis, 'heteronomy' means that the laws of society are perceived to come from a source external to the populace, whether God, ancestors, nature or Founding Fathers. Castoriadis contrasts heteronomy with autonomy, whereby members of a community acknowledge that they are ultimately the source of the laws of society and therefore take control of creating and sanctioning those laws.

7. Cornelius Castoriadis, "Value, Equality, Justice, Politics: From Marx to Aristotle and from Aristotle to Ourselves," id. *Crossroads in the Labyrinth*, translated by Kate Soper and Martin H. Ryle, Brighton, UK, The Harvester Press, 1984. Hereafter, *VEJP.*

8. Many contemporary Marxists insist that this understanding of Marx's theory of value is incorrect and that Marx understood value as thoroughly social. There are a number of problems with this assertion, not the least of which are the essentialist descriptions of labor-value that Marx uses and which will be described below. However, even if Castoriadis is wrong, and Marx's value theory has no trans-historical interpretation, this does not invalidate Nitzan and Bichler's theory of capital or the empirical results it uniquely makes possible.

9. Thorstein Veblen, "On the Nature of Capital," *The Quarterly Journal of Economics* 22, no. 4 (1908), 104–36; Thorstein Veblen, "On the Nature of Capital: Investment, Intangible Assets and the Pecuniary Magnate," *The Quarterly Journal of Economics* 23, no. 1 (1908), 517–32. In the present text, reference to "On the Nature of Capital" is mainly to the first of these articles, which was mistakenly published without its intended subtitle, "The Productivity of Capital Goods." Hereafter, *ONC1* and *ONC2.*

theory of capital transforms our understanding of accumulation and capitalism.

Marx and Value Theory

Since a theory of capital begins with a theory of value, we must understand the source of value and the processes of valuation before we can separate out capital as a particular valued 'thing,' let alone develop a theory of capitalism. The meaning of capital can then be articulated in terms of its relationship to valuation. This is precisely the approach of both neoclassical and Marxist theories of capital.[10] These theories postulate that value begins with *utility* or *labor*, respectively, and *capital* is that portion of valuation embodied in productive machinery. The question is: where does this portion (i.e., capital) of valuation come from? Neoclassicists are differentiated from Marxists by the way in which they answer this question. For neoclassicists, profits, i.e., the returns to capital, are returns to the productivity of the capital that owners make available for production. For Marxists, profits are the appropriation of the value created by labor above and beyond what is required for the subsistence of the workers. This appropriation is made possible as a consequence of the capitalists' ownership of the means of production. Both the neoclassicists and the Marxists agree that capital accumulation occurs through the return of profits to the system of production in the form of more productive machinery. Hence, capital has two sides: productive and financial.

Both the Marxist and the neoclassical conceptions of value begin with the postulation of transcendent and unobservable entities that nonetheless are conceived of as 'real': utility and abstract labor. This 'reality' is then privileged over the observable, nominal realm, which is conceived as a distorted reflection. This shared conceptualization provides the foundations for both theories of capital. Rarely acknowledged among adherents of these theoretical systems, the Marxist and neoclassical theories of value and capital permeate their understanding of the field of political economy and their discussions of the actual, unfolding,

---

10. Due to considerations of the intellectual backgrounds of Castoriadis and Veblen, I will focus on critique of the Marxist theory of value.

observable political economy. Consider discussions of market 'bubbles,' in which the underlying claim is that *nominal prices* deviated from *real values*. What would the neoclassicist's concept of 'productivity' mean without the notion of utility informing the prices of goods and inputs, including capital goods and labor? How could we understand Marx's concept of 'exploitation' without the notion of abstract labor informing surplus value? The fact that the prices of goods and inputs, including capital goods and labor relies on utility, or the fact that surplus value relies on abstract labor means that the philosophical objections to the concepts of utility and abstract labor must be taken seriously. If these objections are valid, then they threaten the entire theoretical structures on which these schools of thought are based.

In the LToV, which constitutes a theory of exchange and distribution, Marx distinguishes between the use-value and the exchange-value of a good. He wants to know what makes two goods 'equal' in exchange. How do humans determine that one table exchanges for two chairs? Marx's answer: the labor involved in the production of each item. Although he recognizes that translating labor value into the price of an item is a messy, social process, he nonetheless believes that these objective labor values ground the process of exchange and inform the distribution of the social product. Since the worker must sell herself in the capitalist economic system – or more specifically, she must sell her labor-power – to the capitalist, the output of her labor, i.e., labor value, is owned by and hence controlled by the one who has purchased her labor-power, namely, the owner of production, the capitalist. In a working day, a worker can produce enough value to sustain herself, but she also produces a surplus. Under capitalism, according to Marx, the capitalist captures the surplus that the worker has produced, while it compensates the worker with a mere subsistence wage. The captured surplus is then transformed into more productive machinery – becomes capital – that contributes to the further usurpation of surplus labor value. Marx did not believe that machines themselves created any value; machines are 'dead labor.' Since only workers create value, the capitalists' expropriation of value is an unjust and unnecessary social process.[11] Ultimately and fortunately, "capitalist production begets, with the inexorability of a law of Nature, its own negation."[12] Following its own logic of accumulation, constantly transforming expropriated surplus value into machinery and driving a process of proletarianization, capitalism sows the seeds of its own destruction. Since profit rates are understood by capitalists as the ratio of expropriated surplus to the value of 'constant capital' – machinery – under their control, their continual reinvestment of the surplus into more constant capital drives down the rate of profit. To countermand this tendency, capitalists turn on each other and capital becomes more and more centralized: "One capitalist always kills many."[13] This, combined with more and more individuals being drawn into the productive process, would mean an eventual clash:

> The monopoly of capital becomes a fetter upon the mode of production... Centralization of the means of production and socialization of labor at last reach a point where they become incompatible with their capitalist integument. Thus integument is burst asunder. The knell of capitalist private property sounds. The expropriators are expropriated.[14]

---

11. This would prove to be one of the most dangerous outcomes of Marx's theory and one directly challenged by early American neoclassicist J. B. Clark, who declares that if the claims of 'exploitation' are correct, meaning that workers are not remunerated their full contribution to value, then "every right-minded man should become a socialist." Of course, Clark would go on to 'prove' that every component in production – land, labor and capital – is remunerated according to its marginal contribution to the value of the output, or would be if free markets were allowed to function (J. B. Clark, *The Distribution of Wealth: A Theory of Wages, Interest and Profit*, Library of Economics and Liberty, 1908, http://www.econlib.org/library/Clark/clkDW.html, Ch.1).

12. Karl Marx, *Capital: A Critical Analysis of Capitalist Production*, edited by Friedrich Engels, translated by Samuel Moore and Edward Aveling, 3 vols, vol. 1, New York, International Publishers, 1967, 715.

13. *Capital* vol. 1, 714.

14. *Capital* vol. 1, 715.

The entire process is necessitated by the idea that every product is understood in terms of its labor value, i.e., the units of labor required to produce it.

In August and November of 1908, *The Quarterly Journal of Economics* published two articles by Veblen, both of which bear the title "On the nature of capital"; the second of which was subtitled "Investment, Intangible Assets, and the Pecuniary Magnate." Although Veblen mentions neither Marx nor the thinkers of the neoclassical school, his articles are a rejection of these, then and still, dominant concepts of value and capital. It has been said that during his time Veblen had most likely read more of the works of Marx and his followers than anyone else in the United States.[15] He had also been a student of J. B. Clark, one of the leaders of the emergent neoclassical school. Veblen's alternative conception of capital must, therefore, be considered a deeply informed and critical position. Further, given the institutional milieu in which he was writing, compared to Marx, it was also a very current position. While Marx's theory emerged in the context of the competitive capitalism of 'Little Britain,' Veblen's ideas developed among the increasingly monopolistic capitalism of 'Big America.' Additionally, Veblen was actively engaged with the foundational thinkers of the neoclassical justification for capitalism, and these thinkers were motivated, at least in part, by a need to rescue *laissez-faire* markets from Marx's inversion of the labor value-based, classical justification provided by Adam Smith and David Ricardo, among others. While Marx's classical predecessors subscribed to a labor theory of value, they were also advocates of markets as a mechanism that allowed the laws of supply and demand to generate a free and fair outcome. Marx took their idea, reinterpreted the labor theory of value to consider the role of the ownership class, and demonstrated the exploitation inherent in capitalism. The neoclassicists responded with an entirely new hedonic theory of value based on utility. Therefore, while the neoclassicists were

---

15. Douglas Fitzgerald Dowd, "Thorstein Veblen: The Evolution of Capitalism from Economic and Political to Social Dominance; Economics as Its Faithful Servant," in *Understanding Capitalism: Critical Analysis from Karl Marx to Amartya Sen*, edited by Douglas Fitzgerald Dowd, Sterling, VA, Pluto Press, 2002, 39.

not on the radar of Marx's critical analysis of political economists, they certainly were one of the subjects of Veblen's critique;[16] indeed, if any thinker could be considered the early 20th century intellectual heir to Marx's prescient critique of mainstream political economy, it would be Veblen. His response to the neoclassicists is both aligned with Marx and an important update of Marx's ideas. Yet, despite his engagement with a capitalism that resembles more closely the functioning of contemporary capitalism, including those aspects of the capitalist system supported merely for ideological reasons, Veblen's unique take on capital has rarely been considered in its own right.

Although to my knowledge Veblen never dealt explicitly with the LToV, he must have been aware of the various criticisms to which the theory had been subjected by both those opposed to Marx and avowed Marxists. The first criticisms pertained to the 'transformation problem' and emerged shortly after the first volume of *Capital* was published. Reams of paper have been produced on the transformation problem. The basic issue is that it is unclear how labor-value translates into observed prices or how one would identify labor-values based on prices. Friedrich Engels promised that this difficulty would be resolved in the third volume of *Capital*; indeed, he even proposed a contest to see if anyone could anticipate Marx's solution to the problem.[17] The contemporary transformation problem based criticisms of the LToV argue that the theory is inconsistent, redundant and/or impossible.[18] Even among Marxists,

16. The only mention of neoclassical thinkers or concepts in Marx's work is in a preface to the third volume of *Capital*, penned by Engels. This is not an indictment of Marx. The founding works of neoclassicism, although written during the later years of Marx's life, were marginal compared to the towering classical thinkers like Smith and Ricardo. However, this lack of engagement does create problems for those trying to use Marx's criticism of political economists as a relevant critique of current mainstream economic thought. See *Capital: The Process of Capitalist Production as a Whole*, edited by Frederick Engels, translated by Ernest Untermann, 3 vols., vol. 3, New York, International Publishers, 1967, 10.

17. Michael C. Howard and John Edward King, *A History of Marxian Economics, 1883–1929*, 2 vols., vol. 1, Princeton, NJ, Princeton University Press, 1989 (*HME*).

18. Concerning *inconsistency*, see Ladislaus von Bortkiewicz, "Value and Price in

the proposed solutions, as well as the one offered by Marx, are less than decisive.[19] Both criticisms and defenses of the LToV, with claims to have solved the transformation problem, continue to this day.[20]

One response to the problems with the LToV is simply to ignore both the theory and its problems. Most of these attempts can be considered descendants of Paul Sweezy, who understood the problems with the LToV as well as anyone. [21] However, he thought that it would be possible to drop the quantitative aspects of the theory, while retaining its qualitative insights, namely that labor is the source of all value and therefore, capitalism is exploitative on the basis of its appropriation of value. He remained acutely aware throughout his intellectual life of the difficulties this posed for attempts to understand accumulation, namely that it left discussions of the nominal values of capitalism without clear meaning. He assessed any failures with his work as stemming from the fact that "its conceptualization of the capital accumulation process is one-sided and incomplete."[22] Contrary to Sweezy, most contemporary presentations of Marx's labor theory, minus the quantitative claims, make little effort to grapple with the long and extensive debate on the matter.

The best known contemporary example of an attempt to retain Marx's qualitative discussions of labor value, while excising the quantitative ele-

---

the Marxian System," translated by J. Kahane, *International Economic Papers* 2 (1952 [1907]), http://classiques.uqac.ca/classiques. On *redundancy*, see Paul Samuelson, "Wages and Interest: A Modern Dissection of Marxian Economic Models," *American Economic Review* 47 (1957), 884–912. *Impossibility* is dealt with in Ian Steedman, "Positive Profits With Negative Surplus Value," *Economic Journal* 85 (1975), 114–23. Nitzan and Bichler (*CP*, 99–102) synthesize these criticisms, as well as others.

19. Nitzan and Bichler, *CP*; E. K. Hunt and Mark Glick, "Transformation Problem" in *Marxian Economics*, edited by John Eatwell, Martin Milgate, and Peter Newman, New York, W. W. Norton & Company, 1990.

20. See Andrew Kliman, *Reclaiming Marx's 'Capital': Refuting the Myth of Inconsistency*, Lanham, MD, Lexington Books, 2006.

21. Paul M. Sweezy, *The Theory of Capitalist Development*, New York, Modern Reader, 1942.

22. Paul M. Sweezy, "Monopoly Capital After Twenty-Five Years," *Monthly Review* 43, No. 7. (1991), 52–57.

ments is in the works of Michael Hardt and Antonio Negri. Hardt and Negri maintain that the theory, although valid during Marx's time, ceased being applicable with the move of capitalism out of 'large-scale industry'; thus, the quantitative features of the LToV are invalid not because of inherent flaws in the theory itself, but because of a historical change that makes measurability itself an impossibility.[23] Such a contention of the historical invalidation of the LToV echoes an earlier argument that attempted to save the theory from the 'transformation problem.' Writing to Werner Sombart in 1895 about his concerns regarding the theory, Engels states, "When commodity exchange began ... [products] were exchanged approximately *according* to their value ... Thus value had a *direct and real existence* at the time. We know that this direct realization of value in exchange ceased and that it now no longer happens."[24] Like Engels, Hardt and Negri seek to retain Marx, while avoiding the difficult work of addressing the problems with the LToV and the consequences of those problems for Marx's conception of capital. They want to eliminate the LToV but at the same time they also want to continue to use Marx's concepts, maintaining that, despite the inapplicability of the LToV, labor remains the source of value. "It is not possible to imagine (let alone describe) production, wealth, and civilization," Negri writes, "if they cannot be traced back to an accumulation of labor."[25] In this assertion, however, he confuses necessity with sufficiency. While I doubt anyone would deny the necessity of labor for production, wealth, and civilization, labor is not, on its own, sufficient for understanding all the complexities of Western civilization or any other civilization for that matter. If Negri wishes to encapsulate all of the necessary and sufficient ingredients for production, wealth, and civilization within the concept of 'labor,' then he is stretching the concept to the point of uselessness.

23. Michael Hardt and Antonio Negri, *Empire*, Cambridge, MA, Harvard University Press, 2000, 354–56.
24. Cited by Howard and King, *HME*, 48; emphasis in original.
25. Antonio Negri, "Twenty Theses on Marx" in *Marxism Beyond Marxism*, edited by Saree Makdisi, Cesare Casarino and Rebecca E. Karl, New York, Routledge, 1996, 152.

Furthermore, as we shall see, value, whether understood as labor or in some other form, does not objectively determine 'production, wealth, and civilization'; rather, these factors, as part of the social-historical reality, determine value. The problems of the LToV represent not a historical shift toward immeasurability, as Engels, Hardt or Negri would have it, but an epistemological flaw in Marx's paradoxical claims regarding labor and value.

Castoriadis on Value

Unlike Hardt and Negri, Cornelius Castoriadis recognizes the metaphysical contradictions inherent in the LToV. These contradictions undermine not only the theory, but also the claim that labor remains the source of value. Furthermore, the metaphysical critique of the LToV renders moot both the 'transformation problem' and attempts to resolve the problem. Whether Marx's transformation of values into prices is mathematically impossible or not does not matter if the units involved are metaphysically impossible. Castoriadis suggests that a return to Aristotle opens a different perspective on value. He begins his discussion in "Value, Equality, Justice, Politics" with a lengthy quote from Marx's criticism of Aristotle's conception of value. Marx first commends Aristotle for his observation that the ability to exchange diverse goods requires that they are equal – "5 beds = 1 house" – and that they are commensurable: "on what basis can a bed be compared to a house?"[26] However, he then chastises the ancient Greek thinker for his conclusion that this equality is foreign to the "real nature" of the goods in exchange and is merely, in Aristotle's words, "a makeshift for practical purposes."[27] Marx explains that there is indeed something inherent in Aristotle's example of the beds and the house that makes them equal and commensurable, namely, human labor. According to Marx, despite the qualitative diversity of labor's use-value "[t]he labor ... that forms the substance of value, is homogeneous human labor, expenditure of one uniform labor-power."[28] However, as

26. *Capital,* vol 1, 55–59.
27. *Capital,* vol 1, 59, where Marx cites Aristotle.
28. *Capital,* vol 1, 39.

Castoriadis argues, Marx never clearly explains whether:

– capitalism actually *transforms* diverse individuals into something homogeneous and commensurable;

– capitalism simply *makes visible* an eternal and underlying homogeneity; or

– the sameness of 'abstract labor' is only an *appearance* of commensurability resulting from capitalism's commodification of labor.

In other words, Marx "is unable to decide whether Labor Value is a trans-historic Substance/Essence, a particular phenomenalization of that Substance/Essence brought about by capitalism, or an Appearance which capitalism has created."[29] Castoriadis blames these contradictions on an inexact, incomplete, or confused conception of the relationship between the *nomos* – social norms and principles – and the *physis* – natural norms and principles: "Is the 'equality' of men, and the commensurability of men's labor, a matter of man's *physis* ... or [is it] of the *nomos* ...; or is there a *physis* of history, by which this particular *nomos* must come to be posited and imposed at a particular moment?"[30] This confusion is related to what Castoriadis calls "the antinomies of Marx's thought."[31] According to Castoriadis, Marx prominently advances two incompatible elements throughout his works: The first is the idea that people acting within society are the force of history. The second is his effort to discover the laws of society and history, of social formation, of 'capitalist economy.'[32] These opposing conceptions cannot be resolved; either laws govern the motions of society and history or these motions are the product of indeterminate human creation. Marx's labor theory is a fundamental

---

29. *VEJP*, 327.

30. *VEJP*, 284–85.

31. *VEJP*, 266; Cornelius Castoriadis, "Marx Today: An Interview," *Thesis Eleven* 8, no. 1 (1984), 124–32.

32. "Marx Today", 124; Cornelius Castoriadis, *The Imaginary Institution of Society*, translated by Kathleen Blamey, Cambridge, UK, Polity Press, 1987, 56–70 (hereafter, *IIS*).

component of his 'laws of society and history.' Therefore, an agreement with Marx's assertion that humanity is responsible for its own history requires rejection of Marx's LToV leaving us uncertain 'what we talk about when we talk about capital.'

Castoriadis is not unaware of contradictions in Aristotle, and carefully explains that like Marx, Aristotle confuses the question of society as being of the *nomos* or of the *physis*. In fact, Castoriadis writes that contradictions and aporias are the hallmark of great thinkers because such thinkers are always trying to break out of the inherited thought within which they find themselves. Although they attempt to think beyond this tradition, they cannot escape it completely. Like adventuresome explorers, these thinkers, charting new intellectual territory, are wont to make wrong turns; they go astray. This is equally true, he says, of both Marx and Aristotle.[33] Castoriadis never provides an explicit name for his theory of value based on Aristotle. However, its basic premise is that, far from being determined by an impossible trans-historical substance – i.e., abstract labor, value is determined socially and historically, as part of the *nomos*, in accordance with whatever values the society elevates as primary. This also means that value is not determined materially, but at the juncture of the material elements that allow a society to function and the immaterial significations that give the society its unique characteristics.

Valuation, Castoriadis notes, is a matter of distribution, and distribution is a matter of justice: who gets what? In the distribution of the social product, or of products that become social in the act of exchange/distribution, a relation is established between the individuals involved.[34] This relation involves a proportionality. If we denote the objects exchanged as a and b and the individuals involved in the exchange as A and B, then the act of exchange implies that $A/B = a/b$. Rearranging, this becomes $A/a = B/b$. According to Aristotle, "this conjunction of A with a and of B with

---

33. *VEJP*, 328.
34. *VEJP*, 294. Although Castoriadis is explicitly criticizing Marx's LToV, the influence of Marx on his thought is still very evident, just as the influence of Aristotle on Marx is evident.

b is what is just in distribution."[35] When we confront this relationship, the question arises concerning the commensurability not only of objects *a* and *b*, but also of individuals *A* and *B*. To what common units can *a* and *b*, *and*, *A* and *B* be reduced? According to Marx, the answer is 'abstract, socially necessary labor.' Aristotle, however, claims that the proportionality among men occurs because "all men agree that what is just in distribution must be (established) according to worth [*axia*] in some sense, though they do not all specify the same sort of worth."[36]

Castoriadis states that this *axia*, or proto-value, serves as the attribute that determines the 'weight' of each individual in the distribution of the social product:

> each party declares justice in distribution to be relative to what the individual already is/has with respect to a 'value' which, for its part, is not 'relative' to anything, not defined 'with respect to' anything – a value that is posited absolutely, which is the origin of justice, which is the basis of reference whose only possible reference is to itself.[37]

The criterion of valuation is the proto-value that forms the basis of justice: "[D]emocrats identify it with freedom, supporters of oligarchy with wealth, or with noble birth, and supporters of aristocracy with virtue."[38] Castoriadis asserts what Aristotle never could; namely, the proto-value, and the commensurability it establishes, is entirely a product of the *nomos*, existing only as a convention with no necessary counterpart in *physis*. The proto-value (*axia*), of the community, as the basis for valuation, orders the distribution of the social product. Those deemed worthy according to the society's criteria – whether virtue, wisdom or God's grace – get access to more of the social product. We should not regard this product as solely material since the esteem of community members and the knowledge produced within the community is also

---

35. *VEJP,* 293, where Castoriadis cites Aristotle.
36. *VEJP,* 296, where Castoriadis cites Aristotle.
37. *VEJP,* 297.
38. *VEJP,* 296, where Castoriadis cites Aristotle.

distributed in favor of the worthy.

What, then, is the convention (*nomos*) of capitalism? What serves as the proto-value that determines valuation in capitalist societies? As will be explained below, Veblen offers a partial answer to these questions in both articles of "On the Nature of Capital": control. However, in these works, Veblen argues that the convention has a long history and is not unique to capitalism.[39] In fact, where Aristotle sees a value determining *axia* based on virtue, I would argue that he is actually seeing an *a posteriori* justification for distribution based on control, which we can understand as the right to exclude others from access. Control is the true proto-value, made acceptable with claims of virtue, divinity, or wisdom. Any non-egalitarian *axia* – justifying an unequal distribution of the social product – ultimately rests on the plausible threat of violence. What is unique about capitalism as a social-historical system is not the *axia* that forms the basis of its valuation but that it has turned valuation back on the proto-value itself, quantifying control in the form of ownership and making it vendible. This takes us to the heart of Nitzan and Bichler's theory – capital as the valuation of power. First, we will turn to the partial answer provided by Veblen, concerning the role that ownership and control have played in human societies. He also takes the first step toward an understanding that capital represents the quantification of ownership. The completion of that step, including locating the quantitative possibilities in this definition, will require the work of Nitzan and Bichler, who invigorate Veblen's thought and clearly articulate the relationship among ownership, control, capital and accumulation that defines capitalism.

Veblen on Value

While Marx's theory of capital begins with production, Veblen's theory begins with assets. A community's assets, Veblen claims, even those produced and employed by an individual, depend upon the entire social order within which that individual lives and acts. The community's assets must be understood in this context; they have meaning and contribute to

---

39. *ONC1*, 535.

the social product only as part of the particular circumstances in which the community finds itself. Veblen criticizes the then, and still, "current theories of production" – meaning both the Marxist and neoclassical theories – for being "drawn in individualistic terms."[40] Man, he writes,

> ... has never lived an isolated, self-sufficient life as an individual, either actually or potentially ... The life-history of the race has been a life history of human communities ... with more or less of group solidarity, and with more or less of cultural continuity over successive generations.[41]

In direct challenge to Marx's emphasis on the material, he continues, the "continuity, congruity, or coherence of the group is of an immaterial character. It is a matter of knowledge, usage, habits of life and habits of thought, not a matter of mechanical continuity." He calls this collective body of knowledge the community's "intangible assets." This knowledge, however, should not be thought of in entirely functional terms; rather, it constitutes what Castoriadis would call the 'social imaginary signification' – the means by which the community makes sense of its world, including its mythology and religious practices, its familial organization and sexual rules, its understanding of leadership and processes of decision-making, etc. Although not every part of the community's social imaginary signification will be strictly functional in a utilitarian sense, it must, as Castoriadis emphasizes, function. If it did not, then the community would cease to exist.[42] Intangible assets accumulated and developed during the

---

40. *ONC1*, 517.

41. *ONC1*, 517–18. This assertion suggests an affinity between Veblen and the anarchist biologist Peter Kropotkin, who demonstrated the dependence of human communities upon sociability and cooperation in *Mutual Aid: A Factor in Evolution* (available through *Project Gutenberg*: http://www.gutenberg.org/etext/4341). For more on the similarities between the two, see William M. Dugger, "Veblen and Kropotkin on Human Evolution," *Journal of Economic Issues* 18 (1984).

42. Cornelius Castoriadis, "Done and to Be Done," id., *The Castoriadis Reader*, edited and translated by David Ames Curtis, Oxford, UK, Blackwell, 1989, 363–65; see also id., *IIS*, 42–45; and id., *Philosophy, Politics, Autonomy: Essays in Political Philosophy*, translated by David Ames Curtis, New York, Oxford University Press, 1991, 40–42.

community's prior life-history, make possible the individual's contribution to the social product and infuse that contribution with meaning.[43] Therefore, while the labor of the individual is necessary, it is not useful or valuable in isolation. Although value and capital were understood by Marx to be social institutions, within the LToV the creators of labor-value must be capable of analytical isolation. This was part of Marx's effort to mimic the powerful natural sciences of his era. Contrary to the transcendent and commensurable labor that grounds Marx's value theory, Veblen recognizes that labor's use and value is dependent upon the circumstances of the particular material and immaterial assets of the community, including the other qualitatively different labors. While knowledge of aerodynamics, for example, translates into valuable skills within the aerospace industry, it has little if any use or value among the sheep herders of New Zealand. The community's interdependence and reliance on circumstance-dependent assets means that the reduction of all products to their labor value presupposed by and necessary for the practical application of the LToV is not only an epistemological impossibility, as demonstrated by the 'transformation problem,' but an ontological absurdity.[44]

Early societies, according to Veblen, were relatively egalitarian because

---

43. Veblen's emphasis on the importance of the immaterial for even the earliest human communities challenges the supposedly new and important concept of 'immaterial labor.' Although entirely unacknowledged, Veblen anticipates the attention given to 'immaterial labor' by the Autonomist Marxists. Maurizio Lazzarato, for example, writes that "immaterial labor constitutes itself in forms that are immediately collective." Veblen's early 20th century explication of the concept of 'intangible assets' undermines the idea that an immaterial component of labor represents a unique development of capitalism (Maurizio Lazzarato, "Immaterial Labor," *Generation Online* (n.d.) http://www.generation-online.org/c/fcimmateriallabour3.htm).

44. Marx states that "[t]he total labor-power of society, which is embodied in the sum total of the values of all commodities produced by that society, counts here as one homogeneous mass of human labor-power, composed though it be of *innumerable individual units*" (*Capital*, vol. 1, 39). In order to maintain his reductionism Marx asserts that "Skilled labor counts only as simple labor intensified, or rather, as multiplied simple labor" (*Capital*, vol. 1, 44).

of the community's interdependence that made material and immaterial assets productive. As long as everyone had relatively free access to the assets of the community, it was difficult, if not impossible, for domination to become entrenched. Efforts at domination through proprietary claims to one's particular assets and attempts to exercise hegemonic control of the community's assets would result in ostracism and isolation. Inequality and domination emerges,

> ... so soon, or in so far, as the technological development falls into shape as to require a relatively large unit of material equipment for the effective pursuit of industry ... so as seriously to handicap the individuals who are without these material means, and to place the current possessors of such equipment at a marked advantage, then the strong arm intervenes, property rights apparently begin to fall into definite shape, the principles of ownership gather force and consistency, and men begin to accumulate [productive] goods and take measures to make them secure.[45]

An ownership class emerges that proclaims rights over the community's material assets. Their reward, although made possible by the existence of a surplus, *is not* equal to that surplus. Rather, the owners are able to demand a subjectively determined tribute in exchange for allowing access to the assets. The tribute demanded is a function of the relative bargaining power of the asset-controlling 'owners' and the asset-using community. The power gained will depend on such factors as the means of control, the importance of the asset and the ease of substitution: no tribute will be paid for control of a forest if other forests are accessible, while control of a quarry may generate a massive reward if it is the only available source of stone required for the community's practices. Over time, each member of society will be reduced to making claims on the social product based on what small portion of the community's assets fall under their control. For most, that will be little more than his or her own body's capacity for labor-power. Thus, control becomes the proto-value of the society and

45. Veblen, *ONC1*, 524.

distribution of the social product is based on that control. In contemporary communities this is expressed as profit and wages. Ownership bestows control over the community's assets and allows owners to exclude the rest of the community. In order to access these assets, a portion of the social product is distributed to the owners. The profits of Exxon-Mobil, as one example, are achieved for the provision of access to the oil extraction and distribution assets under their control. The wages of a doctor are earned for giving the community access to the medical skills and knowledge she controls. The earnings, either profits or wages, depend upon the extent of control and the desirability of the asset, both of which are contingent and inter-related among the entire social-historical reality in which they unfold.

Domination is not limited to control of the material assets. Some community knowledge can only be exercised in association with its material assets, and domination can extend to choosing who gets to utilize what knowledge: knowledge of flint shaping is useless without access to flint, just as access to flint is worthless without knowledge of flint shaping. Moreover, in order to augment and entrench their control, 'the strong arm' exerts influence over the further development of the immaterial assets; *de facto* domination generates *de jure* justification through the manipulation of myth; hence, the emergence of virtue and other *axia* that determined distribution. Changes in the control of the community's material assets, and the forms and content of its immaterial assets, influence the ways communal productivity will be employed. Completely distinguishing between the control exerted through material ownership and immaterial influence becomes impossible.[46] It is here in the history of assets, ownership, and control that we find Veblen's conception of capital.

---

46. Egyptian kings were powerful in part because of their deification, but also through the command of hundreds of thousands of workers whose collective power was mobilized to produce massive edifices, justified by the God-status of the king. See Lewis Mumford, *Myth of the Machine: Technics and Human Development*, New York, Harcourt, Brace & World, 1934, Ch. 9§1.

Marx's notion of capital has two sides: 1) a financial side: the realized profits from the surplus of previous production, and; 2) a material side: the reinvested profits realized as means of production.[47] The productive assets of the capitalists are the agglomerated 'dead labor' of invested surplus value. Veblen uses the term 'capital goods,' not to denote that the assets themselves are capital, but rather, that the assets are *capitalized*: "Capital goods ... are capital in the measure, not of their technological serviceability [read: productivity], but in the measure of the income which they may yield to their owner."[48] Veblen's notion of capital is, therefore, solely a financial entity.[49] Notice that deals among capitalists rarely involve the actual mobilization of the means of production; rather, it is control over these assets that is bought and sold through these financial transactions.

Marx holds that the return of profits to circulation as constant capital is the means by which accumulation is achieved.[50] Temporally, accumulation occurs after production. The relationship between production and profits has been stylized as M-C-P-C'-M' where money (M) is transformed into commodities (C) that, through the process of production (P) become more commodities (C') – properly, more valuable commodities – that can then be turned into more money (M'); and the cycle begins anew. For Marx, capital could take two forms, first, as money and, second, as inputs to production. However, "it functions just once and produces profits just once."[51] Veblen, on the other hand, recognized that

---

47. "The same capital appears in two roles — as loanable capital in the lender's hands and as industrial, or commercial, capital in the hands of the functioning capitalist" (Karl Marx, *Capital*, vol. 3, 364).
48. *ONC2*, 111.
49. An important element of their theory of capital, Nitzan and Bichler repeatedly stress, is that "capital is finance and *only* finance" (Jonathan Nitzan and Shimshon Bichler, "Capital Accumulation: Breaking the Dualism of 'Economics' and 'Politics'" in *Global Political Economy: Contemporary Theories*, edited by Ronen Palan, New York, Routledge, 2000, 78, and Nitzan and Bichler, *GEPI*, 36).
50. "The never-ending augmentation of exchange-value, which the miser strives after, by seeking to save his money from circulation, is attained by the more acute capitalist, by constantly throwing it afresh into circulation" (Karl Marx, *Capital*, vol. 3, 153).
51. Karl Marx, *Capital*, vol. 3, 364.

accumulation is not achieved by way of production itself, but as a result of changed *expectation* of future earning streams. Such a change can be achieved not only by increasing the stock of productive machinery or the actual quantity of output, but also through a reorganization of existing systems of production that is viewed favorably by market participants. Therefore, accumulation does not occur after production but prior to it; it is expectations that matter. This fits with Castoriadis's emphasis on valuation as a process of the *nomos*. It is individuals taking stock of every feature of society, or at least every feature they deem relevant, with a view toward the future unfolding of society. The prior round of production has meaning only with regard to capital and accumulation in as much as it influences the expectations for the next round. As one example, consider the rise and fall of the now maligned Pets.com. Based on the growing hype over internet based companies, the growing pet market in the U.S., and the company's own rapid sales growth in the previous year, Pets. com achieved a market capitalization as high as $324 million (US) at its initial price offering. At the time, it had total sales of just over $5 million with operating losses of more than $61 million. Of course, the company failed to live up to these expectations, was reassessed and dropped in value to about $6.5 million before its eventual liquidation. However, the eventual failure of Pets.com does not mean that eventually the market 'got it right' and its earlier hype driven valuation was, somehow, not real. Its accumulation and eventual liquidation were redistributionary, with both a material and immaterial impact.

For Veblen it is not solely the material industrial assets of the community that generate income for their controlling owners. Intangible assets are also capitalized in as much as they are judged to contribute to their owners' earnings streams. Intangible assets, Veblen notes, consist of both 1) those that come from the community, including superstitions, customs and norms, government regulations, and contractual concessions, and; 2) those generated by capitalist enterprises themselves, primarily 'goodwill.'[52] Any intangible entity that can be both turned to accumulatory advantage

---

52. Veblen, *ONC2*, 113–14.

and can be transferred among owners, becomes an asset under capitalist control, and thereby contributes to capital.

Veblen provides a social-historical understanding of the relationship between control and assets, as well as an opening to the relationship between control and capital. Combined with the argument by Castoriadis for an immanent conception of value based upon a shared *axia*, we can return to the claim made in the introduction that 'what we talk about when we talk about capital' is *quantified, vendible ownership claims over groupings of tangible and intangible assets that are expected to generate streams of earnings*. This is simply putting into words the formula for capitalization, used by business to estimate the present value of an asset. It is in the theoretical developments of Nitzan and Bichler that capitalization can be understood as much more than a simple pricing operation. As noted above, what particularizes capitalism is not that control is the basis of valuation. Rather, it is that the translation of control into earnings is then quantified in the form of capitalization, which makes ownership itself vendible.

Nitzan and Bichler draw out the importance of capitalization as "the central institution and key logic of the capitalist *nomos*."[53] Critical consideration of how the members of business view their own functioning, and how this view translates into engagement with the world, is true to the spirit of Veblen who writes, "A theory of the modern economic situation must be primarily a theory of business traffic, with its motives, aims, methods, and effects."[54] The groupings of assets within contemporary capitalism take the form of the capitalist enterprise – primarily the corporation. These groupings cannot be understood in terms of productivity as they are frequently unrelated, with no clear industrial intersection. For example, what 'efficiency' gains are there for General Electric to own both NBC Universal and GE Aviation? Further, groupings are constantly changing as capitalists seek an accumulatory advantage. Consider the sale by Canadian firm SNC-Lavalin, primarily an engineering company, of its Quebec-based weapons-production unit

---

53. *CP*, 153.
54. Thorstein Veblen, *The Theory of Business Enterprise*, New York, Mentor Books, 1904, 8.

SNC-Tec to the US arms giant General Dynamics in 2007. Both firms hoped that the move would be viewed favorably by market participants. The value of the ownership claims are based on the subjective and contingent judgments made by participants in the debt and equity markets. Nitzan and Bichler note that these judgments are based upon *everything* that is *expected* to contribute to future income streams for the two enterprises including, but not limited to, labor. Therefore, labor's relationship to capital is not as *the* bottom-up, determining totality theorized by Marx, whereby the expenditure of labor-power generates commensurable units of socially-necessary, abstract labor value and serves as the source of all value. Instead, labor is *part of* a top-down, contextualized assessment by market participants, who continually price and re-price ownership claims on the basis of the expected future earnings of assets controlled by virtue of that ownership. The part labor plays may be extremely important, but it is not the only determining institution that must be considered.

Capital and Accumulation

Nitzan and Bichler note that "any power arrangement, institution, and process that systematically affect the flow and temporal pattern of earnings is a potential facet of capital."[55] It is impossible to distinguish contributions to accumulation as clearly 'economic.' Instead, social institutions that cut across the distinctions of 'economy,' 'politics,' 'culture,' 'family,' etc. are factored into assessments of earning potential; a government may employ nationalistic rhetoric to justify land concessions favorable to transportation companies; manufacturers may exploit racist and sexist social norms to pay minorities and women lower wages; makers of consumer goods may foster anomie to entice individuals to spend.[56] Positive assessment by market participants of these institutionalized activities will result in an increased valuation of the enterprises expected to benefit in the form of increased earnings. Capitalists exert control within relevant communities in order maintain the status quo and protect

55. Jonathan Nitzan and Shimshon Bichler, "New Imperialism or New Capitalism?" *Review* 29, no. 1 (2006), 57.
56. Nitzan and Bichler, *Capital Accumulation*.

the value of the assets they own, or they seek to provoke changes in order to generate and divert earnings.

As Veblen notes, and Nitzan and Bichler emphasize, accumulatory outcomes are not absolute – there is no absolute register against which accumulation may be judged as successful or unsuccessful – but are rather a matter of *differential comparison*. Success can only be determined against market benchmarks that measure accumulatory efforts in aggregate. For example, a corporation whose capitalized value grows 10% will judge its efforts a failure if the market as a whole grew by 15% over the same period of time. On the other hand, a decline of 5% is a differential success if the market shrank by 10%. In other words, capitalists seek to 'beat the average.' The most cursory of glances at the business press will reveal the prevalence of this differential appraisal.

Nitzan and Bichler's call for evaluation of accumulatory efforts in terms of a differential process directs attention towards the intra-capitalist struggle that marks day-to-day political-economic interactions. The redistribution of current capitalized assets through trades, takeovers, and mergers, together with the pursuit and capture of assets not already capitalized is possibly *the* defining feature of capitalism. None of the particulars that constitute these practices can be reduced either to productive efficiency, or to the exploitation of labor. Instead, the redistribution and capture of assets involves complex efforts at multiple scales – the individual, the city, the market segment, the government agency, etc. – that feed upon human creativity in nearly every aspect of life. Evaluation occurs within markets as participants buy and sell on the expected ability of the vested interests to turn their social control into earnings. Markets therefore constitute empirical representations of control. 20th century capitalism has driven this process of capture and redistribution of assets to an unprecedented scale and pace. These activities are aimed at achieving an advantage over fellow combatants rather than over the general population. As long as the capitalist system itself is not threatened, capitalists fear each other.

The differential assessment of value as a quantification of ownership and control provides us with an important picture of the distribution of power among what Nitzan and Bichler have termed 'dominant capital' – "the largest power coalitions at the centre of the political economy."[57] It is these groupings within dominant capital whose actions have the greatest influence on political economic developments. Their struggles for differential accumulation are massive exercises of power that continually order and reorder society. As capital is a quantification of the relative control exercised by capitalists, measure continues to be both possible and extremely relevant. This quantitative picture provides a topology of changing capitalist power as diverse social events, even those that have no clear 'economic' meaning, affect accumulatory efforts. More importantly, from the perspective of human life, it highlights patterns of accumulatory struggle as it begets diverse social events.

Let us consider a cursory empirical application of Nitzan and Bichler's theory. Recent political economic events have drawn much attention to the *financial intermediaries* (FIRE).[58] The lower line (Fig. 1) shows FIRE's share of corporate earnings from January, 1973 to July, 2009 while the top line is the Bank of America Corporation's (BAC) share of FIRE's earnings over the same period. [59] FIRE's share of corporate earnings increased from 6% in 1973 to more than 35% in 2004. Since then, its share has dropped to just over 10%. From the perspective of 'capital as power,' this represents a rebalancing of power in favor of FIRE, while the recent decline demonstrates a loss of social control. At the same time, power within FIRE was shifting in favor of BAC. Interestingly,

---

57. Shimshon Bichler and Jonathan Nitzan, "Dominant Capital and the New Wars," *Journal of World-Systems Research* 10, no. 2 (2004), 256. This analysis also reveals how power is distributed between 'dominant' and 'peripheral' capital.

58. FIRE actually includes finance, insurance and real estate firms. However, it will serve as an acceptable proxy for the financial intermediaries.

59. Both FIRE and the corporate aggregate are restricted to publicly traded firms. Both series represent the ratio of monthly earnings for the named entities, Bank of America (BAC), finance, insurance and real estate (FIRE), and all publicly traded corporations. We owe the bottom series to Jonathan Nitzan and Shimshon Bichler, see "Imperialism and Financialism: A Story of a Nexus," http://bnarchives.yorku.ca/267

BAC appears to have outperformed FIRE when the latter was under-performing the market. Furthermore, while the seizure of credit markets in the wake of the subprime mortgage meltdown shifted power away from FIRE relative to other corporations, it strengthened BAC relative to FIRE.

Figure 1: Setting FIRE to the Market Profit, Power and Redistribution, 1973–2009

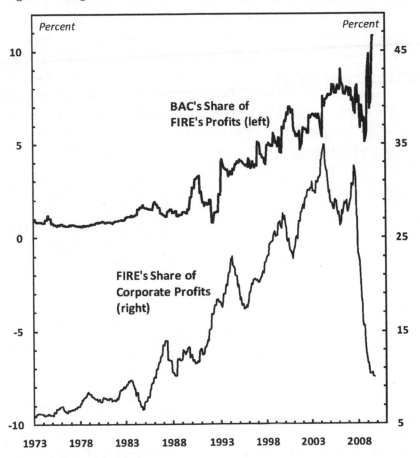

Figure 1: DATA: Datastream

This raises questions about how FIRE and BAC managed to make their relative gains. Although I am unable to explore the gains of BAC in this brief example, I can give a partial answer in the case of FIRE generally. Figure 2 shows the month-over-month percentage point change in FIRE's share of corporate earnings against the inverse change in the Fed Fund rate – the key lending rate of the U. S. Federal Reserve.[60] Gains in FIRE's share of corporate earnings correspond to cuts in the Fed Fund rate while losses correspond to increases in the rate. This means that the U. S. Federal Reserve has some capacity to redistribute earnings within capital. We cannot definitively claim that changes in the Fed Fund rate are motivated by a desire to redistribute profits toward FIRE. However, the relationship is striking and demands further analysis. Once we reject the standard theories of value, only deeper empirical research can illuminate such redistributions and the processes to which they are conjoined, as we no longer have recourse to either 'productivity' or 'exploitation' as ready-made explanations.

60. Both series calculated as the month-over-month change in percentage points. Series are smoothed as 24-month moving averages. The Fed Fund series is inverted (note right hand axis) to show more clearly the relationship between the two series.

Figure 2: Coordination and Redistribution: FIRE and the Fed, 1973–2009

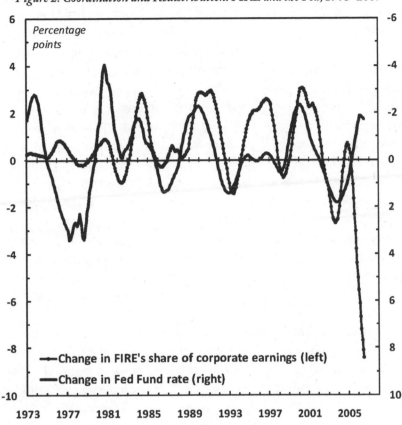

Figure 2: DATA: FIRE and corporate earnings: Datastream; Fed Fund rate: Global Insight

Closing remarks

For critics of capitalism, it would be easy to dismiss theorizing about the concept of capital as overly rooted in capitalism itself. What does it matter what 'capital' means if our hope is to supersede capitalism, destroying capital in the process? However, once we do away with Marx's teleology it is important to understand, as precisely as possible, just how business operates day-to-day; why it does what it does and how. Although Marx is considered a theorist of resistance, one side of his antinomy – the seeking of historical laws of motion – undermines the purpose and possibilities of resistance; if the materialist engine of history makes socialism inevitable, what contribution could resistance possibly make? To be sure, struggle could hasten the arrival of liberation, but ultimately it could not change the course of history. Of course, the other side of his antinomy – we make our own history – means that struggle is vital if we seek liberation. In the LToV we find Marx's determinism, which then infuses his categories and the forms of struggle they inform, even if most Marxists have long abandoned the particular program he and his followers laid out. Both Veblen and Castoriadis explicitly reject any conception of deterministic social-historical 'progress.' Instead, they place responsibility for our institutions, including those of value, squarely on us. At the same time, both share with Marx the recognition that vested interests enforce a punitive and damaging power structure. They also emphasize a need to understand the institutions of value and capital if we are to understand this structure. The relationship between the existing power structure and struggle is revealed anew in Nitzan and Bichler's theory of capital as power.

Castoriadis wants to return to an immanent conception of value as a "make-shift for practical purposes" that was found in Aristotle, and criticized by Marx. He resolves confusion found in both Marx and Aristotle due to their attempts to locate value as simultaneously a product of the *nomos* and the *physis*. His solution is to place it entirely within the sphere of the *nomos*. Valuation, he argues, emerges from a proto-value, or *axia*, that determines the distribution of the social product. However, he refrains from developing what this 'make-shift' valuation looks like within capitalism and how it might differ from earlier forms. Veblen develops a political-economic history based on the control of assets, from which I argue that control actually constitutes the *axia* of every non-egalitarian society, with other values serving as an *a posteriori* justification for a distribution that favors the powerful. Veblen, further developed by Nitzan and Bichler, argues for an understanding of capital and capitalization as the valuation of control itself. This, I claim, is what makes capitalism unique. While the *axia* of control, justified as virtue, or wisdom or divinity, was the determinant of distribution in earlier social orders, capitalism has turned valuation back on the *axia* itself. Never before could the vested interests assign a value to control, allowing them to then buy and sell power itself. As Nitzan and Bichler argue, capitalization, as the mechanism that allows for this valuation, becomes not only an instrument by which assets are continually priced and repriced, but the central, organizing logic of the social order.

As accumulation depends on the ongoing interactions of social assemblages at every scale, resistance can and must confront capitalists within multiple and diverse social arenas. This contrasts with the forms of resistance that were informed by the LToV, which included clichéd practices of consciousness-raising among the workers and efforts by a intellectualist vanguard – those privy to the laws of historical motion – to lead the proletariat in its workplace struggles against the bourgeoisie. In an example of theory catching up to practice, even Marxists largely abandoned such efforts as limited, at best. Nitzan and Bichler's conception of capital gives theoretical coherence to the diverse examples of resistance to capitalism around the world.

The concept of differential accumulation highlights the lacunary reality of capital. The formation and reformation of capitalist entities and coalitions through innovation, reorganization, and capture creates points of tension and division, i.e., interstices in the structure of capitalist ownership. These are available for exploit by dissidents. Since each capitalist entity judges its own success in terms of its assessment of expected future income flows, each entity is vulnerable to any real or perceived threat to these flows, even if such threats never materialize. As is evident from recent history, even the perception of uncertainty can reduce the capitalized value of a corporation. Although an increased awareness that a threat will not come to fruition may or may not return the value to its previous heights, volatility is undesirable and itself creates uncertainty among market participants. Moreover, given the differential nature of success, capitalist enterprises are more than willing to undermine other players in the capitalist system if it appears to favor their own interests. This can be seen in the contrariwise lobbying efforts of various capitalist coalitions.[61] Without having to resort to the reformist notion of 'good' and 'bad' corporations – appealing to the former to waylay the latter – it should be possible to turn the accumulatory self-interest of one enterprise against another. Consider the anti-vivisection campaign 'Stop Huntingdon Animal Cruelty' (SHAC). Participants in the campaign have specifically targeted capitalist entities with ties to Huntingdon's Life Sciences (HLS), including investors and financiers; even Staples has been targeted for providing office supplies to HLS. The campaign has managed to get every market-maker to stop handling trades of Huntingdon's shares and all but two institutional investors to divest. The isolation of HLS has had the effect of reducing their capital through a reduction in the assessment of expected future profits. The company was forced to plead with financiers to take on their shares or extend it loans. Since a move to the USA and the neutralization of the SHAC campaign through indictments and convictions, the valuation of HLS – now called Life Sciences Research – has dramatically increased.[62] We can acknowledge that none of these efforts inherently constitute a challenge to capitalism. On this point, dissidents informed by a theory of capital as power converge with the Marxists in the recognition that resistance to capitalism requires the overthrow of the institution of private property, which makes capitalization possible. However, we are likely further away from such a challenge than ever before. In the meantime, we must be able to insert ourselves in the processes of accumulation if we hope to prevent

---

61. For example, Wal-Mart is increasingly lobbying in Washington in the hopes of being approved for a license to provide financial services, something they already offer in Mexico. However, existing banking enterprises perceive this as a threat and have, so far, successfully lobbied against granting Wal-Mart a banking concession.

62. For more on how Nitzan and Bichler's theory of capital can inform resistance efforts, see D. T. Cochrane and Jeff Monaghan, "Fight to Win!: Tools for Confronting Capital," in *An Economy of Sustainability: Anarchist Economics*, edited by Deric Shannon, Anthony J. Nocella II, and John Asimakopoulos (Oakland, CA, AK Press, forthcoming).

certain outcomes of capitalist reordering that make people's lives worse and encourage others that make them better. Such outcomes will always be re-distributionary, favoring some capitalists over others. Recognition of this as a necessary outcome of the accumulatory process means we can stop lamenting efforts as 'unrevolutionary.'

Resistance to capitalism and the hope of creating alternative political economies to replace it demands a clear understanding of capitalist institutions. Although most radical and dissident thinkers do not subscribe to Marx's *telos*, they either fail to acknowledge the LToV as a fundamental component of that *telos*, or they simply excise the theory from Marx. The latter approach is theoretically shortsighted as many of Marx's concepts – including capital – lose their validity in the absence of a value theory. This solution also strips quantitative analysis of all meaning,[63] thus, sacrificing an important tool for empirical research.

The lingering influence of the LToV has blinkered political economists and other theorists to the importance of business in all its complexity. If we believe that human activities are responsible for our society and history, then, in the words of Castoriadis, "the task of theory will not be directed to discovering 'laws', but to the elucidation of the conditions within which human activity unfolds."[64] One of the primary tasks of such an elucidation must be articulating 'what we talk about when we talk about capital.'

---

63. Labor value was Marx's way of explaining how market prices were determined. If the LToV is excised from Marx, then there is no longer any explanation of prices, which is the foundation of important capitalist quantities, such as wages, profits, etc.
64. "Marx Today", 125.

From Market Economy to
Capitalistic Planned Economy[1]

Anders Lundkvist

John H. Dunning, nestor within the study of transnational corporations (TNCs), concluded his great work on the subject with the following words:

> [The English economist Dennis Holme Robertson] once described firms as 'islands of conscious power in this ocean of unconscious cooperation, like lumps of butter coagulating in a pail of buttermilk.' However, the modern large firm, particularly the large [Multi-National Enterprise], is not an island set within an ocean of unconscious cooperation – except in so far that it is set apart from (i.e., can be identified as being different from) other firms (islands). Between the islands are a series of causeways which are linked to each other by mutual self-interest; these causeways help forge the conscious, rather than unconscious, cooperation.[2]

---

1. This article is a slightly revised version of a similarly titled article in *"Forum for Development Studies,"* issued by the Norwegian Institute of International Affairs, No. 1, 2006. The main points of the analysis were first presented in Anders Lundkvist, *Hoveder og Høveder. En demokratisk kritik af det private samfund.* Vol. 1: *Privatejendom og markedsøkonomi;* Vol. 2: *Kapitalisme;* Vol. 3: *Demokrati og økonomisk demokrati,* København, Frydenlund, 2004.
2. John H. Dunning, *Multinational Enterprises and the Global Economy,* Addison-Wesley, Wokingham 1993, 610. Hereafter, *MEGE.*

Modern corporate capitalism is a far cry from Adam Smith, for whom the market – in the form of the famous 'invisible hand' – disciplined the firms and coordinated their relations. Today, the TNC is often so big that *it* can discipline the market, and arm's length competition gives way to capitalistic cooperation between these corporations. The objective of this article is to demonstrate empirically that this trend within the global economy has strengthened since Dunning wrote in 1993, and to draw a few theoretical and political inferences.

The article is organized in the following way: The 'islands' themselves are predominately TNCs, which are defined as firms having one or more foreign affiliates. The relations between parent company and its affiliates are coordinated in ways that have nothing to do with market economy and competition. These units of conscious planning tend to merge and thus become bigger. Some evidence is presented concerning this increased *concentration* of economic power. Relations between the TNCs increasingly take the form of *strategic alliances* and tacit cooperation in *oligopolies*. Old fashioned competition still exists, of course, but on the global level it seems to be abating. Capital has grown so big and concentrated that it can avoid or control competition – and competition is, after all, the main enemy of capital, since it erodes profits.

Next, the subordination of formally independent *sub-contractors* under the regime of the TNCs (outsourcing) is briefly considered. A small company in Vietnam is no match for a TNC. A genuine market presumes that all agents are so small that no one can determine prices: hence, the notion of the invisible hand of the market. But the TNC dominates its market; it has 'market power'. It is then noted that this whole development stems from the fact that the *public authorities* have liberalized capital and given up on controlling and hampering the innate tendency of capital to concentrate. Simultaneously, the transfer of power from democracy to capital has made it possible to transform the public sector into mimicking the private, making it more market oriented. The heart of the article is the ensuing quantitative analysis of *the weight of the TNCs in the global economy*. Evidence is given for the increased role of capitalistic cooperation on the level of international trade and production.

The last section concludes, and also suggests some lessons to be learned from the marginalization of the market mechanisms that have been identified in the article. Politically speaking, many critics of the ruling global economic system have not realized that the liberal world view, according to which liberalization and deregulation has given us a world dominated by market economy and competition, is defunct. The political left should argue that the main threat to a more just and democratic economy is *corporate capital* rather than 'free trade.' Demands for *genuine* free trade could, indeed, be a potent weapon against the protective walls which the TNCs are building around themselves. In the long run, however, the alternative to capitalistic planning is not the market, but the visible hand of democratic planning.

Today, market economy is getting ready for a place among the great economic systems of the past. At the same time, we hear and read more and more about the market – the 'emerging market economies' and so forth. This is because 'the market' is associated with efficiency, economic freedom, and decentralization of economic power, making market economy an appropriate cover (ideology) for capitalistic planned economy.

Concentration of TNC-Activity

Since 1980, deregulation has been a global trend, from lower custom duties over greater freedom for firms to invest where and in what they want, to the crumbling of public monopolies. The general argument has been that deregulation encourages competition and thus improves the quality of the economy, since inefficient production will be weeded out. Monopoly profits disappear and prices will fall, to the benefit of consumers. And perhaps most importantly: economic power centers can be challenged, giving us a more free and equal economy. This is neither completely true nor completely false.

It is obviously true that more free trade exposes domestic producers to foreign competitors; allowing for more competition at the national level. It is also true that competition within a given branch intensifies when protective borders are abolished and firms are allowed to invest in whatever line of production they want. And no one can deny that genuine market economy is strengthened when a public monopoly – or, seen from another point of view, democratic decision making – is exposed to private competition or privatized and thus turned into a market player. But it is equally true that competition breeds its own opposite, monopoly or oligopoly, because economic freedom also means the freedom of the big fish to eat the small ones.[3] This trend towards concentration tends to manifest itself at the higher level, the wider market: Not within the nation but in the global market, and not within a narrow branch but within the wider sector. Why this is so can be shown by taking the financial sector in United States of America as an example.

US banking has traditionally been decentralized, with thousands of independent banks spread out over the states, cities, and towns. This structure was kept in place by laws prohibiting interstate banking and laws mandating a separation between old-fashioned commercial banks and investment banks that cater to corporations. Since the 1980s, these regulations have been abolished, while in the same period control over mergers and acquisitions has in all effects ceased, allowing for example the merger of Citicorp and Travellers in 1998. As a result, the number of US banks fell from about 14,000 until 1980 to about 8,000 in 2001, while the 10 largest banks increased their share of total bank assets from 21% to 45% in the same period.[4] At the local level, urban or rural, concentration

---

3. This trend was first analyzed by Marx in *Capital*. Standard neoclassical theory has always treated this tendency as a deviation from the alleged normal case where production becomes inefficient after reaching a certain level, due to managerial complexities ('decreasing returns to scale'), implying that competitive capitalism is a stable system, i.e., does not develop into monopolistic or oligopolistic capitalism. The argument overlooks that such technical limits can be overcome by product diversification and managerial decentralization and therefore do not limit the size of the firm, only the size of the plant.

4. Kenneth Spong, "The US Financial Sector: Regulatory Issues," in *Alliance Capitalism for the New American Economy*, edited by Alan M. Rugman and Gavin

was stable or falling, because the local monopoly – one bank per town – was now exposed to competition from the big national banks.

At the same time, financial deregulation tended to transform the earlier separate markets for banking, insurance, real estate, and securities into one big market by turning banks, insurance companies, real estate firms and brokerage houses into huge multipurpose financial supermarkets like Citigroup. A specific financial function like insurance thus faces new intruding competitors. The smaller, specialized market turns more competitive, while the larger and more general market becomes more concentrated, because the large players in whatever branch now enjoy freedom to merge and devour smaller competitors.[5]

At the global level – our main interest – liberalization of the international movements of finance capital has allowed the big players to merge or spread out over the globe, undermining smaller national players in the process; in 1998, 15% of US banking assets were placed overseas. According to the logic described, we must expect a definite trend towards increased concentration globally, and this is in fact what we can observe. In many countries, entry of foreign banks has increased competition, at least in the first round, but worldwide concentration has increased rather dramatically, helped by two great international merger waves around 1995 and 2000.

Financial services are not unique: Globally, there has also been a definite trend towards higher concentration within oil, retail, textiles, and garments.[6] An examination of the knowledge-based industries is more

---

Boyd, Cheltenham, Edward Elgar 2003, 86. This increase in concentration must, however, be moderated by increasing exposure to competition from foreign banks; the share of US banking assets held by foreigners increased from 12% in 1980 to 20% in 2001 (Spong, 90).

5. The economy of the United States is analyzed in Anders Lundkvist, *Bush, Neokonomien og Dollaren – en bog om USA's politiske økonomi*, København, Frydenlund, 2006.

6. See Peter Dicken, *Global Shift. Reshaping the Global Economic Map in The 21st Century*, 4. ed. London, Sage, 2003 (hereafter, *GS*), 317ff (on clothes), 355ff (cars), 399ff (semiconductors), 437ff (financial services) and 470ff (retail). The car industry is traditionally very concentrated, but there seems to have been a slight decrease in concentration from 1989 to 2000; however, if we take mergers and alliances into

interesting, since they are said to represent the future. Here the degree of concentration also seems to be increasing, as noted by UNDP: "Indeed, across all knowledge-intensive industries, a select group of corporations controls ever-growing shares of the global market."[7] This is evident for *medicine*, where the number of companies on the list of the 100 largest companies fell from thirteen to eight in a single year (1997), because of world-wide consolidation;[8] in 1998 the ten largest pharmaceutical companies controlled 35% of sales. Within *telecommunications*, this percentage was 86.[9]

As for the *media* sector (TV, radio, film, newspapers, music etc.), consolidation has been exceptional, due to deregulation. In the US, the number of important independent news sources shrank from 50 in 1983 to 5 in 2004, namely AOL Time Warner, News Corporation (i.e., Rupert Murdoch), Disney, Viacom, and Vivendi; who control about 90% of the information flow in USA.[10] In this sector, foreign competition is insignificant, while the influence of US media on the global scene is well-known; AOL Time Warner, Disney, and News Corporation dominate.[11] The trend is the same on the *Internet*: In 1999 60% of the Internet-users' on-line time was spent on the homepages of 110 companies, but in 2001 only 14 companies had this market share.[12]

---

account, it is evident that concentration has increased substantially. The oil industry has seen a number of mega-mergers, especially Exxon (US) and Mobil (US), BP (UK) and Amoco (US) and Total, Petrofine, and ElfAquitane (French, Belgian, and French); all took place in 1998/99.

7. United Nations Development Program (UNDP), *Human Developmental Report 1999*, Oxford, Oxford University Press, 1999, 67 (hereafter, *HDR*).
8. United Nations Conference on Trade And Development (UNCTAD), *World Investment Report 2000, Cross-border Mergers and Acquisitions and Development*, 78. Available at www.unctad.org. Hereafter: *WIR 2000, 2001*, and so forth.
9. UNDP, *HDR*.
10. William R. Clark, *Petrodollar Warfare*, Canada BC, New Society, 2005, 162f.
11. Robert W. McChesney, *Rich Media, Poor Democracy*, New York, The New Press, 2000, 91ff.
12. Serge Halimi, "Deregulation Concentrates Media Ownerships," *Le Monde Diplomatique*, English edition, June 2003.

For the *IT industry*, the evidence is somewhat conflicting, perhaps because the boundaries of the industry change every year. Concentration is very high – in 1998 the ten largest companies accounted for nearly 70% of the global market for computers – but it decreased between 1985 and 1997; on the other hand, Microsoft's share of the market for operative systems has increased every year since the beginning of the 90s so that now it is at least 95%. In the semiconductors market, the share of the ten largest corporations fell from 57% in 1989 to 54% in 1999, but the number one company in 1999 (Intel) had 15.9% while number one in 1989 (a Japanese company) had only 8.9%.[13]

In general, it is more difficult to find statistics and other information for the global level than for countries or regions. Within the European Union the market share of the 100 largest firms in manufacturing and energy increased from 14.8% in 1982 to 20% in 1988. According to Tsoukalis, the trend continued into the 90s, "especially in technologically intensive industries" and industries "closely related to public procurement, such as telecommunication and transport, and also in food industries and mass consumer goods. These are sectors that have been particularly affected by the internal market programme and its liberalizing effects."[14]

Although liberalization was intended to increase competition, it seems – ironically – to have had the opposite effect. Public monopolies have been challenged, but deregulation has also freed big capital to devour smaller capital. Thus, a number of indications suggest that concentration has increased in the global market place; fewer and bigger players will in general mean less competition.

Mergers and Acquisitions

The obvious way to gain a greater market share, thus greater control, is through *mergers and acquisitions* (M&A). At the international level,

13. *HDR*, 67; *WIR 1999*, 105ff; Richard B. McKenzie and Dwight R. Lee, "How Digital Economics Revises Anti-trust Thinking," in *Measuring Market Power*, edited by Daniel J. Slottje, Amsterdam, Elsevier, 2002, 180.
14. Loukas Tsoukalis, *The New European Economy Revisited*, Oxford, Oxford University Press, 1997, 76 (*NEER*).

M&A form an important part of *foreign direct investments* (FDI). Until around 1980, US authorities in particular were hesitant to allow M&A, but the ensuing liberalization resulted in a huge increase, for example in Latin America where TNCs took over privatized public companies. Between 1980 and 1999, the value of M&A increased on the average by 42% *each year*; while there was a drop due to the global recession during the next few years, M&A picked up after a few years. In 1999 the total value was $2.3 tri (trillion), of which a little less than 30% was cross-border.[15] M&A form an increasing part of FDIs, from 52% in 1987 to 83% in 1999 (the non-M&A part of FDI is called Greenfield investment, where the capital export results in new plants and production, rather than in a simple transfer of ownership).

M&A imply increased concentration, since they result in fewer players at the market, but increased concentration does not automatically result in less competition. If we have an industry with ten players, one of which completely dominates the market, i.e., is a 'market leader,' effective competition might increase if the nine smaller companies merge – unless the new duopoly engages in cooperation. In most cases, however, it is true that competition weakens as the number of players diminishes. If a TNC that is not represented in Argentina merges with or takes over an Argentinean firm, concentration in this country is unchanged, but at the global market there will be one player less. The degree of competition is also diminished by the fact that M&A increasingly take place within the same industry – for example a soft drink producer taking over another soft drink producer (horizontal M&A) – rather than between firms in different markets (vertical and conglomerate M&A). The relative share of the horizontal type increased from 59% of all cross-border M&A in 1989 to 70% in 1999.[16]

---

15. *WIR 2000*, 106. 1 trillion = 1,000 billions = 1,000,000 millions.
16. *WIR 2000*, 101.

Intra-Firm Trade

Any capitalistic enterprise is internally a planned economy, but the TNC extends this planning process across national borders and thus includes international trade. UNCTAD estimates that *33% of global export is intra-firm trade* – that is, trade that takes place between different sections of the same TNCs, whether between a *foreign affiliate* (FA) and the parent company or between two FAs.[17]

This part of international trade is shielded from the market economy and its competition, since the same agent – the TNC – is sitting on both sides of the table, as both importer and exporter. The prices are decided solely by the corporation, often so that the surplus is placed in the country with the lowest taxation. The authorities have tried to prevent this tax-evasion, but without much success; basically, what would be needed is cooperation between the states to set rules for the corporations, but competition between the states for greater shares of the TNC business has proved more powerful.

This intra-firm trade represents a significant element of capitalistic planned economy within the global economy. It differs from the Soviet-style planned economy in three ways. It has only one purpose, namely to maximize profits (while the Soviet economy sought to achieve politically defined – and often contradictory – purposes); there are as many plans as

---

17. This figure is on the conservative side. The EU Commission believed that the share had risen to 'at least 40%' in 1995, see Amit Bhaduri, "Implications of globalization for macroeconomic theory and policy in developing countries" in *Globalization and Progressive Economic Policy*, edited by Dean Baker, Gerald Epstein, and Robert Pollin, Cambridge University Press, 1998. Dicken (*GS*, 53) mentions the 33%, but adds that this 'could well be a substantial underestimate'. For an individual country such as the US, intra-firm export is the sum of export from US parents to their FA's and export from foreign FA's in the US to their parents (or other FA's) abroad. The US has by far the best statistics on TNCs, and for this country intra-firm export of goods constituted 36% of total US export in 1994 while the proportion was 43% for intra-firm import; both figures are virtually unchanged since 1977 (William J. Zeile, *U.S. Intra-firm Trade in Goods*, U.S. Department of Commerce, Bureau of Economic Analysis, 1997; available at www.bea.doc.gov).

there are TNCs conducting intra-firm trade – that is, there is no macro-plan as in the communist system; and the planning is global, not restricted to a certain geographical area.

Mainstream economic theory argues that unplanned coordination – the "invisible hand' – is more effective than planned coordination. If that is the case, why do we have firms – that is, entities that coordinate consciously and hierarchically? This simple question was posed in 1937 by Ronald H. Coase.[18] His answer was that the market involves a number of transaction costs, which often make firm-coordination cheaper. I would rather say that from the point of view of the firm the market does not have failures, but *is* a failure. It implies threats from competitors and lack of control of deliveries and sales; hence, an inability to control prices of inputs and finished goods. It is an expensive and uncertain device. In the words of Dunning, arms length transactions are imprecise instruments, because they imply prices and conditions which are based on aggregate demand and supply; the market cannot micro-coordinate.[19]

The market is a crude way of coordinating because the dissatisfied agent is left with only the 'exit' option. The firm prefers a system where there is room for 'choice' – a positive alternative – and this requires cooperation between two or more parties. What the TNC needs is fine-tuning through specific, individual contracts, where the price does not depend upon the anonymous market but on known trading-partners – allowing the big corporation, incidentally, to get the upper hand. Therefore, the company dislikes the market. In the best of worlds it is alone in selling the commodity (monopoly), and alone in buying the inputs (monopsony) – or it owns the firms producing the inputs so that it can dispense altogether with this market. This latter option is called *internalization* of the market, where unplanned market coordination is substituted with planned company coordination; thus competitive prices are substituted with administratively decided prices.

---

18. Ronald H. Coase "The Nature of the Firm" [1937], id. *The Firm, the Market and the Law.* Chicago, University of Chicago Press, 1988.
19. John H. Dunning, *Alliance Capitalism and Global Business,* London, Routledge, 1997, 68ff. Hereafter, *AC.*

A corporation becomes transnational when it exports capital (FDI) in order to establish an FA that is engaged in production. Instead of exporting to an independent importer in a foreign country, the TNC produces on the spot, thus dispensing with the uncertainties connected to the export price and rate of exchange; the purpose is to get more controlled market access. Or, instead of importing raw materials and components from independent producers it imports from its own FAs; where the purpose is to gain a more controlled and efficient division of labor. Dunning has summarized the basic hypothesis in the theory of internalization thus:

> [M]ultinational hierarchies represent an alternative mechanism for arranging value-added activities across national boundaries to that of the market ... [F]irms are likely to engage in FDI whenever they perceive that the net benefits of their joint ownership of domestic and foreign activities, and the transactions arising from them, are likely to exceed those offered by external trading relationships.[20]

Coordination between Transnational Corporations

We have now seen that a competitive, global market economy seems to be under threat from increasing concentration; referring to the image in the Introduction, the important 'islands' have become more dominating. Now we turn to the threat emerging from the growth of non-market relations between the TNCs.

Strategic alliances

The system of forming strategic alliances is a method of limiting competition and gaining more control over the market. Dunning believes these alliances to be so important that he has termed the present economic system 'Alliance Capitalism'. Their number has increased fast, from a little more than one thousand in 1989 to around seven thousand in 1999, and the value of each alliance is now much larger than earlier.[21] The

20. Dunning *MEGE*, 75.
21. Dicken, *GS*, 258.

one thousand largest American companies increased the part of earnings originating from alliances from 2% in 1980 to 18% in 1997.[22] Airline companies were divided into three alliances: Sky Team (including among others Dutch KLM and Air France), Star Alliance (SAS, Lufthansa, American United Airlines and nine others), and One World (eight companies); in a similar way, the computer industry in 1996 consisted of four alliances.[23]

The partners in an alliance cooperate in specific, limited areas; often these concern Research and Development or marketing. Partners can contribute capital (equity) to a certain project, thus establishing a 'joint venture' which is a sort of partial and time-limited merger, or form an alliance that can be 'non-equity' and less formalized. The involved corporations normally present alliances as if they are of a purely technical nature, benefiting all parties, consumers included. However, where there is cooperation there is not competition. The firms can compete in other areas, especially pricing, where the trust laws normally forbid explicit agreements. But price is only one parameter in competition, and today rivalry in developing new products or new marketing techniques might be just as important. Agreements on common standards inside the IT-area certainly make sense (e.g. 'Wintelism' which homogenizes Microsoft's Windows and Intel), but they tend to put other firms at a disadvantage; therefore it was earlier considered a public responsibility to establish such standards.

If the cooperating companies were to operate on unrelated markets (wheat and computers), there would be no competition to reduce. But the majority of alliances are within the same market, between direct competitors.[24] This is natural, since cooperation presupposes a certain degree of common problems and common interests.

22. Marina von Neumann Whitman, *New Worlds, New Rules; the Changing Role of the American Corporation*, Harvard Business School Press 1999, 155.
23. Dicken, *GS*, 259.
24. Harbison and Pekar set the percentage to 52, (John R. Harbison and Peter Pekar, *Cross-Border Alliances in the Age of Collaboration*. Booz-Allen & Hamilton, 1997, 17), while Dicken (*GS*, 258) put this share to 70% in 2000. According to Dunning, most alliances involve "large firms competing as oligopolies in global markets" (*AC*, 75).

Strategic Alliances are often the answer to intolerable competition. By standing together, a group of companies can achieve better deals with sub-contractors, customers, trade-unions and governments.[25] Thereby, they force other companies to form counter-alliances, transforming the old, more atomistic competition into what has been called "collective competition".[26] In the words of UNCTAD, "... global markets increasingly involve competition between entire production *systems*, orchestrated by TNCs, rather than between individual factories or firms."[27]

The TNCs do not form a harmonious family. There are still fierce struggles about markets and resources, but they tend to be between corporations allied in groups. Since it is not the anonymous market, but the conscious strategies of the groups, based on their relative economic power, which determine the outcome, perhaps 'rivalry' is a better term than 'competition'. Thus, cooperation vies with internecine struggle, but the trend seems to be that cooperation gets the upper hand, since the common interests between the separate capitals triumph more easily with fewer players in the global market.

Oligopoly

Oligopoly means that there are few players in a certain market; cars, semiconductors and oil are clear examples of oligopolistic markets. How does such a market work? Mainstream theory explains that the result will be too little production and too high prices, the standard being output and prices under perfect competition (where we have innumerable players), while Schumpeter, Galbraith and others argued that companies have to be big – thus few – in order to be effective.[28] In any case, oligopoly seldom

---

25. Dunning, *AC*, 240.
26. Benjamin Gomes-Casseres, *The Alliance Revolution, The New Shape of Business Rivalry*, Cambridge Mass., Harvard University Press, 1996, 2.
27. *WIR 2002*, 121.
28. While it is obvious that certain industries like cars demand a minimum size of firm in order to be effective, it is not in general clear whether the big company is effective because of technological reasons or because size gives it control of the market and its prices ('profit-effective'). Efficiency might predominantly be a function of profitability, rather than the other way around, because the profitable firm can afford

leads to fierce competition. The individual company realizes that it will not increase its market share by lowering prices since the other companies will respond by also lowering prices. The result will be the same market share, but lower prices, thus smaller profits for all. If companies are rational, they take account of the other companies' reaction, realizing that competition is a mutual disadvantage; their common interest is therefore to establish a formal or tacit agreement not to compete. Formal price agreements are illegal today, but the tacit variety is more difficult to prevent. It is difficult to establish empirically just how widespread this informal cooperation is; only indirect evidence – looking at development of prices and sales – is available. Susan Strange believes that these agreements eliminate competition in a number of industries:

> In steel, in shipping, and probably in most chemicals, aluminium, electrical products, authority of the market is exercised by associations of firms organized in overt or covert cartels to rig prices in favour of the members ... [29]

The degree of oligopoly depends on which market we are considering. It might increase for coffee, but decrease for organic coffee. Also, we might get more competition, with more players, on most national markets, but more oligopoly on the global market, since fewer and bigger global corporations could be in a better position to challenge national near-monopolies.

To evaluate the degree of concentration and coordination it is necessary to take account of ownership. From the point of view of consumers there is no competition between refrigerators and furniture. But these two industries are engaged in a global competition for capital; e.g. if the rate of profit is low in producing refrigerators, capital will move to other industries, like furniture. This presupposes, however, that competition on the capital market is free, which is not the case. Capital is increasingly

to invest in technology, marketing etc.
29. Susan Strange, *The Retreat of the State*. Cambridge University Press, 1996, 160. Hereafter, *RS*.

concentrated in huge funds (pension funds, insurance, mutual investment funds, hedge funds, and lately so-called capital funds). The power of these funds – that is, of finance capital – has been demonstrated in the financial markets, where their speculation has unleashed or aggravated a number of financial crises. The funds also invest in corporations, and sometimes control them; in 1994, for example, they owned 57% of the US American shares, up from 16% in 1965.[30] In later years, institutional investors like pension funds have been seen to follow a more active policy towards companies in which they have an interest. The funds are in a position to coordinate activities in specific industries and between widely different industries, directly through active representation in the boards of directors, indirectly through allocation of capital to different companies.

Sub-Contracting

We now turn from the cooperation between TNCs to their less-than-competitive relation to smaller firms. As mentioned above, internalization of the market through establishing FAs has important advantages. There is, however, also a disadvantage. When the TNC itself invests and produces, it bears the risk if the line of production turns out to be a failure. By outsourcing production to independent firms – often in the poor countries – the risk is shifted to these sub-contractors; if sales fail the corporation can simply discontinue the contract. Flexibility is increased. Now, the 'trick' is that this *externalization to the market* can often be done without jeopardizing the advantages of internalization. The reason is that the relation between the TNC and the sub-contractor is only formally a market relation between two independent agents.

In a pure market economy, the firms produce for an anonymous market, where the price is determined by demand and supply; no one can dictate a certain price. In sub-contracting, however, the price is negotiated between the two parties, so it depends upon their relative economic and political power. Here it is obvious that the TNC has the upper hand; it has market power: that is, power over the market. Its resources are huge compared to

---

30. Michael Useem, quoted in Whitman, *New Worlds*, 30f.

the sub-contractor, and it has more options. If a firm in the Philippines is too expensive, the TNC can move to Vietnam, while we never hear of an unsatisfied sub-contractor who replaces Nike with another TNC; often, its production is geared to a certain corporation, from whom it receives design and equipment, perhaps even financing.[31] Put in another way, there is little competition between TNCs for securing contracts, while there is intense competition among the sub-contractors for orders:

> Even when international production is highly externalized, TNCs typically exert powerful authority through their control of key functions, such as brand management and product definition, as well as through the setting and enforcing of technical, quality and delivery standards throughout a network of formally independent producers.[32]

So, indirectly – between the subcontractors – there is a lot of competition, but it is a competition which weakens the small and strengthens the big. The whole system is "a kind of half-way house between complete internalization of procurement on the one hand and arm's length transactions on the open market on the other."[33] In sum, through intra-firm trade, strategic alliances, tacit cooperation and sub-contracting the TNCs form what has been called the *Integrated International Production system* (IIP), a construct to which we will return below.

Competition between Poor Countries and in the Public Sector
In addition to the failures of the market noted above, however, the market can also count some success stories. Between poor countries competition for capital has increased, and market principles have entered the public sector. As Marx realized, capitalism, when left to itself, breeds monopolization and inter-capital cooperation, since competition erodes profits and therefore is the natural enemy of capitalism. This tendency, however, does not manifest itself empirically if it is counteracted by pub-

31. Dicken, *GS*, 254f.
32. *WIR 2002*, 123f.
33. Dicken, *GS*, 254.

lic authorities that prohibit trusts and monopolies and in general keep a critical eye on infringements of competition. In the US, this was more or less the case in the Progressive Era before 1914, and during the Golden Era from 1945 to the 1970s.

The essence of neoliberalism is the freedom of capital to invest where and in what it chooses. Since 'freedom' here is the nicer word for 'power' the liberalization of capital around 1980 transferred power from democratically elected politicians to capital. Public authorities in the US and EU gave up efforts to hamper mergers and acquisitions, allowing virtually all. The EU Commission has 'generally welcomed, if not encouraged', M&A, approving 99% of the applications in 1995 and 99.5% in 1999.[34]

In the poor countries,[35] the debt crises after 1980 made structural adjustment programs possible, forcing the states to give up the earlier, more equitable negotiations between states and TNCs and submit to the demands of the companies. Barriers to globalization of capital were thus removed, which at the same time furthered global concentration and increased competition for capital among the poor countries.

In so far as the state is democratic, the changed power relation between state and capital implies a weakened democracy. In principle, the public sector is the democratic sector, because decisions ultimately are based on the principle 'one person, one vote', as opposed to the private sector where influence is proportional to money owned. With the unfolding of neoliberalism, the national state has retreated from efforts to regulate capitalism. Moreover, the public sector has increasingly been subsumed under the interests of private capital; education is either privatized or asked to conform to the needs of corporations, provision of health and

34. Tsoukalis, *NEER*, 88, and *Financial Times*, November 3. 1999. Susan Strange is of the opinion that even the fight against cartels, which are formally forbidden, is "pretty much of a farce" in the US, Japan, and the EU; when cartels are disclosed, the fines are insignificant (Strange, *RS*, 147f and 158f).

35. I choose the neutral categorization of countries in 'rich' and 'poor,' in preference to 'developed' versus 'developing' countries. While everyone can agree that poor countries should become richer, the latter categories imply that poor countries are children that should be brought up, namely brought up to 'us.' This language presents corporate capitalism as the ideal.

pensions is turned into business for medical corporations and finance capital, many public activities are outsourced, and so forth. Still, the public sector cannot, like the private, be ruled completely by the dictates of profit maximization, since it has to provide some basic services, whether profitable or not, and since it is financed by taxes; decisions on these matters are still made by 'competing' political parties. While the provision of services in the public sector has become a source of profit, it is only partially ruled by profit. But it is safe to say that the methods of providing these services have become more market oriented. So, in this area the market economy *is* thriving.

Global Corporate Capitalism

We now turn to the general picture, asking: What power do TNCs hold in the global economy, and how did it develop? There is no doubt that the volume of the TNCs in the global economy has increased substantially. All indicators point in this direction:

– The number of TNCs has increased from 33,000 (with 150,000 FAs) in 1990 to 65,000 (with 850,000 FAs) in 2001.[36] While global export has increased only with the factor 1.7 (see Table 1), the number of TNCs has doubled and their FAs have grown by a factor of almost 6.

– FDI outflow, which per definition is performed by TNCs, has in the same period increased from \$233 bio (billion) to \$621 bio, relatively from 4.8% of global gross fixed capital formation in 1990 to 9.3% in 2001 (see Table 1).

Is it possible, on the global level, to give more comprehensive empirical evidence for the trends outlined above? Indeed it is, though there may be a significant element of uncertainty about the figures.[37]

---

36. *WIR 1992*, 15, and *WIR 2002*, 14. These two years have been chosen for the following reasons: 1990 is the first year for which *WIR* has more comprehensive data. Since we have to compare peak with peak, or through with through, over the economic cycle, and since 1990 was a rather bad year globally (though 1991 was worse), it is appropriate to use the recession year, 2001, as a point of comparison.
37. Normally, the official statistics for the different countries have no interest in

When we are estimating the 2001 weight of the TNCs in the global economy as well as the trend from 1990 to 2001, two indicators are used: Share of global trade and share of value added. Since the TNCs are the big companies of this world, the higher their share the higher must be the concentration of global economic power.[38] Still, these figures do not tell the whole story. It is also important to look at the concentration within the TNC family. Have the very large corporations increased their share of economic activity? We can measure these matters with some degree of confidence. Yet the power stemming from more cooperation and coordination between the corporations (strategic alliances and oligopoly), as well as from increased subordination of smaller firms (subcontractors), is much harder to estimate empirically. In 1997, Dunning's estimate was that we have a global economy "where upwards of one-half of trade is either within the same organizational entity (i.e., intra-firm trade) or between parties which engage in some kind of medium- to long-term co-operative relationship (e.g. subcontracting, strategic alliances)."[39] If we add the tacit cooperation in oligopolies, the Integrated International Production system must control more than 50% of world trade.

Dunning is among the best informed researchers on TNCs, and certainly neither an alarmist nor unduly critical of the corporations. His estimate means that around half of global trade in the mid-90s was dominated by the planning and cooperation of corporations, leaving the other half to the competition of the market economy. Let us try to be more specific, especially about the trend.

---

distinguishing between TNCs and other firms when estimating trade, production, etc. The figures we do have are mostly estimates made by UNCTAD in the yearly *World Investment Reports*. The problem with these numbers is that they normally concentrate on the FAs, excluding the activities of the parent company.

38. A TNC can be a small firm with only one FA, but as a matter of fact most are very big compared to non-TNC firms; when a firm reaches a certain size, limited responsibility and other favours bestowed by the state make the corporate form an obvious advantage. In the US, small and medium TNCs only constituted 28% of all TNCs in 1990 (and they could have up to 500 employees), see *WIR 1993*, 22ff.

39. *AC*, 120.

Global trade

The estimates and calculations are based on the following table from UNCTAD, 2002.[40] The figures are in billions of dollars, the real increases are thus exaggerated, but since inflation was modest in the 90s, this is not very important. Anyway, the TNC-share of global trade and production is not affected.

Table 1

	1990	2001
FDI outflow	233	621
FDI outward stock	1,721	6,582
FA sales	5,479	18,517
FA export	1,169	2,600
License fees	27	73
FA assets	5,759	24,952
Export (world)	4,375	7,430

---

40. *WIR 2002*, 4.

From the table we see that world trade, as measured by global export (in principle equal to global import), in 2001 was a little less than $7,5 trillion (tri). Dunning's estimate of upwards of one-half of all trade refers to the mid-90s and only includes intra-firm trade, subcontracting, and trade based on strategic alliances; all other TNC trade – other trade between TNCs or between TNCs and non-TNCs – is excluded. When this is taken into account, we reach 67%: i.e., TNCs were responsible for an estimated two-thirds of world trade. About half of TNC trade takes place between parent firms and their affiliates abroad, or among affiliates.[41] World trade around 2001 was thus nicely divided into three parts of equal size:

a) 33% or $2.5 tri is intra-firm trade and thus directly controlled by a TNC; this part is pure capitalistic planned economy.

b) 33% or $2.5 tri, namely half of the TNC share of 67%, is also controlled by the TNCs, but in this case the trade is between a TNC and some other firm (perhaps another TNC); this part is a mix between genuine market economy (competition) and capitalistic cooperation and planning (oligopolies, strategic alliances and sub-contracting).[42]

c) 33% or $2.5 tri is the residual global trade, where TNCs are not involved. Here the market forces have more of a say.

Let us now try to compare with the year 1990, when global export was $4.4 tri. How big of a share did the TNCs account for in that year? The export from the FAs were a little less than $1.2 tri (see again Table 1), while export from parent companies can be estimated at $1.4 tri.[43] Total

41. *WIR 2000*, 17. We also find the estimate of two-third in *WIR 2002*, 153. Unfortunately, WIR does not explain the basis for this estimate. For the US, TNCs took care of 57% of US export in 2003, but to this must be added the export from foreign FAs, situated in the US, see Raymond J. Mataloni Jr., *U.S. Multinational Companies, Operations in 2003*, U.S. Department of Commerce, Bureau of Economic Analysis, July 2005; available at www.bea.doc.gov

42. If we square Dunning's and *WIR*'s estimates (disregarding that Dunning refers to the mid-90s), half of the share b) must be exports in the context of strategic alliances or subcontracting; thus we reach Dunning's 50%. Again, we might add the effects of oligopolies.

43. We do not have a direct figure for the export conducted by the parent companies,

TNC export ($1.2 tri + $1.4 tri) would then have constituted *59% of the global export in 1990*, as compared to 67% in 2001. A rather dramatic increase in a short period of a little more than 10 years.

In 2001 intra-firm export constituted 33% of global export. Probably this share of capitalistic planned economy was lower in 1990,[44] so a global percentage of around 30 seems realistic.

Let us finally look at the development in the degree of concentration within the TNC family – have the very large companies increased their relative weight? The merger-waves between 1990 and 2001 suggest such a trend. Calculations indicate that the 500 largest TNCs have

---

but we can overcome that difficulty. In 2001 TNC export was $5 tri, out of which the FAs exported $2.6 tri, leaving $2.4 tri to the parent companies. From 1990 to 2001, FA export increased 2.2 times (from $1.2 tri to $2.6 tri), and if the rate of increase were the same for the parent companies their export would have been $2.4 tri/2.2 = $1.1 tri in 1990. Total TNC export ($1.2tri + $1.1 tri) would then have constituted 52% of the global export of $4.4 tri. But corporations have become more international, shifting activity from the parent company to the FAs. This is indicated, first, by the fact that the number of FAs has increased three times as much as the number of TNCs (see above) and, second, by the increase in *WIR*'s transnationality index for the 100 largest corporations from 51% in 1991 to almost 56% in 2000 (*WIR 2002*, 96). The American experience is that export from US parents and total US export increased with the factor 1.9 and 1.8, respectively, from 1989 to 1999 (calculated from Table 14 in R. J. Mataloni Jr. and D. R. Yorgason, 2002, *Operations of U.S. Multinational Companies, Preliminary Results From the 1999 Benchmark Survey*, U.S. Department of Commerce, Bureau of Economic Analysis, March 2002; available at www.bea.doc.gov). Let us therefore assume, conservatively, that the global export from the parent companies has grown only with the same pace as world export (from $4,375 billion to $7,430 billion), i.e., 1.7 times. Parent company exports would then have been $2.4 tri/1.7 = $1.4 tri in 1990.

44. UNCTAD's overall estimates for the beginning of the 1990s have varied from 25% to 33% (*WIR 1992*, 53; *WIR 1995*, 37), but the last figure is based on the high US proportion and is surely too high for the world average. As mentioned above, the share for US export and import of goods did not change between 1977 and 1994, but the intra-firm share of US import of services increased from 30% in 1986 to 47% in 2002 (*WIR 2004*, xxii), suggesting that the share of intra-firm trade has increased since 1990.

had an unchanged share of total TNC sales,[45] but since the number of TNCs has doubled between 1990 and 2001 this means that the degree of concentration, thus measured, has doubled: In 1990 1.52% of the TNCs (500 of 33,000) had the same share as 0.77% (500 of 65,000) had in 2001. If we look at the 100 largest TNCs, however, the degree of concentration is unchanged. The top within the TNC family has become more economically powerful, but the top has flattened.

Global production

Let us now turn from trade to production as an indicator of the economic power of the TNCs. What is the share of these companies in global production? UNCTAD gives yearly figures for world-GNP, that is, total global income or – what amounts to the same thing – value of global production; this value is also called value-added or gross product. These figures must be compared to the gross product of the TNCs, but unfortunately we have only direct figures for the FAs. See Table 2;[46] again, the figures indicate billions (bio) of dollars in current prices.

Table 2

	1990	2001
Gross product (FAs)	1,423	3,495
World GDP	21,672	31,900

The FA's contribution to world production (or income) thus increased from 6.5% in 1990 to 11% in 2001. To calculate the percentages for total TNC activity we need to estimate figures for the parent companies.

For the 100 largest TNCs the activity was almost equally distributed

45. My calculations are based on the information in *WIR 2002*, 90, namely that "the sales of the 500 largest firms in the world nearly tripled between 1990 and 2001."
46. Taken from *WIR 2002*, 4.

between home countries and foreign countries in 2001, whether we look at assets, sales, or employment;[47] assume that the same goes for the value of production. The other – smaller – TNCs are without a doubt less globalized; a general FA share of 40% is probably realistic. That gives us a total TNC production of $3,495 bio/40 x 100 = $8,737 bio in 2001, i.e., 27.4% of world GNP. This proportion is much less than we saw for trade; since TNCs are international per definition it is not surprising that they dominate international trade more than world production (which is still predominately sold in the country where the production takes place).

In 1990 corporations were less globalized. For the 100 largest corporations, FA assets then constituted only 37.5% of the assets of these TNCs.[48] Again, when we take into account the fact that the rest of the TNCs are less globalized, we end up with a somewhat lower proportion. I choose 31.5%, since this is Dunning's figure for 1988: He estimates total TNC assets in this year to be $9–10 tri, out of which the FAs had $3 tri.[49] Assuming that the proportions are the same for production as for assets, we conclude that total TNC production in 1990 was $1,423 bio/31.5 X 100 = $4.517 bio, i. e. 20.8% of world GNP. This means *that the TNCs have increased their share of world production from 20.8% in 1990 to 27.4% in 2001*. Again a rather dramatic development.

The End of Market Economy?

Now, I do not wish to minimize the elements of uncertainty in the above calculations. UNCTAD's and Dunning's figures are rough estimates, and a couple of informed guesses are necessary in order to reach my conclusions, both concerning trade and production. To my knowledge this is the first attempt to establish trends for the economic weight of the TNCs; let us hope that better and more comprehensive data, especially about the activities of the parent companies, will allow us greater accuracy in the future.[50] I would add, however, that we should trust the figures for

47. *WIR 2003*, 5.
48. *WIR 1993*, 22f.
49. *MEGE*, 16.
50. Also, there is a great need for a comprehensive, quantitative analysis of global

the trends more than the figures for the structure in particular years, the reason being that if there is a bias in the structure it will often be present both in 1990 and 2001, thus tending to cancel out when we calculate trends. With these reservations, the weakening of old-fashioned market economy and the strengthening of global corporate capitalism seems rather certain.

However we define market economy, it must include competition as the principle of organization, as opposed to the socially conscious coordination characteristic for a planned economy. It is competition which harmonizes demand and supply, needs and production, through the famous invisible – or socially unconscious – hand. The market determines the prices to which the agents have to adjust. In a market economy, the market rules.

When agents are able to determine the prices, *they* set the rules. It is no longer the market which has power over the agents, but the agents who have power over the market ('market power'). When this becomes the predominant condition, market economy ceases to exist. Products are still bought and sold for money, but that was also the case in Soviet-style economies and cannot therefore be the defining characteristic, though it can create the illusion of a market economy. The liberalization since 1980 has certainly increased competition within some areas: Sub-contractors compete for contracts, states compete for capital from the TNCs, and wage-earners compete for jobs.[51] Competition decentralizes economic power and has therefore in this case the function of weakening those players who potentially could constitute a counter-power to the corporations.

We have also noted that liberalization tends to increase competition

---

finance capital. This capital is organized in huge banks, pension funds, insurance companies, and mutual funds (e.g., hedge funds). It has already been indicated that banks tend to concentrate and the same probably is true for the other funds, but how strong has the tendency been? How international is finance capital? What power does it have compared to the reserves of the states, and how does it interact with productive capital (the TNCs)?

51. The labor market has become more flexible, with more individualization and less trade union influence, and wage-earners in different countries find themselves indirectly competing against each other because capital now has the freedom to choose the country with the lowest wages.

at the lower level: In the special rather than the general market, in the local rather than the national market, and in the national rather than the global market. At the commanding heights of the global economy, however, competition has become weakened. First, because the TNCs have increased their separate, private empires, where they can operate their planned economies shielded from the market economy. Second, because in the relation *between* the TNCs, competition tends to be substituted for conscious coordination, whether formally in strategic alliances or informally (tacitly) in oligopolies.

We tend to form our conception of the world by generalizing from our close experiences, and these experiences suggest that competition is thriving; often, the market close to your home has become more competitive. This might explain the common but wrong belief that market economy every day becomes more predominant as the ruling principle of the global economy. The controversy over 'free trade' is a case in point. In a much used textbook on international economics, the scene is thus set:

> Countries engage in international trade for two basic reasons, each of which contributes to their gain from trade. First, countries trade because they are different from each other. Nations, like individuals, can benefit from their differences by reaching an arrangement in which each does the things it does relatively well. Second, countries trade to achieve economics of scale in production. That is, if each country produces only a limited range of goods, it can produce each of these goods at a larger scale and hence more efficiently than if it tried to produce everything. In the real world, patterns of international trade reflect the interaction of these motives.[52]

So, countries trade, and they do it in order to obtain efficiencies. Both wrong. The subjects of international trade are not 'nations', but private importers and exporters, two-thirds of which happens to be TNCs; half of 'China's export' is in fact taken care of by American FAs in China.

52. Paul Krugman and Maurice Obstfeld, *International Economics*, 6.ed., Boston, Addison-Wesley, 2003, 10 (*IE*).

It was in the communist systems that nations, represented by their ministers of trade, decided what to import and export; and up until 1959, this was also partly the case in Western Europe, since the lack of foreign currency (dollars) induced a system where import had to be approved by the authorities. But the freer the trade, the less the nations are involved as such. It follows that the 'reason' for trade is not the gain of the nations.

Nor is the purpose of trade to 'obtain efficiencies'. Since trade is taken care of by private capital (mostly the TNCs), it follows that its purpose is maximum profit, efficiency being a means and a possible side-effect. It is not a foregone conclusion that the well-being of a TNC is identical to the well-being of the nation and its inhabitants. In the Yeltsin years, Russian importers used the scarce foreign currency to buy luxurious cars, since they were the most profitable to sell, while what Russia needed as a nation was Western technology and basic consumption goods.

'Free trade' means private trade, i.e., trade which democratically elected politicians are unable to direct in the general interest of the country. It should here be noted that the standard argument for 'free trade', Ricardo's theory of comparative advantages and Hecksher-Ohlin's extension of the theory to factors of production, is nothing of the sort. It is a – very good – argument for the advantages of trade, but it does not say that private agents are best positioned to realize these advantages. Nobody denies that division of labor, within a country or between countries, increases efficiency and welfare, but to reach the conclusion that this division should be effectuated by the market one has to activate an altogether different theory, namely the neoclassical general equilibrium theory (including Pareto's welfare theory) that purports to show that private agents, when left free, will generate the optimal economic system. Whatever the merits of this theory, it does not seem to be valid when it comes to international trade. In the 50s, the Russian-American economist, Leontief, found that US export was more labor intensive than the import, though the Heckscher-Ohlin theory stipulated that the capital-rich USA should specialize in selling capital intensive products. Economists inferred that there must be something wrong with the theory. But the theory was quite right in pointing out that a country should take advantage of the abundant factor of production: It was the US capitalistic trading system which was wrong, since it was unable to create a rational pattern of trade. But that is not all. The two theories mentioned are only valid if a number of conditions are fulfilled, among them that only goods, not capital, can move from country to country. This was indeed the case at Ricardo's time, but not today, making the two theories irrelevant when analyzing the actual working of the global economic system. Unfortunately, textbooks in international economics fail to mention this.

The liberalization of capital has increased the possibility of a divergence between the interests of capital and those of the country. Chad has oil, and one should therefore think that the country had profited from the high oil prices in recent years. Not so. The oil is produced and exported by foreign TNCs, who send the profit back to their headquarters; the money will appear in Chad's balance of trade as income from export, but the inhabitants will never see it. Thirty–forty years ago, the authorities might have demanded the money invested in their own country, but not today when capital is free.

Today, 'free trade' actually means freedom for the TNCs to trade as they please, since the traders mainly are these companies; 'free trade' is but an aspect of the liberalization of capital. And abolition of custom duties actually means a transfer of money from the public purse to the TNCs (this is especially a problem for poor countries such as India).[53]

'Free trade' does *not* mean trade on a competitive market; on the contrary. As we have seen, liberalization of trade tends to undermine a genuine market economy and substitute it for a capitalistic planned economy. One-third of global trade is intra-firm and thus clearly outside the market while capitalistic cooperation (strategic alliances and oligopolies) and the domination of smaller firms by the big corporations

---

53. Krugman and Obstfeld devote exactly 8 out of 754 pages (169–77) to multinational firms. Their economic weight in the world trade is not mentioned and their impact on competition is not discussed. This might be the reason that the authors can conclude that "multinational corporations probably are not as important a factor in the world economy as their visibility suggest" (*IE*, 175).

(sub-contracting) accounts for a further one-third of global trade. As mentioned, it has been estimated that the organization of the global economy is split fifty-fifty between plan and market. New waves of liberalizations will probably weaken the market further.

It is not strange that liberal politicians and economists present the global economic system as market oriented. 'The market' is a functional ideology for the emerging capitalistic planned economy, because it hides this reality under a veil of economic freedom. The more curious point is that critics of this system overlook that capitalism tends to destroy the competitive market. It is often accepted that neoliberalism implies freer trade, and that societies therefore should protect themselves from the rough assaults of the market through duties and other means. This certainly makes sense in many cases, especially for poor countries. Protection could take the form of a global extra-duty of, for example, 1% on corporate trade – exempting coffee cooperatives in Central America, for example – in addition to a so-called 'Tobin tax' on finance capital. However, by uncritically taking over the liberal world-view, the political Left overlooks the main arguments and the main lines of conflict.

Today, protectionism is predominately capital protecting itself from the market, and fighting *this* protectionism should therefore be the top of the agenda. Correspondingly, thinkers and activists on the political Left could demand that TNCs implement *effective* free trade, by prohibiting mergers and perhaps by breaking up bigger TNCs into smaller units. The monopolization of intellectual inventions in patents and copyrights – overwhelmingly the property of Western corporations – should also be targeted; the efforts of WHO and the TNCs to extend private intellectual property rights is in strict contradiction to the idea of free trade. In such battles the political Left can join hands with genuine liberals – and expose the dominant, hypocritical variety.

For the time being, such battles are important, but in the long run a return to a competitive economy is probably a reactionary dream. There is more promise in arguing that since history is about to leave market economy behind, the real choice will be between a *capitalistic* and a *democratic planned economy.* Since the invisible hand is defunct, and the economy in any case is going to be planned, why not leave the planning to the people and their democratically elected politicians rather than to a limited number of capital owners and Chief Executive Officers?

The Transcendental Power of Money

Karl Marx's Argument in the *Grundrisse*[1]

J. F. Humphrey

Above all things, good policy is to be used that the treasure and moneys in a state be not gathered into few hands. For otherwise a state may have a great stock, and yet starve. And money is like muck, not good except it be spread. This is done chiefly by suppressing or at least keeping a strait hand upon the devouring trades of usury ... [2]

The recent economic crisis has raised a number of questions about the conception of free markets, and the neoconservative economic theories on which the capitalist nations have relied. Free marketeers like former Federal Reserve Chairman, Alan Greenspan, have acknowledged that unregulated markets have enormous costs and in the end could be damaging to the welfare of citizens, the financial health of economic institutions, and to the fiscal strength of nation states. For example, *New York Times* journalist Edmund L. Andrews writes:

---

1. An earlier version of this paper was published in *Nordicum-Mediterraneum: Icelandic E-Journal of Nordic and Mediterranean Studies*, vol. 5, no. 1 (March 2010), 124 (http://nome.unak.is). I would like to thank the editor, Giorgio Baruchello, for his kindness and encouragement in my efforts to develop this piece.
2. Francis Bacon, "Seditions and Troubles," id., *Major Works*, Oxford University Press, 2002, 369.

Almost three years after stepping down as chairman of the Federal Reserve, a humbled Mr. Greenspan admitted that he had put too much faith in the self-correcting power of free markets and had failed to anticipate the self-destructive power of wanton mortgage lending. "Those of us who have looked to the self-interest of lending institutions to protect shareholders' equity, myself included, are in a state of shocked disbelief," he [Greenspan] told the House Committee on Oversight and Government Reform.[3]

In a National Public Radio interview, Greenspan even calls this current crisis a "credit tsunami," admitting that "the free market ideology may be flawed."[4] Still, despite this painful admission, Greenspan had very few suggestions for regulating or correcting the failures of the free-market system. Andrews notes that "despite his [Greenspan's] chagrin over the mortgage mess, the former Fed chairman proposed only one specific regulation: that companies selling mortgage-backed securities be required to hold a significant number themselves."[5] In the same article, Greenspan expresses his continued belief in the market: "Whatever regulatory changes are made, they will pale in comparison to the change already evident in today's markets. ... Those markets for an indefinite future will be far more restrained than would any currently contemplated new regulatory regime."

Other observers of global capitalism – both supporters and critics of capitalism – have been concerned for some time about the boding dangers of the free market system. Already in 2002 'the sage of Omaha,' Warren Buffet, Chairman of Berkshire Hathaway, for example, warned against the perils of derivatives, calling them "financial weapons of mass destruction, carrying dangers that, while now latent are potentially lethal."[6] And in

3. Edmund L. Andrews, "Greenspan Concedes Error on Regulation," New York Times, October 23, 2008.
4. See Brian Naylor's October 24, 2008 interview with Alan Greenspan, "Greenspan Admits Free Market Ideology Flawed," http://www.npr.org/templates/story/story.php?storyId=96070766.
5. Andrews, NYT.
6. Warren Buffet, "Chairman's Letter," in Berkshire Hathaway, Inc., 2002 Annual Report, 15. http://www.berkshirehathaway.com/2002ar/2002ar.pdf.

an interview with the British Broadcasting Corporation [BBC], Buffet said, "Large amounts of risk have become concentrated in the hands of relatively few derivatives dealers ... which can trigger serious systemic problems."[7] Indeed, Buffet concludes, derivatives are like "hell ... easy to get into and almost impossible to exit."

John McMurtry, who traces the origins of capitalism to the works of John Locke and Adam Smith, however, reminds us that both of these thinkers developed their economic theories out of their ethical philosophies. But how has economic thought moved so far from ethical and moral considerations? Presumably, the free market was justified because, according to classical liberal economists, it led to human happiness. As reviewer Mary Rawson asks, "If the market system was to bring a better life to all, why can we find everywhere armaments, killing fields, malnutrition, brown water, and the disappearance of species? Why do we find, not life, but death?"[8] Citing Robert Lane's *The Loss of Happiness in Market Democracies*, McMurtry argues that, although most current economic theory would not agree, "human satisfaction actually declines as income and commodity consumption rise beyond need."[9] Furthermore, insofar as government leaders are tied to large corporate interests, the public interest is completely ignored:

> As Governments decline into 'the best democracies that money can buy' there is no public authority left to protect the common interest. Our political leaders assume market growth is essential to society's development. So public welfare is sacrificed to 'more global market competiveness' – and more life-system depredation. To name the causal links remains taboo.[10]

7. BBC News, "Buffet Warns of Investment Time Bomb," Tuesday, March 4, 2003. http://news.bbc.co.uk/2/hi2817995.stm
8. Mary Rawson, review of *Unequal Freedoms: The Global Market as an Ethical System* by John McMurtry, *Peace Magazine* 15, 3 (May–June 1999), 31.
9. John McMurtry, "Myths of the Global Market," *New Internationalist*, issue 301 (June 2007), 1. Hereafter, *MGM*.
10. *MGM*, 2. One cannot help thinking of the United State Supreme Court ruling

Although recent economic theory has claimed that the market is 'objective,' 'value-free,' McMurtry complains of those economists who expound 'free market' private enterprise and democracy as if together they were a god." As former investor George Soros argues, however, "by claiming to be value free, market fundamentalism has actually undermined moral values."[11]

The ever controversial multibillionaire George Soros, who is known for breaking the Bank of England as a currency speculator, for founding the Soros Fund Management, for cofounding the Quantum Fund, for being convicted of insider trading, as a financial backer of US Major League Soccer, and now as a philanthropist has been called everything from a corporate raider to a leftist. While he has obviously benefitted from the capitalist system, as an author, Soros has warned of the dangers of the system; indeed, he argues that the current global economic problems have fundamentally harmed the global financial system itself and indicates the end of free market capitalism.[12] While he distinguishes the current crisis from the collapse of the Japanese economy (1990s) because the current problems are not confined to one country, Soros also distinguishes it from the 'Great Depression' (1929) because the world economic system has not been allowed to collapse completely; it has been propped up by various national governments. He predicts that a "new world order … will eventually emerge" and it "will not be dominated by the United States to the same extent as the old one."[13] Summing up his position, Soros maintains that "a global economy demands global regulations." Echoing these concerns, Nobel prize winning economist Joseph Stiglitz asserts that "the truth is, most of the individual mistakes boil down to just one:

(January 21, 2010) that gave corporations the right to contribute unlimited funds to political campaigns; thus a pseudo-democracy has officially become a plutocracy. See, for example, Adam Liptak, "Justices, 5–4, Reject Corporate Spending Limit," *New York Times*, January 21, 2010.

11. George Soros, "The Way Forward," *Financial Times*. October 30, 2009 (*TWF*).
12. Walid el-Gabry, "Soros Says Crisis Signals End of a Free-Market Model," *Bloomberg.com*, February 23, 2009.
13. *TWF*.

a belief that markets are self-adjusting and that the role of government should be minimal."[14]

For good reason, those who have suffered from this crisis are angry; many want to know: Who is going to jail? For how long? And when? While those who have been personally affected by this recession have suffered loss of jobs and homes with foreclosures, taxpayers have been bailing out the large Western banks that, according to John Lanchester, have been allowed to become "Too Big to Fail."[15] Indeed, this was "the most important lesson" of the failure of the investment bank Lehman Brothers. Truly, we are living with a "monstrous hybrid," Lanchester continues, "in which bank profits are privately owned, but are made possible thanks to an unlimited guarantee against losses, provided by the taxpayer." He agrees with German Chancellor Angela Merkel, "no bank should be allowed to become so big that it can blackmail governments."[16] If capitalism is about assuming risk, i.e., "about 'creative destruction,' and the freedom to fail," then we no longer have free market capitalism, but an economy dominated by the "banksters"; or, to speak precisely, Lanchester concludes "the most accurate term would be 'bankocracy.'"

Others argue that the recent crisis is not an exception to the rule, but that these kinds of crises are endemic to the nature of capitalism. Stiglitz, for example, claims that instead of free markets providing "a calm ocean of economic stability," or equilibrium, "they have delivered us a financial crisis, on average, every year or two."[17] Indeed, financial crises belong to the logic of the capitalist system because when money, once a means of exchange, becomes capital, it becomes an end in itself. In other words, the economic system no longer serves to produce various products required to make human beings happy, but the system serves to produce one com-

---

14. Sean O'Grady, "The Money Man: Super-economist Joseph Stiglitz on How to Fix the Recession," *The Independent*, February 9, 2010.
15. John Lanchester, "Bankocracy," *London Review of Books*, 31, 21 (November 5, 2009), 35–36.
16. "Bankocracy," 35–36. Lanchester cites Merkel's comments after meeting with French president Nicolas Sarkozy.
17. O'Grady, "The Money Man."

modity, i.e., money or capital, and the problem for the corporations and the banks is how to produce, control, and accumulate capital.

There are two questions here. The first is the historical question: *when* in the development of the capitalist economic system was there a concentration of production and the emergence of monopolies that led to the enormous accumulation of capital in the hands of a few large banking concerns? Citing the German economist, Otto Jeidels' *Relation of the German Big Banks to Industry with Special Reference to the Iron Industry* from1905, Vladimir I. Lenin answers this question: "Thus, the twentieth century marks the turning-point from the old capitalism to the new, from the domination of capital in general to the domination of finance capital."[18] Clearly others would answer this question differently; most would probably look more specifically to contemporary problems relevant to the current capitalist system. This paper, however, is not concerned with these historical matters; rather, it is concerned with a second question: *how*, according to the logic of capitalism, did money – which served as a means of exchange – become capital? In other words, how did money or capital replace products as the goal of capitalist production? My paper will address this question by examining Karl Marx's argument concerning the logic of capitalism in the *Grundrisse*.

Written during the winter of 1857–58, the *Grundrisse*[19] was authored by Karl Marx between the 1848 publication of the *Manifesto of the Communist Party* and the 1867 publication of the first volume of *Capital*. The text is a series of seven notebooks in which Marx strives to gain conceptual clarity on a number of fundamental economic concepts, including production, distribution, exchange, consumption, and money. Although the *Grundrisse* was not published during his own lifetime –

18. Vladimir Illyich Lenin, "Imperialism, the Highest Stage of Capitalism," id., *Selected Works*, Moscow, Progress Publishers, 1963, http://www.marxists.org/archive/lenin/works/1916/imp-hsc/
19. Karl Marx, 1973, *Grundrisse: Foundations of the Critique of Political Economy*, translated with a foreword by Martin Nicolaus, New York, Vintage Books. For the particulars regarding the writing and publication of the *Grundrisse*, see Martin Nicolaus, "Foreword," 7–66.

indeed, the work was not even published in the nineteenth century[20] – this work is essential for our understanding of the nineteenth century, because in it Marx articulates one of the most important transitions for modern bourgeois capitalism, namely, the transition from money as a medium of exchange to money as a commodity. In this paper, I shall examine Marx's argument for this transition under the heading of the 'transcendental power of money.' To achieve this end, I have divided my discussion into three parts. The first part is a brief consideration of what Marx calls "the scientifically correct method" of political economy.[21] Before exploring the concept of production in general, I shall consider how Marx justifies beginning his reflection with this concept. Then, I shall reconstruct the way in which Marx understands the concepts of production, distribution, exchange, and consumption in his introduction to the *Grundrisse*. Finally, I intend to identify the conceptual or logical – and not the historical – moments of money as it moves from a mere medium of exchange to a commodity necessary for the productive process.

"The Method of Political Economy"[22]

Reflecting on the method of political economy, Marx distinguishes two approaches to this 'science': the historical method of the seventeenth century political economists and "the scientifically correct method," i.e., "the theoretical method." Marx criticizes seventeenth century political economists for beginning scientific reflection with an indeterminate abstraction like "population." For if we begin with population, we must "move analytically towards ever more simple concepts [*Begriff*], from the imagined concrete towards ever thinner abstractions until [we reach] the simplest determinations." In other words, if we begin with population, we shall have to consider the classes that constitute the given population. But according to Marx, the concept of 'classes' has no content unless we understand "the elements on which they rest" such as "wage, labor,

20. Nicolaus, "Foreword," n. 1, 7. Nicolaus reports that a limited edition, consisting of two volumes, was published in the 20th century, one in 1939, the other in 1941.
21. Grundrisse, 100.
22. Karl Marx, The Method of Political Economy, *Grundrisse*, 100–08.

capital, etc." And since "these concepts in turn presuppose exchange, division of labor, prices, etc.," those political economists who start with the concept of "population," make the mistake of beginning with "a chaotic conception [*Vorstellung*] of the whole."[23]

Rejecting this confused approach, Marx claims that "the scientifically correct method" of political economy is one that begins by sorting out "a small number of determinant, abstract, general relations" – and here Marx is thinking of "labor, money, value, etc." – which he calls "the simplest determinations." These determinations, however, are not yet concrete. Once "these individual moments [have] been more or less firmly established and abstracted," Marx writes, "there [begin] the economic systems, which [ascend] from the simple relations, such as labor, division of labor, need, exchange value, to the level of the state, exchange between nations and the world market." This is not the mistaken historical method of the seventeenth century political economists that begins with the "*imagined concrete*" (e.g., population); rather, according to the scientifically correct method, the concrete is something to be attained. "The concrete," Marx argues,

> is concrete because it is the concentration of many determinations, hence unity of the diverse. It appears in the process of thinking, therefore, as a process of concentration, as a result, not as a point of departure, even though it is the point of departure in reality and hence also the point of departure for observation [*Anshauung*] and conception.[24]

Reality is not transparent to the understanding; it is not immediately accessible to political economists. To attempt to comprehend reality in terms of the most immediate determinations only serves to confuse; reality is over-determined, i.e., as having so many determinations that we cannot sort them all out in theoretical discourse. Instead, reality must be understood. Beginning with the simplest determinations, the political economist brings to conceptual clarity chaotic conceptions by identify-

---

23. *Grundrisse*, 100.
24. *Grundrisse*, 101.

ing "a small number of determinant, abstract, general relations" which "lead towards a reproduction of the concrete by way of thought." Hence, political economists do not produce reality as the product of thought; rather, they proceed correctly by conceptualizing reality in thought.[25]

Reconstruction of Production, Distribution, Exchange, and Consumption

Marx employs this 'scientifically correct method' in his own work when he takes up the concepts of 'production,' 'distribution,' exchange,' and 'consumption'. In preparation for an understanding of his argument for the 'transcendental power of money,' I shall reconstruct his understanding of the relations between these notions. Since I am aware that Marx's detailed analysis presents a challenge to the reader, I have attempted to sketch out his argument as clearly as possible. While these concepts are not identical, Marx argues that production is the dominate moment and that distribution, exchange, and consumption must be understood in the context of production. We shall begin by examining the way in which Marx understands 'production in general' in his introduction to the *Grundrisse*.[26] After considering production in general, we shall explore three identities that Marx distinguishes in the spheres of 'consumption and production.' Next, we shall examine the spheres of 'distribution and production'. While these two spheres may seem to be independent, Marx argues that distribution not only belongs to the sphere of production, but it is also determined by production. Then, we shall consider 'exchange and production.' Again, Marx argues that production is the dominate sphere because it determines the form of exchange and the way in which exchange is organized. Once we have worked out these relations in the sphere of production, we will examine the various logical moments of money and we will be positioned to understand 'the transition of money as exchange to money as commodity.' There are two important points to keep in mind here. First, for Marx, production is the predominate sphere to which 'consumption,' 'distribution,' and 'exchange' belong as

25. *Grundrisse*, 100, 101.
26. *Grundrisse*, 85–88.

logical moments of one activity. Second, when money, once a medium of exchange, becomes a commodity, money, not products, becomes the end or the goal of production. Hence, the discussion of money assumes an understanding of production.

Production in General

Reminding his readers of his discussion of the 'scientifically correct method,' Marx turns to the concept of "production." In any reflection on production, we always refer to "production at a definite stage of social development production by social individuals." Because of this, Marx argues, there would seem to be two ways to speak of production. If we are to "talk about production at all we must either pursue the process of historic development through its different phases, or declare beforehand that we are dealing with a specific historic epoch such as[,] e.g.[,] modern bourgeois production." But to start in this manner would once again lead us down the thorny path of the historical method; beginning with "the chaotic conception of the whole," we would have to search for the simplest determinations that constitute production.[27]

Alternatively, Marx suggests that we can begin with "a rational abstraction," i.e., *production in general* because "all epochs of production have certain common traits, common characteristics." The difficulty, however, is that production as it appears has many determinations. In fact, it could be characterized in its specificity as being over-determined. Furthermore, not all of these determinations belong to every epoch as identifiable moments. "Some determinations belong to all epochs, others only to a few. [Some] determinations will be shared by the most modern epoch and the most ancient." If we are to develop this kind of theoretical discourse, Marx argues, we must allow certain determinations to be stripped away and removed from this process of abstraction, the residuum, albeit an abstraction will not be an *indeterminate* abstraction; rather, it will be a *concrete* abstraction. And the 'scientifically correct method' demands that we begin our theoretical reflection with a concrete

27. *Grundrisse*, 85–88.

abstraction, i.e., a concept of production which includes just those clearly articulated, essential moments that all specific instances of production have in common. Consequently, we shall begin the present discussion with the concrete abstraction of production in general.

If we simply consider the concept of production in general, it appears in the first instance to be the making of products. In production, human beings appropriate nature "within and through a specific form of society."[28] Production in its immediacy, however, assumes the three following moments: 1) human activity, i.e., work; 2) the subject of the work, i.e., the material worked on, and 3) the instruments through which the work is accomplished, i.e., the instruments of production.[29] Moreover, the products of production belong to someone; they are properties that fulfill human needs. "An appropriation which does not make something into property," Marx writes, "is a *contradictio in subjecto*."[30] Since production (i.e., bourgeois production) involves property, since property assumes a distinction between 'mine' and 'thine,' and since there is a need for a mechanism whereby 'mine' can be made 'thine,' according to Marx, bourgeois economists have assumed that the introduction of property demands certain specific legislative and juridical frameworks to protect private property. But "history," Marx notes, "shows *common property* (e.g. in India, among the Slavs, the early Celts, etc.) to be the more original form, a form which long continues to play a significant role in the shape of communal property."[31] Furthermore, Marx argues, "every form of production creates its own legal relations, form of government, etc." [32] "All the bourgeois economists are aware of," he writes,

> is that production can be carried on better under the modern police than e.g. on the principle of might makes right. They forget only that this

---

28. *Grundrisse*, 87.
29. *Grundrisse*, 87. See *Capital* vol. 1 where Marx calls these "the elementary factors of the labour process." Karl Marx and Frederick Engels, *Collected Works, Volume 35. Karl Marx, Capital*, Vol. I, New York, International Publishers, 1996, 188.
30. *Grundrisse*, 88.
31. *Grundrisse*, 88; italics added.
32. *Grundrisse*, 88.

principle is also a legal relation, and that the right of the stronger prevails in their 'constitutional republics' as well, only in another form. [33]

"In production the members of society appropriate (create, shape) the products of nature in accord with human needs"; Marx calls this "the obvious" or "trite notion" of production. Furthermore, "production, distribution, exchange, and consumption," according to Marx, "form a regular syllogism: production is the generality, distribution and exchange the particularity, and consumption the singularity in which the whole is joined together."[34] However, this does not mean that "production, distribution, exchange, and consumption are identical, but that they all form the members of a totality; they are distinctions within a unity. Production predominates not only over itself, in the antithetical definition of production, but over the other moments as well."[35] What then is the relationship of each of these determinations distribution, exchange, and consumption to production?

"Consumption and Production"[36]

Marx distinguishes three "identities between consumption and production"[37]: "Production is consumption, consumption is production." In this first identity, which he calls "*immediate identity*," he distinguishes "consumptive production" or "reproduction" which involves "productive or unproductive labour," and "productive consumption," which involves "productive or non-productive consumption."[38] In the second identity, Marx claims, that production "appears as a means for" consumption and consumption "appears as a means for" production.[39] In other words, "production creates the material, as an external object, for consumption; consumption creates the need, as internal object, as aim, for production."

33. *Grundrisse*, 88.
34. *Grundrisse*, 89.
35. *Grundrisse*, 99.
36. *Grundrisse*, 90–94.
37. *Grundrisse*, 92.
38. *Grundrisse*, 93.
39. *Grundrisse*, 93.

For this reason, Marx insists on the "mutual dependence" of production and consumption and, at the same time, he claims, because of the "material," i.e., "the external object," that they are "external to each other." And finally in the third identity, "Each of them ... creates the other in completing itself, and creates itself as the other." [40] In other words, consumption brings the product to completion by using and consuming it and thus "accomplishes the act of production" by creating the "inclination" to produce. Only in being consumed does the product – the external material form of production – truly become a product. Simultaneously, "production produces consumption by creating the specific manner of consumption" and the need to consume. While Marx does not name the last two mentioned identities, in keeping with the Hegelian vocabulary he employs here, I shall refer to the second and third identities as *mediate identity* and *self-mediated identity*, respectively. Since the end of production is to produce products for consumption, we must understand the complex relation between consumption and production in order to comprehend how money *qua* means of exchange, becomes the end of production. Let us take up each of these identities in turn.

Production which appears immediately as consumption, Marx maintains, is "twofold consumption"; it is both "subjective and objective." It is subjective because the producer "develops his abilities in production"; it is objective because the producer also "expends" these abilities "uses them up in the act of production." In producing the product, "the means of production" are consumed; they "become worn out through use" in the productive process. To illustrate his point, Marx appeals to the image of combustion. While fire and heat are produced in combustion, the material that supports combustion is consumed. Similarly, in production "the raw material" surrenders "its natural form and composition by being used up." "The act of production," Marx argues, "is therefore in all its moments also an act of consumption. Production as directly identical with consumption, and consumption as directly coincident with production, is termed ... *productive consumption*."[41]

---

40. *Grundrisse*, 93.
41. *Grundrisse*, 90.

At the same time, "consumption is also immediately production." Drawing an image from nature, Marx argues that just as a plant produces itself by consuming certain nutriments, so too a "human being produces his own body" by consuming nourishment. And this, Marx continues, "is true of every kind of consumption which in one way or another produces human beings in some particular aspect." Consumption that is immediately production, according to Marx, is *consumptive production.* Consumptive production, however, is "secondary" because it involves the "destruction of the prior product" in the productive process. In production, "the producer objectified himself"; in consumption "the object he created personifies itself." Hence, productive consumption is to be distinguished from "production proper." For although production is immediately consumption and consumption is immediately production, their "immediate duality" remains unaltered; each process retains its unique character and is independent of the other.[42]

According to Marx, a "mediating movement" occurs between the two processes of production and consumption. These two processes are "related to" and "indispensable to one another"; Marx insists on "their mutual dependence" that "still leaves them external to each other."[43] Each process is "a means for the other" – each "is mediated by the other." "Consumption," Marx argues, "mediates production" because "it alone creates for the products the subject for whom they are products."[44] "Without production, no consumption; but also, without consumption, no production; since production would then be purposeless." Indeed, "consumption," Marx argues, produces production in two ways. First, consumption produces production because it is only by being consumed that a product "becomes a real product." A product achieves its "'last finish' in consumption." A product that is not consumed is not *actually* a product at all; it is only *potentially* a product. For example, "a railway on which no trains run, hence which is not used up, not consumed," Marx

42. *Grundrisse*, 90–91.
43. *Grundrisse*, 93.
44. *Grundrisse*, 91.

insists, "is a railway only δυναμει [potentially], and not in reality." This means that a product is quite different from a natural object. While a natural object simply is what it is, the product "*becomes* a product only through consumption." "Only by decomposing the product," Marx maintains, "does consumption give the product the finishing touch; for the product is production not as objectified activity, but rather only as object for the active subject."

Second, consumption produces production "because consumption creates the need for new production, that is, it creates the ideal, internally impelling cause for production which is its presupposition." In other words, consumption produces production by creating 'need' that will be satisfied by production. As the object of production, however, need is not external to the productive process; rather, need is understood "as internal object of production, as aim"; the goal of production is to fulfill need created by consumption. Hence, according to Marx, consumption is understood as "the aim of production"; consumption motivates production by creating "the object which is active in production as its determinant aim."[45] If it is true that production "offers consumption its external object," then it is equally true, Marx contends,

> that consumption *ideally* posits the object of production as an internal image, as a need, as drive and as purpose. It creates the objects of production in a still subjective form. No production without a need. But consumption reproduces the need.[46]

At the same time, Marx identifies three ways that production mediates the process of consumption. First, production "produces the object of consumption." In production, products are produced for no other reason than to be consumed; "production creates the material, as external object, for consumption."[47] Without an object to be consumed, consumption would not be consumption at all. It is by supplying the material to be

45. *Grundrisse*, 93, 91.
46. *Grundrisse*, 92.
47. *Grundrisse*, 93.

consumed that "production produces consumption."[48]

Second, production produces "the manner of consumption." Previously, we observed that only in consumption does the product achieve its final finish. Similarly, production does not merely create a product for consumption; rather, it "also gives consumption its specificity, its character, its finish." Production does not create just any object or "an object in general." In the productive process, specific objects are produced. Because production produces the product, and because the product is the product that it is, i.e., a specific product, production also produces the way in which the product is to be consumed. Hence, "the object," Marx argues, "is not an object in general, but a specific object which must be consumed in a specific manner." For example, Marx considers satisfying one's hunger. The need to gratify our hunger is the same in any context. After all, "hunger is hunger." But there is a difference between our "bolt[ing] down raw meat with the aid of hand, nail, and tooth," and our satisfying our hunger "by cooked meat eaten with a knife and fork." Since production produces a specific product, and since production produces the manner in which the product is to be consumed, Marx argues that "production thus creates the consumer."[49]

Finally, production produces "the motive of consumption." Motivated by need, production creates the material to satisfy need. But production also "supplies a need for the material." As it first appears, consumption exists in its immediacy – "a state of natural crudity." However, consumption is "mediated as a need for the object" produced by production. Hence, production not only creates the *material object* for consumption, and it not only creates the *manner in which the material object is to be consumed*, but it also creates the *need* for the material object. In other words, production creates "the perception" of need. Borrowing an example from the arts, Marx maintains that in this there is no difference between an "object of art" and any other product. For just as an artifact produces "a public which is sensitive to art and enjoys beauty," so too, in the creation of every other product, production produces a perceived need. "Production thus

48. *Grundrisse*, 92.
49. *Grundrisse*, 92.

not only creates an object for the subject, but also a subject for the object," i.e., the consumer.[50]

In addition to the two previous identities – the *immediate identity* of production and consumption and the *mediate identity* of production and consumption – production produces consumption and consumption produces production, and in so doing "each of them … creates the other in completing itself as other."[51] For its part, consumption creates production because in consumption the product is consumed. If the product were not consumed, it would not be what it is, namely, a product, i.e., a particular product that is intended to fulfill a need or a desire. In the activity of the product being consumed, consumption not only brings the product to completion, but it also produces the need for production and re-production. Insofar as the process of consumption brings the product to completion, and insofar as the process of consumption produces the inclination for production and reproduction, consumption completes the process of production by producing the producer. "Consumption," Marx argues,

> accomplishes the act of production only in completing the product as product by dissolving it, by consuming its independently material form, by raising the inclination developed in the first act of production, through the need for repetition, to its finished form; it is thus not only the concluding act in which the product becomes product, but also that in which the producer becomes producer.[52]

Hence, consumption creates production by bringing itself to completion; and in this way consumption is distinguished from production.

For its part, production completes the productive process by producing consumption. Insofar as production produces both "an object for the subject" and "a subject for the object," production creates consumption (1) by creating the material for it; (2) by determining the manner of

50. *Grundrisse*, 92.
51. *Grundrisse*, 93.
52. *Grundrisse*, 93.

consumption; and (3) by creating the products initially posited by it as objects, in the form of a need felt by the consumer. It thus produces the object of consumption, the manner of consumption and the motive of consumption.[53]

Furthermore, besides producing the material or object, the manner, and the motive for consumption, "production produces consumption ... by creating the stimulus of consumption, the ability to consume, as a need."[54] In other words, when Marx writes that production produces the subject for the object of consumption,[55] he means that production not only produces the product that is to be consumed, but it also produces the consumer that needs the product.[56] Production thus creates consumption by bringing itself to completion; and in this way production is distinguished from consumption.

Marx, however, stresses that while each of these moments – production and consumption – "creates the other in completing itself, and creates itself as the other," still the moments articulated here *belong to production in general*. Production and consumption "appear as moments of a single act."[57] In other words, production must be understood as "one process" to which all of the identities and the moments constituting them belong. Hence, production in general is the "predominant moment."

With a single subject, production and consumption appear as moments of a single act. The important thing to emphasize here is only that ... they [production and consumption] appear in any case as moments of one process, in which production is the real point of departure and hence also the predominant moment. Consumption as urgency, as need, is itself an intrinsic moment of productive activity. But the latter is the point of departure for realization and hence also its predominant moment: it is the act through which the whole process again runs its course. The individual produces an object and, by consuming it, returns to himself, but returns as

---

53. *Grundrisse*, 92.
54. *Grundrisse*, 93.
55. *Grundrisse*, 92.
56. *Grundrisse*, 92, 93.
57. *Grundrisse*, 94.

a productive and self-reproducing individual. Consumption thus appears as a moment of production.[58]

"Distribution and Production"[59]

Marx begins his discussion of the distribution of products with the following question: "Does distribution stand at the side of and outside production as an autonomous sphere?" Although he will answer this question in the negative by arguing that production does indeed include distribution, there are a number of reasons to think that distribution does not belong to the sphere of production. From the standpoint of the individual, distribution of property seems to be prior to production because it establishes his or her place in the process of production. According to this point of view, Marx writes, "distribution appears as a social law" because it fixes the individual's place in the social system, i.e., "the system of production."[60] Since the individual's place within this system is determined prior to his or her participation in the process of production, it would stand to reason that distribution does not belong to the sphere of production; rather, distribution would seem to precede production. "To the single individual," Marx argues,

> distribution appears as a social law which determines his position within the system of production within which he produces, and which therefore precedes production. The individual comes into the world possessing neither capital nor land. Social distribution assigns him at birth to wage labor. But this situation of being assigned is itself a consequence of the existence of capital and landed property as independent agents of production.[61]

The individual comes into this world without capital or land; he or she possesses only his or her own body which may be sold in the form of

---

58. *Grundrisse*, 94.
59. *Grundrisse*, 94–98.
60. *Grundrisse*, 96.
61. *Grundrisse*, 96.

the individual's labor power for wages. But Marx emphasizes that it is the mode of production that determines the individual's place in the system of production. Hence, distribution is not an autonomous sphere existing outside of production; rather, distribution belongs to the sphere of production.

From the standpoint of whole societies, Marx mentions four historical examples that provide reasons to think that distribution precedes production, i.e., "that distribution is not structured and determined by production, but rather the opposite, production by distribution." When one nation or people, for example, conquers another and divides the land among themselves, they force a certain mode of "distribution and form of property in land" on those who have been defeated; thus, production would seem to be determined by distribution. Again, if a conquering nation enslaves those it has defeated, and if, as a result, production were founded on slave labor, distribution would appear to be both prior to production and to determine the mode of production. Or, in the case of a revolution when a people revolts against the land owners or the landed gentry and redistributes the land by dividing their holdings into smaller tracts of land, distribution would appear to change the features of production. Similarly, in a caste system in which a legal system distributes, as a result of "a hereditary privilege," property to some, land to others, and still others are restricted to the caste of laborers, distribution would seem to be prior to production, to determine production, and, hence, to stand outside of production as an entirely autonomous sphere.[62]

Marx, however, rejects the notion that distribution belongs to an autonomous sphere; rather, he argues that "in all cases, the mode of production ... is decisive."[63] While the process of production involves appropriation, i.e., involves making something into property, "the producer's relation to the product, once the latter is finished, is an external one"; in other words, the producer does not take possession of the product immediately.[64] In production, the producer does not intend the immediate

62. *Grundrisse*, 96.
63. *Grundrisse*, 97.
64. *Grundrisse*, 94.

appropriation of the products; the producer does not produce products for his or her own personal consumption. Rather, the producer can only take possession of the product insofar as the product is distributed to others. Distribution depends on the producer's relation to other individuals. Hence, distribution, Marx argues, like consumption, belongs to the sphere of production. "*Distribution* steps between the producers and the products, hence between production and consumption, to determine in accordance with social laws what the producers share will be in the world of products."[65] At the most immediate level distribution and production appear independently of one another. Distribution seems to be the mere distribution of products according to certain social laws which first appear as natural laws. However, "this distribution of products" is a moment in production realized as: "1) the distribution of the instruments of production, and … 2) the distribution of members of society among the different kinds of production."[66] For its part, production produces distribution, and different modes of production require different forms of distribution. "The structure [*Gliederung*] of distribution," Marx writes,

> is completely determined by the structure of production. Distribution is itself a product of production, not only in its object, in that only the results of production can be distributed, but also in its form, in that the specific kind of participation in production determines specific forms of distribution, i.e., the pattern of participation in distribution.[67]

In other words, while the structure of distribution appears as the naturally determined distribution of products, actually, the distribution of products is the result of this structure of distribution which is in turn the result of production as it changes the natural determinants to "historic determinants." "At the very beginning," Marx continues,

---

65. *Grundrisse*, 94.
66. *Grundrisse*, 96.
67. *Grundrisse*, 95.

these may appear as spontaneous, natural. But by the process of production itself they are transformed from natural into historic determinants, and if they appear to one epoch as natural presuppositions of production, they were its historic product for another.[68]

Thus, distribution belongs to the sphere of production and Marx calls it "production-determined distribution"; as production-determined distribution, distribution appears as one moment of production.

"Exchange and Production"[69]

Exchange appears as a moment mediating "production with its production-determined distribution on one side and consumption on the other ... ."[70] Because of this mediation, exchange makes a threefold appearance, each logical moment of which is either determined by, or appears in, the sphere of production:

1. It is within production "that exchange of activities and abilities [division of labour] takes place."[71] This moment of exchange is the essential constitutive moment of production.

2. Exchange as the 'means' of bringing a product to its concrete reality, i.e., exchange preparing the product for consumption, is also determined by production. It is exchange that brings the product to consumption wherein the product is completed. In other words, production determines the way in which consumption receives its object by means of exchange.[72]

3. The form of exchange, i.e., the way in which exchange is organized "between dealers and dealers ...," is "itself a producing activity" while at the same time being "entirely determined by production ...," i.e., the mode of production.[73] In other words, the organization of exchange which

68. *Grundrisse*, 97.
69. *Grundrisse*, 98–100.
70. *Grundrisse*, 99.
71. *Grundrisse*, 99.
72. *Grundrisse*, 99.
73. *Grundrisse*, 99.

is determined by production determines the intensity and extensity of exchange. And, only in this last instance "where the product is exchanged directly for consumption" does exchange begin to appear separately from production.[74]

Thus, exchange, like distribution and consumption, appears not as an autonomous activity, but "as either directly comprised in production or determined by it." Each of these concepts – production, distribution, exchange, and consumption – exists as a moment within a complex whole where each mediates and is mediated by the others, but the *determinate* concept is that of *production in general*. Thus, distribution, exchange, and consumption always return us to production.

The Transition of Money as Exchange to Money as Commodity

Thus far, I have sketched out the concepts Marx presents in the "Introduction" to the *Grundrisse*. The question that must now be answered is: what are the conceptual moments of money as it moves from a mere medium of exchange to a commodity necessary for the productive process? Marx provides us with a clue to answer this question when he writes "circulation itself [is] merely a specific moment of exchange, or [it is] also exchange regarded in its totality."[75] One of the specific moments of circulation, however, is money that in turn exists in its concreteness in so far as it is seen in its determinate nature, i.e., as having certain specifiable determinations. Money can be understood to have the four following moments: The properties of money as (1) measure of commodity exchange; (2) medium of exchange; (3) representative of commodities (hence object of contracts); and (4) general commodity alongside the particular commodities, all simply follow from its character as exchange value separated from commodities themselves and objectified.[76] Let us consider each of these moments.

If commodity A and commodity B are to be exchanged, then there

---

74. *Grundrisse*, 99.
75. *Grundrisse*, 98.
76. *Grundrisse*, 146.

must be an existent measure or standard to which both A and B may be related or compared in order to determine the feasibility of exchanging A for B. This process of quantification takes place in thought as "both commodities to be exchanged are transformed ... into exchange values and are thus reciprocally compared."[77] This would even be true in barter. If, for example, a banana farmer wishes to trade a hundred pounds of bananas for coconuts, she will have to be able to determine how many coconuts a pound of bananas is worth. Since coconuts and bananas are obviously different and since there is no one-to-one correspondence between bananas and coconuts, she will have to appeal to some existent measure or standard to which bananas and coconuts may be related so as to judge whether the exchange of bananas for coconuts is fair.

Money takes on a character of its own independent of the products to be exchanged. In other words, in order to obtain commodity B, we no longer need to exchange commodity A for commodity B – for example, bananas for coconuts. All that need be done is to exchange a socially determined representation, i.e., exchange value, which, as it is attached to commodities A and B, appears as the price of these commodities, for commodity B. This socially determined representation, i.e., symbol (money as it appears as coin or paper) of the price of commodity B, may be obtained by exchanging commodity A for money. Thus, at this moment money mediates exchange because money may be exchanged for commodities, or commodities may be exchanged for money.

Money comes to represent commodities as it attains a character of its own. When this happens it is no longer necessary to think in terms of exchanging one commodity for another, i.e., exchanging commodity A for commodity B. At this moment it is simply possible to purchase either commodity A or commodity B, or both commodities A and B for that matter, with a socially determined amount of money. Or looking at this purchasing process from another point of view, it is possible to sell commodities A and B for a certain amount of money. Hence, commodities are said to have an exchange value that appears as a *price*,

---

77. *Grundrisse*, 144.

in terms of a specific quantity of money. At the same time, money, too, has an exchange value that appears as a price in terms of commodities. In short, a commodity is said to have a price that is attached to the commodity in terms of money.

Thus, as money takes on a character of its own, it becomes an object, i.e., a thing-in-itself. It becomes completely separated from specific commodities while taking on the characteristics of a commodity. It is in its commodity character that money is borrowed and lent, and generates interest. Hence, money has the capacity to produce money and money *qua* commodity takes on the character of capital. By virtue of its property as the general commodity in relation to all others, as the embodiment of the exchange value of the other commodities, money at the same time becomes the realized and always realizable form of capital; the form of capital's appearance which is always valid.[78] Therefore, money in its four moments appears as a process in which the exchange value of a product *qua* commodity "obtains a material existence separate from the commodity" and in so doing becomes a commodity itself;[79] money is produced not for its use value, but for its exchange value.

At the same time, Marx distinguishes four contradictions corresponding to the four properties of money. First, the commodity has a double existence: On the one hand, it exists as the product, i.e., "as a specific product whose natural form of existence ideally contains (latently contains) its exchange value."[80] Marx uses the term 'ideally' or 'latently' to indicate that, considered as a specific product, the exchange value exists only potentially; it is not realized. On the other hand, the commodity exists "as manifest exchange value (money)."[81] Considered as money, the commodity, i.e., the product is not considered in its specificity – "all connection with the natural form of the product is stripped away."[82] In

---

78. *Grundrisse*, 146.
79. *Grundrisse*, 145.
80. *Grundrisse*, 147.
81. *Grundrisse*, 147.
82. *Grundrisse*, 147.

other words, the commodity exists *qua* commodity and *qua* money, i.e., exchange value. And it is because of the double character of the commodity "that these two separated forms in which the commodity exists are not convertible into one another."[83] In that money has now attained a character of its own, it exists independently of the commodity. At the same time the commodity exists independently of money. As money comes to exist independently of the commodity, the commodity is no longer *necessarily* exchangeable for money because, as Marx writes, "the exchangeability ... is abandoned to the mercy of external conditions ... which may or may not be present." Thus, exchangeability becomes "something different from and alien to the commodity, with which it first has to be brought into equation, to which it is therefore at the beginning unequal; while the equation itself becomes dependent on external conditions, hence a matter of chance."[84] *Secondly*: Just as the exchange value of the commodity leads a double existence, as the particular commodity and as money, so does the act of exchange split into two mutually independent acts: exchange of commodities for money, exchange of money for commodities: purchase and sale.[85] There is no necessary correspondence between purchase and sale which often appear "temporally and spatially separate" and for this reason their "immediate identity ceases." *Thirdly*: With the separation of purchase and sale, with the splitting of exchange into two spatially and temporally independent acts there further emerges another new relation. Just as exchange itself splits apart into two mutually independent acts, so does the overall movement of exchange itself become separate from the exchanges, the producers of commodities. Exchange for the sake of exchange separates off from exchange for the sake of commodities.[86] Exchange for the sake of exchange, according to Marx, is commerce. The purpose of exchange is the object for which the exchange exists, but "the purpose of commerce is not consumption, directly, but the gaining of

---

83. *Grundrisse*, 147.
84. *Grundrisse*, 148.
85. *Grundrisse*, 148.
86. *Grundrisse*, 148.

money, of exchange values."[87] *Fourthly*: Just as exchange value, in the form of money, takes its place as the *general commodity* alongside all particular commodities, so does exchange value as money therefore at the same time take its place as a *particular commodity* (since it has a particular existence) alongside all other commodities.[88] In other words, money, as it comes to exist independently of commodities, becomes a commodity itself. On the one hand, money is a commodity just like any other commodity. But on the other hand, it is different from other commodities: "it is not only the general exchange value, but at the same time a particular exchange value alongside other exchange values."[89] Therefore, money exists in contradiction with itself. But "money does not create these antitheses and contradictions; it is, rather, the development of these contradictions and antitheses which creates the seemingly transcendental power of money."[90] Consequently, money is a specific moment of circulation which in turn is "a specific moment of exchange, or ... exchange regarded in its totality."[91] From the point of view of production, we see that production no longer produces products for consumption, i.e., products that are to be complete in consumption, but rather, production produces exchange values. Consumption seems to slide out of the picture. Production comes to be determined by exchange values as money which first appeared as a means of exchange comes to be the end of exchange.[92]

Conclusion

According to Marx's argument in the *Grundrisse*, then, the logic of capitalism turns precisely on this point: the end of production is no longer to produce products to satisfy needs or desires, no longer to produce products for consumption; rather, production produces exchange values. An automobile corporation, for example does not produce automobiles

---

87. *Grundrisse*, 149.
88. *Grundrisse*, 150.
89. *Grundrisse*, 151.
90. *Grundrisse*, 146.
91. *Grundrisse*, 98.
92. *Grundrisse*, 146, 151.

so that the owners may have a vehicle to drive; the corporation produces vehicles to sell or, which is the same thing, vehicles are produced to be exchanged for money. The difficulty is that once the accumulation of money becomes the end of production – rather than the satisfaction of wants and needs – producers become more concerned with the maximization of their returns; accumulation becomes the principle that guides production. While there are a number of problems here, certainly an important one is that good products are not distinguished from bad products or, as John McMurtry writes, "no principle of business or economics has been developed to distinguish commodities that cause disease from goods that enable people's lives."[93] Additionally, in the same place McMurtry maintains that those who support the idea of a "global market" because it is "productive and efficient" are mistaken:

... supporters [of the global market] argue that the global market is both 'productive and efficient.' This assumption does not hold up either. The global market system produces many times more waste than any economic order in history. In his world-renowned text *Economics*, Paul Samuelson defines economic efficiency as 'absences of waste'. But, like all economists of the dominate paradigm, Samuelson includes only wastes that cost private enterprises money. So as long as pollution and damages to others can be externalized, it is 'more efficient' – even if gluttonously wasteful. These 'externalities' are kept off the books. That is why depredation of the most basic means of human life – breathable air, water aquifers, the oceans, soil fertility – are ignored by both governments and corporations, both of which operate with the same life-blind model.[94]

Assuming McMurtry is correct, it would seem that if we could determine

93. *MGM*, 1.
94. *MGM*, 1. The issue of internalizing externalities has been raised and discussed in the discipline of business ethics at least since the mid-1970s. See, for example, Keith Davis, "Five Propositions for Social Responsibility," *Business Horizons* (June 1975), 18–24; also, see Melvin Anshen, "Changing the Social Contract: A Role for Business," *Columbia Journal of World Business* 5 (November–December 1970).

which products should be produced because they enhance life and which products should not be produced because they do not enhance life –and may even be harmful to human beings and the environment – and if businesses were forced to internalize their externalities, capitalism could be reformed to function in the interests of the common good. He concludes his discussion of the myths of the free market by suggesting a "set of goods required by all peoples without which they suffer or die":

• Atmospheric goods – breathable air, open space and light

• Bodily goods – clean water, nourishing foods and waste disposal

• Home and habitat – shelter and a life-enhancing environment

• Care through time – love, safety and healthcare

• Human vocation – meaningful work of value to others

• Economic justice – right to enjoy these life goods and an obligation to help provide them[95]

However, if McMurtry's list guides in distinguishing between products that should and should not be produced, will the resulting system still be capitalism? If not, then what will it be, and how will it function to provide goods and services in keeping with McMurtry's list?

Reflecting on the 2008 world-wide economic crisis, Joseph Stiglitz distinguishes five decisions that brought on the financial difficulties in the US from which, even at the time of this writing, we continue to suffer. He singles out: (1) the Regan administration's 1987 decision to replace then chair of the Federal Reserve Board Paul Volcker with Alan Greenspan because Volcker was not perceived to be committed to deregulation, (2) the November 1999 US Congress's decision to repeal the Glass-Steagall Act that had forced the separation of the banking and financial-services industries, (3) the Bush tax cuts that, contrary to laissez-faire ideology, did next to nothing to stimulate the economy, (4) stock options and incentive

---

95. *MGM*, 3.

pay that encouraged falsifying the corporate records of profits and losses because bonuses were not tied to performance, and (5) the October 2008 bailout package whereby Treasury Secretary Henry Paulson purchased bad assets and shifted the costs to US taxpayers,[96] while US businesses paid their employees bonuses. Like McMurtry, Stiglitz emphasizes the importance of regulation or reregulation: "Self-regulation is preposterous, as even Alan Greenspan now concedes, and as a practical matter it can't … identify systemic risks."[97] Most importantly, Stiglitz insists, governments must tackle "the underlying problems – the flawed incentive structures and the inadequate regulatory system."[98]

While he understands the advantages of free-market economies, George Soros also sees the dangers of the recent laissez-faire ideology: "Too much competition and too little cooperation can cause intolerable inequities and instability."[99] He contends that "laissez-faire ideology … is just as much a perversion of supposedly scientific verities as Marxism-Leninism is." Indeed, Soros argues that "laissez-faire ideas can pose a threat to the open society" in three ways. First, while laissez-faire ideology claims that free markets will result in economic stability, in fact "market values served to undermine traditional values."[100] Markets do not respond to peoples' wants, needs, and preferences; they attempt to shape them. "What used to be a medium of exchange has usurped the place of fundamental values, reversing the relationship postulated by economic theory. What used to be professions have turned into businesses. The cult of success has replaced a belief in principles."[101] Second, Soros argues against what he calls "social Darwinism," because it "is based on an outmoded theory of evolution" that embraces a simplistic view of "the survival of the fittest."[102] Indeed,

---

96. Joseph E. Stiglitz, "Capitalist Fools," *Vanity Fair* (January 2009), 1–6 (*CF*).
97. *CF*, 3.
98. *CF*, 5.
99. George Soros, "The Capitalist Threat," *Atlantic Monthly* vol. 279, no 2 (February 1997), 3 (*TCT*).
100. *TCT*, 5.
101. *TCT*, 5.
102. *TCT*, 5, 6.

Soros claims, social Darwinism misrepresents the fact that "cooperation is just as much a part of the [economic] system as competition."[103] Most importantly, Soros writes: "The laissez-faire argument against income redistribution invokes the doctrine of the survival of the fittest. The argument is undercut by the fact that wealth is passed on by inheritance and the second generation is rarely as fit as the first." Finally, laissez-faire ideology is a threat because it is too much like "geopolitics" which argues that "states have no principles, only interests ... and those interests are determined by geographic location and other fundamentals." Soros holds that geopolitics is "deterministic" and "rooted in an outdated nineteenth-century view of scientific method." In particular, he notes two problems with geopolitics:

> One is that it treats the state as the indivisible unity of analysis, just as economics treats the individual. There is something contradictory in banishing the state from the economy while at the same time enshrining it as the ultimate source of authority in international relations.[104]

Still, Soros insists, "there is a more pressing practical aspect of the problem. What happens when a state disintegrates? Geopolitical realists find themselves totally unprepared." The second problem with geopolitics, according to Soros, "is that it does not recognize a common interest beyond the national interest."[105] While Soros levels his criticism at geopolitics, he argues that these same criticisms apply to laissez-faire ideology, although not with the same force. Marxism-Leninism, Nazism, and laissez-faire ideology have one thing in common; "they all try to justify their claim to ultimate truth with an appeal to science" – dialectical materialism, a distorted genetic theory combined with a vulgar racialized social Darwinism (i.e., 'pure' Aryan blood as opposed to 'degenerate' Semitic, Slavic, or Roma types), and laissez-faire economics.[106] While

---

103. *TCT*, 6.
104. *TCT*, 6.
105. *TCT*, 6.
106. *TCT*, 3.

lie recognizes that there is no global community, Soros echoes some of McMurtry's suggestions when he says, "there are common interests on a global level, such as the preservation of the environment and the prevention of war."[107] In the end Soros calls for a global open society based on the admission of human fallibility and that means "a society open to improvement."[108] This would require developing an awareness, as Cornelius Castoriadis might say, that citizens create their own social, political, and economic institutions and that since they create these institutions, they may change and improve them.

In the first paper of this volume, Ingerid S. Straume raised the question: "why are there no serious alternatives to the capitalist economic system offered today?" Although McMurtry, Stiglitz, and Soros are not radicals by any means, perhaps a discussion of alternatives to laissez-faire ideology can emerge from a consideration of their suggestions. With the collapse of the Soviet Union, it is difficult to imagine any support for soviet styled communism. At the same time, fascism always looms as a possibility with the fear mongering that has been the response to terrorists' attacks around the world and the massive world-wide migrations brought on by poverty, exploitation, and genocides. Certainly any attempt to offer a serious alternative to the capitalist economic system will have to take into account the various stakeholders in contemporary economic system; this will make any change extremely difficult. Perhaps it is true that certain goods and services are best distributed by regulated markets; perhaps any alternative to capitalism will have to include some sort of regulated markets. In response to Straume's question, perhaps we can take a cue from Cornelius Castoriadis here when he counsels that:

> We cannot, we should not seek ... a 'scientific' theory or even a total theory in the area of society, and still less in any other domain. We cannot for a single instant let ourselves believe that the articles of a political program contain the secret for the future liberty of humanity. We do not have any Good News to proselytize concerning the Promised Land glimmering

107. *TCT,* 7.
108. *TCT,* 8.

on the horizon, any Book to recommend whose reading would exempt one from having to seek the truth for oneself. Everything we have to say would be inaudible if it is not understood from the outset as a call for a critique that is not a form of skepticism, for an opening that does not dissolve into eclecticism, for a lucidity that does not halt activity, for an activity that does not become inverted into a mere activism, for a recognition of others that remains capable of vigilance. The truth with which we are henceforth concerned is neither a possession nor the return of the Spirit to itself. It is the movement of people through a free space within which there are a few cardinal points. But this appeal, can it still be heard? Is it really this truth that the world today desires and is this the one it can attain?[109]

If the truth that concerns us is "the movement of people through a free space within which there are a few cardinal points," we will have to ensure that there is a public space within which social, political, and economic discourse can take place. Surely, however, Castoriadis is correct when he cautions that, "[n]o great collective political movement can be created by the act of will of a few individuals." Still, this does not mean that we are powerless and that we cannot do anything in response to the continual crises brought on by laissez-faire ideology. "What is at stake here, then," Castoriadis writes,

> has nothing to do with tranquilly managing the prevailing consensus, extending the 'spaces of freedom' millimeter by millimeter, or demanding 'more and more rights.' How this can be done is another matter. ... But as long as this collective hypnosis continues, there is a provisional ethical and political stance for those of us who have the weighty privilege of being able to speak up, namely: unmask, criticize, denounce the existing state of affairs. And for everyone: try to be exemplary in one's behavior

---

109. Cornelius Castoriadis, "General Introduction," id., *Political and Social Writings, Volume 1, 1946–1955: From the Critique of Bureaucracy to the Positive Content of Socialism*, translated and edited by David Ames Curtis, University of Minnesota Press, 1988, 35 (*PSW1*).

and acts wherever one finds oneself. Whatever depends on us is our responsibility.[110]

In short, the moral imperative for "those of us who have the weighty privilege of being able to speak up" is to unmask, criticize, denounce the existing state of affairs. As Castoriadis says, "it is not a matter of establishing a foundation, and still less of indoctrination, but rather of an elucidation that will help this new exigency to propagate itself and take shape."[111]

---

110. Cornelius Castoriadis, "*What Democracy?*" id., *Figures of the Thinkable*, translated by Helen Arnold, Stanford, California, Stanford University Press, 2007, 150.
111. *PSW1*, 36.

Part II
Politics

Jacques Rancière and the Question of Political Subjectivization

Kåre Blinkenberg

The philosophy of the contemporary French philosopher Jacques Rancière is an answer to a certain paradox: Why did we – with the so-called 'New Philosophers'[1] – witness the return of 'political philosophy' in France at the exact same time, i.e., the very late 1970s, as its supposed object, politics, seemed to disappear?[2] Moving away from the streets, the factories, and the universities, the locus of politics shifted to the parliamentary state system. While the collective political manifestations of common people were replaced by narcissistic individualism and affirmative aesthetic practices, the economic theory accompanying the expansion of the capitalist world market – a process now dubbed *globalization* – seemed to provide the answers to every social question, i.e., 'There Is No Alternative' (the 'TINA syndrome'). Accordingly, every political disagreement, every attempt to mobilize the people around political issues were *a priori* judged as irrelevant, as nothing but an annoying obstacle, hindering the smooth operation of the political machinery. Given this historical development, we must ask: is there any relation between depoliticizing processes and political philosophy as such? In his most important political work *La*

---

1. Alain Finkielkraut, André Glucksmann, Bernard-Henri Lévy, and others.
2. Although I owe a great deal of thanks to Holger Ross Lauritsen for his comments, and the editors for linguistic support, I take the full responsibility for the final content and form of my paper.

Mésentente[3] from 1995, Rancière endeavors to conceptualize such a relation. His central thesis, on which I shall elaborate in this paper, is that politics involves *political thinking*. The unquestioning adoption (TINA) of neoliberal economic theory and the processes of institutional and ideological depoliticization rest on an entirely different rationality, which Rancière calls 'parapolitics.'

But what is genuine political thinking, if it is not political philosophy? And what is the relation between political thinking on the one hand and social institutions and ideology on the other? To answer these fundamental theoretical questions, I will explore the concept of *political subjectivization*.[4] Invoking Rancière's political theory, I will show that this kind of subjectivization implies genuine political thinking, something which cannot be said of traditional parliamentarian 'politics.' Indeed, a central thesis of my article is that political thinking is located in the interplay between those processes in which various institutions, understood in the broadest possible sense of the word, limit or negate individual participation in the political sphere – thereby *depoliticizing active democratic decision-making* – and those precarious and brief *political* processes where a given social-institutional order is restructured.

My analysis is divided into two main parts. The first part focuses on depoliticizing processes that are to be understood as special configurations of what Rancière calls '*the police.*' Essentially, to Rancière, every institutional configuration of society implies a hierarchical distribution of power, and the role and function of 'the police' is to maintain this hierarchy. The second part treats the more original part of Rancière's work, i.e., his argument that, despite the processes of depoliticization, *politics* is still possible. Here, I shall also examine the theory of *political subjectivization* developed in *La Mésentente* and conclude the discussion of this part by considering the relation between politics and globalization.

---

3. Jacques Rancière, *La Mésentente. Politique et Philosophie*, Paris, Galilée, 1995 (*LM*).
4. 'Subjectivization' is the English translation of the French word 'subjectivation' used by Rancière. This translation is inspired by Slavoj Žižek, *The Ticklish Subject*, London, Verso, 2000 (*TS*).

'Politics' and 'Police'

What is politics? This classical and profound question is the main subject of *La Mésentente*. We have to understand this work as an objection to the 'restoration' in the 1980s and 1990s when politics was reduced to state institutions and government practices. Previously, politics was found in the streets, the factories, and the universities; now we find politics only in the assemblies, in the affairs of the state, and in the higher courts. According to Rancière, the problem is that there is not much to discuss in these spheres because the decisions have already been determined in advance by the demands of the global market. David Easton's classical definition of politics as "the authoritative allocation of values" leads to a similar problem, namely, the reduction of the political to the political *system* and its reactions to 'inputs' (protest movements, organized interests, etc.).[5] Even if we expand the concept of politics to include the 'outputs' (policies, legislation, trade agreements, etc.) of the system, as well as the allocation of values in other areas such as firms and universities,[6] Rancière's point is that we would still be missing something, namely, a certain political 'power game.'

To approach the question of politics, Rancière returns to classical Greece, and specifically to one of the most famous parts of the Aristotle's *Politics*, where the 'human being' is defined as a 'speaking being.'[7] In the same paragraph, Aristotle claims that human beings are the beings who can distinguish the useful from the harmful, and thus good from bad. Hence, human beings are defined as political beings. As Rancière points out, there is a qualitative leap from the level of the useful/harmful to the political level of good/bad. In other words, we are dealing with two types of *justice*: 'arithmetic equality' and 'geometric equality.' The former is the justice of trade and legal matters, a form of justice that distributes social goods without considering the qualities of the concerned persons; the

---

5. Erik Damgaard, "Om en definition af politik og dennes konsekvenser," Politica 3, 2 (1970), 23–29. David Easton's definition is found in id., *A framework for Political Analysis*, Englewood Cliffs, Prentice-Hall, 1965, 103–35.
6. Erik Rasmussen, "En definition med kommentarer," *Politica* 3, 3 (1971), 29–38.
7. Aristotle, *Politics*, 1253a.

latter is the justice of politics proper, where everyone should have a social position, i.e., a certain amount of power, that matches the specific value one has to the community, i.e., what one contributes, in the broadest sense.[8] The classical Greek examples of these claims to power (*axiai*) are of course: the wealth (*plutos*) of the few (*oligoi*), the virtue/excellence (*arete*) of the best men (*aristoi*), and the liberty (*eleutheria*) of the people (*demos*). What defines politics, according to Aristotle and Greek philosophy in general, is this distribution of power between (what is supposed to be) well-defined social groups.

Unfortunately, as Rancière points out, there are three problems with this solution to the qualitative leap from wealth to politics: *First*, it is problematic to argue that wealth is reducible to the logic of arithmetic equality, as the logic of free exchange (power for money) ignores the question of the *quality* of the oligarchs. *Second*, if we take into consideration the concrete historical aristocracies, it is not at all clear what is meant by virtue if it is not wealth. Even Aristotle recognizes this problem.[9] 'Virtue/Excellence' is an ideological construction. The *third* difficulty is that the property of the people is not really the property of the people at all, but the property of *every* citizen in the *polis*; the *demos* has no *proper* value. And this was not even a problem before the democratic revolution in Greece, where a political manifestation of the people's will brought the emptiness or the arbitrariness of the oligarchs' and aristocrats' claims to power to light. While Aristotle essentially attempts to deal with the 'problem' of the people in such a way that the manifestation of their will does not seriously disturb the *hierarchical* distribution of power in the polis, to Rancière such a manifestation of the people's will is what politics is all about.

Thus, there are two very different modes of being-together in a community: one being the manifestation of the people's will; the other being the attempts to deal with this 'democratic scandal' by glossing over the problem, as Aristotle does, in such a way as not to disrupt a particular configuration of the political system and the attempts to justify

8. Cf. Aristotle, *Ethics*, V.
9. *Politics*, 1294a, 17–19.

this configuration by political philosophy. The manifestation of the people's will is a scandal precisely because it shows that every claim to power is contingent and thus cannot be justified. Rancière calls the first of these modes the process of *equality*. The second, that actually comes much closer to what we pointed out above as the 'normal' conception of politics, he calls *'the police'*, because it has to do with everything related to the "authoritative allocation of values." In Rancière's words, it is "the set of procedures whereby the aggregation and consent of collectivities is achieved; the organization of powers, the distribution of places and roles, and the system for legitimizing this distribution."[10]

Thus, what Easton calls 'politics' Rancière defines as 'the police.' Rancière's objection to the 'restoration' of the1980s and 1990s – when 'politics' was restricted to state institutions and governmental practices – and his distinction between the processes of 'the police' and 'equality,' are of course elements in a critique of depoliticization. To anticipate section two – and in order to establish a better understanding of the concept of 'the police' – we shall define 'politics' as the *encounter* between the (heterogeneous) processes of 'equality' and 'the police.' 'The police' is evidently not what we normally understand by the police; rather, 'the police' is essentially what Rancière calls a 'partition of the perceptible' (*partage du sensible*); that is, the symbolic/aesthetic order that constitutes a community and divides it into specialized tasks, each of these corresponding to a certain claim to power. 'The police' is the name of a very broad societal function. Hence Rancière concurs with Michel Foucault in saying that the police order extends itself far beyond the specialized disciplinary apparatuses like prisons and courts. Of course, Rancière has also borrowed the idea of a broader notion of 'the police' from Foucault.[11] Interestingly, however, Rancière actually rejects the Foucauldian notion of *power* because it "assert[s] in advance a smooth connection between the two domains," i.e., between 'the police' and 'politics.'[12] The main problem

---

10. *LM*, 51 (translated by the author, as are all further quotations from this source).
11. Michel Foucault, "La 'gouvernementalité'" [1978] id., *Dits et écrits 1954–1988, III 1976–1979*, Paris, Éditions Gallimard, 1994, 635–57.
12. *LM*, 55.

is the Foucauldian idea that where there is power, there is counter-power or resistance, which would mean that politics is everywhere a form of resistance – an idea that Rancière does not share.[13] Nor does Rancière accept the idea from the 1970s that power is everywhere, even in private homes, and hence that 'everything is political.' In *La Mésentente*, for example, he incessantly invokes an 'exterior' to 'the police,'[14] and more importantly, *politics* is certainly not everywhere – it is indeed rare.[15] In opposition to the Foucauldian conception of power, 'the police' actually does have a repressive function: the principal aim of 'the police' is to make politics disappear; the goal is depoliticization.

This leads us to the conclusion that as long as there are no politics, the hierarchical distribution of power in the community remains intact. 'The police,' including both the disciplinary institutions and the 'ideological' component, is there to make sure that equality does not interfere with the hierarchical distribution of power. As noted, Rancière accepts Foucault's analysis of the disciplinary societal functions, but he makes the point that 'the police' is there to conserve a *hierarchical* distribution of power; hence, the institutions of society, as such, are inegalitarian. Politics, on the contrary, is what interrupts the institutional arrangements that seek to naturalize the right of certain groups to power (due to wealth or excellence or, today, maybe through higher education in, e.g., political science and communication). Rancière also adds an analysis of the role of 'political philosophy' in this 'policing function' in Foucault's theory. I will now distinguish three main philosophical types within the conception of 'the police', i.e., three general philosophical ways to legitimate a specific configuration of the political community: 'arche-politics,' 'para-politics,' and 'meta-politics.'

---

13 Michel Foucault, *Histoire de la sexualité 1. La volonté de savoir*, Paris, Éditions Gallimard, 1976, 125–26 (*VS*).

14. E.g., *LM*, 103.

15 *LM*, 37.

From 'Arche-politics' to 'Meta-politics'

A substantial part of Rancière's work is devoted to a critique of Plato, and especially those parts of *The Republic* where Plato asserts that the good is best served when the members of each of the three classes, the philosophers, the guardians, and the artisans, remains in their proper places, fulfilling their natural functions.[16] Plato's 'polis in speech' is thus a model for the first type of what I shall call *'policing philosophies'* – *arche-politics*. The central point of arche-politics is that politics proper should be a realization and sensibilization of the *arche* (the principle) of the community. Briefly, the idea is to found a political order in which the domination of the virtuous person over the less virtuous is not really experienced as domination at all. The creation of an awareness in the population of the power structure – i.e., the complete sensibilization of power – through a thorough education, assures that the laws of the polis are inscribed directly into the mores of society, and thus when individuals stick to the place and role to which they are assigned, they realize at once both their own essence and the essence of the community. *Politics becomes ethics*. We know that Plato's utopia is developed as a fierce critique of democracy, and, indeed, a polis/'police' where everybody experiences domination as natural would be an inegalitarian 'paradise' where no democratic interruptions would ever occur. Another modern version of this policing philosophy is of course *communitarianism*, as Slavoj Žižek points out in his reading of Rancière in *The Ticklish Subject*.

The second policing philosophy, invented by Aristotle, is called *para-politics*. The central idea is that Plato's ideal is exactly that – just an ideal. Unattainable in reality, the ideal has been stained by the democratic event, and hence the role of 'the police' is to *incorporate* the demos into the polis in such a way that the hierarchical distribution of power is left intact. In short, the idea is to reconcile the domination of the 'best' with the fact of equality, and therefore the best government is actually when the oligarchs think that the polis is an oligarchy, and the demos thinks

---

16. The central passages are 369c–370c (cf. *LM*, 101) and 495d–e (cf. Jacques Rancière, *La nuit des prolétaires*, Archives du rêve ouvrier, Paris, Fayard, 1981, 10).

it is democracy. From this viewpoint, the best democracy is of course a situation in which people are dispersed over a vast territory and thus unable to reach the governmental organs (the 'Assembly' and the courts) because of time and distance.[17]

This idea of the people dispersed as a multiplicity of points has been perfected in much later theories of the state of nature. The freedom of the people as an integral *part of the city* is thus replaced by the freedom of the *individual*. *Right* becomes the main principle of politics. Reducing politics to the question of the rights of the individual, however, hinders the manifestation of the people as a cohesive group. It is by inscribing equality in the formulations of rights that the modern para-political 'police' seeks to deal with politics. Again, we learn about the contemporary forms of this second policing philosophy from Žižek: i.e., procedural ethics, be it Habermasian discursive ethics or Rawlsian distributive ethics, both of which seek to do away with antagonist parts of society by establishing well-known rules of litigation.

In his critique of the Foucauldian notion of power, Rancière does not turn to a Habermasian version of the 'system' that colonizes the free life-world of communicative rationality. One of the main functions of 'the police' is precisely to establish a consensus on what is to be the 'communicative rationality' of the city. In this way 'the police' makes sure that the expressions of the demos are heard as nothing but *noise*. Politics is the manifestation of a dissensus, a *disagreement* about who is to lead the rational political dialogue, and the role of 'the police' is therefore to assure that the discussions are regulated and consensual. So it is 'the police', not politics that endeavors to establish a consensus among the culturally diverse heterogeneous masses. An important argument against Habermas' colonization thesis is that politics is where 'the police' and equality *meet each other* – 'the police' is thus not external to politics. Everything is always already under 'police jurisdiction,' so there is nothing to colonize, which means that everything can become political, but *not* that everything *is* political.

---

17. Cf. Aristotle, *Politics*, 1319a.

The third policing philosophy is Marxist *meta-politics*. In contrast to the two previous models, meta-politics exposes the wrongs inherent in all ethics and rights of the community. According to the Marxist critique of ideology, all principles conceal a domination of the people. Rancière is highly skeptical about this critique, as it has a tendency to absolutize the division between truth and actual politics. Hence, the Marxist critique tends to the view that all political manifestations are false, and consequently that a true political revelation of the falseness of these manifestations exists. Since *everything* is dominated by the capitalist structure (and its legitimizing ideology), true politics consists in revealing the underlying structure, and not in the actual attempts to deal with injustices here and now. On the contrary, in Marxist meta-politics (according to Rancière) these attempts are ideologically suspect (petty bourgeois). Three additional points must be made here. First, this is exactly what happened in the Soviet Union. In the guise of the Marxist science, all manifestations against the hierarchical system were deemed ideologically suspect, and the Stalinist version, where everything was 'political,' assured that everybody was now under threat. Second, the Marxist critique of constitutional and human rights, is, in Rancière's view, equivalent to disdaining the struggles of real workers. In his long critique of his former master, Louis Althusser, *La Leçon d'Althusser* from 1974, Rancière writes sarcastically about the ideological liberation brought to the people by the Marxist intellectuals:

> Happy masses, finally freed from their 'bourgeois' claims and from 'human dignity.' Now they do not risk the same worries as the millions of workers who have been shot or deported to the farthest parts of our world because they put these sorts of stupidities into their heads.[18]

Third, in 1968 Rancière witnessed how Marxist criticism – due to its obsession with the industrial worker – could be turned against the subjectivization processes of the masses. This is another reason for the

18. Jacques Rancière, *La Leçon d'Althusser*, Paris, Gallimard, 1974, 161 (*LA*). Translation by the author.

virulent dispute between Althusser and Rancière. Rancière's central point is that the Marxist critique was turned against the students' uprising by criticizing their 'petty bourgeois' ideas, and consequently their intervention in the much more important general strike of the workers. "It is wrong to revolt"[19] against the professors, seemed to be the viewpoint of (the professor) Althusser and his party, the French Communist Party.

Besides the Marxist critiques, there is yet another contemporary version of meta-politics – *postmodernism*. In short, postmodernism is a critique of ideology without a concept of truth; in postmodernist thought, there is no real object behind the representations.[20] In this version of meta-politics, the hierarchical organization is only there because it is accepted, just as the king is king only because his subjects treat him as king. There is no transcendent foundation of sovereignty (a god or the divine right of kings), but the hierarchical positions in society are accepted anyway, if only with cynicism.[21] This kind of meta-politics excludes politics because its logic goes against any logic of *appearance* and therefore also against the democratic appearance of the people. This appearance has no symbolic efficacy in a world where all images are pure simulacra.

I have now sketched out Rancière's theory of 'the police.' To avoid misunderstanding, one supplementary point must be made. 'The police' as such is, at least according to Rancière himself, a value-neutral notion. One reason is of course that there is always 'a police,' so there is no point in stating that it is bad. The other reason is that there is no politics without 'the police,' since politics is the encounter between 'the police' and an egalitarian process. However, there are better or worse 'polices.' For example, today we are obviously better off than the slaves of antiquity. But the better conception of 'the police' is not, as we have seen, 'the police' that follows the supposed natural order of society or the principles of political scientists/philosophers; it is 'the police' that has most frequently been disturbed by democratic events, i.e., by politics.

Nonetheless, the central point to retain from our analysis of 'the

19. *LA*, 106.
20. Jean Baudrillard, *Simulacres et Simulation*, Paris, Galilée, 1985.
21. Cf. Žižek, *TS*, 192–93 and Rancière, *LM*, 133–65.

police' is that there are two different logics involved in what we normally understand as politics: The one includes all our institutional arrangements and our philosophy as well, and aims at safeguarding the hierarchical distribution of power in society. The other is the democratic event that disrupts this order. I shall now examine the notions of political subjectivization involved in the two logics.

Modes of Political Subjectivization

Once again we take Foucault's work as our point of departure. In his late work Foucault turns from mainly describing the "government of others" to focusing on the "government of one-self."[22] In short, Foucault wants to show that even though power is omnipresent, the individual enjoys a certain freedom – a playfulness regarding the structures of society. This change is accompanied by a shift from focusing on the processes of *subjection* to focusing on different *modes of subjectivization*.[23]

The problem for Rancière is of course that these modes of subjectivization are not political; they are much more about affirmative individualistic aesthetic practices. They concern the individual, and the individual's relation to the whole, whereas politics is about the relation of a certain part to the whole of the community. The postmodern society and its hierarchical organization is not at all disturbed by individualistic practices, since the highest principle of this society is precisely a narcissistic individualism. So what is a *political* subjectivization? In answering this question we must be aware of one thing: Just as Foucault does not make a *theory* of power but an *analysis* of power, Rancière, unlike Alain Badiou,[24] does not have a theory of the subject. Instead, he identifies the different subjectivizations occurring in history, and analyzes their formal similarities. Let us thus turn to the first historical example of political subjectivization.

---

22. Jens Erik Kristensen, "Det moderne subjekts genealogi. Michel Foucaults subjektproblematik," in *Subjektets status. Om subjektfilosofi, metafysik og modernitet*, edited by Hans Hauge, Århus, Aarhus University press, 1990, 110–35.

23. 'Assujettissement,' in Michel Foucault, *VS*, 30, and 'modes de subjectivation,' id., *Histoire de la sexualité 2. L'usage des plaisirs*, Paris, Éditions Gallimard, 1984, 35.

24. Alain Badiou, *L'être et l'événement*, Paris, Seuil, 1988, 429–47.

As we have seen, politics proper begins with the manifestation of the demos in ancient Greece. This is the first of the – historically rare – occurrences of political subjectivization. What characterizes this political appearance? A party belonging to the polis, the demos, asserts itself by claiming entitlement to a share of the power. But their claim to power, legitimated only by the fact that they are free citizens of Athens, is 'void,' because this property of the people – their freedom (*eleutheria*) – is also the property of the oligarchs and the aristocrats; hence, it is not really the specific property of the people. The liberty of the people is actually nothing but a contingent fact of their being born in Athens. Of course, this wrecks the principle of geometric equality that constitutes the political community: If the people actually bring *nothing*, their only property being an *empty property* (their freedom), their claim constitutes a fundamental *wrong* (*tort*). The democratic event thus constitutes Athens as a *litigious community*.

The wrong consists in the fact that a part of society, which is not entitled to a share of power, claims a share of it. Rancière calls this share *the share of the share-less* (*la part des sans-parts*). In this way the political subjectivization of the people, "purport[ing] that their group is identical to the whole of the community"[25] by identifying themselves with that which is common to everybody, divides the community and separates it from itself, i.e., from being only a community of arithmetic trade.

The assertion that the property of the people is in fact an empty property serves to maintain that there is no such thing as a special capacity for politics. The people's capacity to claim power, which enables them to turn the arithmetic trade community into a proper political community, is an empty property. All they need to do is to actualize the principle of *the equality of anyone and everyone* (*l'égalité de n'importe qui avec n'importe qui*). If there is to be politics, this principle must actually exist; hence, another important point is that this 'minimum equality' is always inscribed somewhere.

Rancière's argument is that to understand a commandment there

---

25. *LM*, 169.

must – at a minimum – be in place an equal capacity to speak and to understand; inferiors must at least understand the commands of their superiors, and that commands are to be obeyed. So in giving an order, one presupposes that inferiors are speaking beings. As we have seen, in Aristotle's terms the ability to use language – to speak and to understand – is one of the essential characteristics of humans as political beings. All that is needed is for the demos to take advantage of this recognition from their 'superiors,' and construct the political *scene* where they use their capacity to speak in public about the affairs of the city. In this way we can understand Rancière's rethinking of ideology. The human being (*l'Homme*) of the *Déclaration des droits de l'homme et du citoyen* and the various constitutions is not an ideological veil that conceals the 'real' domination; rather, these declarations of rights are inscriptions of the equality of anyone and everyone. Thus, instead of disavowing the various declarations of rights (Marxist meta-politics), politics *confirms* them. The declarations display a certain power (*puissance*) of the people, and politics is precisely about augmenting this power.

The Reason of the Revolt

> *On a raison de se révolter [it is right to revolt].*[26]
> *Les gens pensent [people think].*[27]

Political subjectivizations, according to Rancière, are about the relation between 'names' and 'social bodies.' Politics, as we have seen, is the manifestation of a social body incorporating nothing but an empty property, which in turn shows that 'underneath' the names of the dominant powers – the 'aristocracy' or the 'oligarchy' – there is no ontological substance. This means that the support of every inegalitarian distribution of power is the empty egalitarian principle that claims all human beings to be equal. This also means that names are not just illocutionary indicators of objects; they have a performative (perlocutionary) character, or a symbolic

---

26. Philippe Gavi, Jean-Paul Sartre, and Pierre Victor, *On a raison de se révolter*, Paris, Gallimard, 1974. Originally a statement by Mao Tse Tung.
27. Sylvain Lazarus, *Anthropologie du nom*, Paris, Seuil, 1996, 11.

efficacy. However, Rancière does not share the language pragmatism of Habermas and other speech act theorist. Politics is not simply about assuring a consensual discussion between well-established partners in the social field; it is not about assuring a communicative rationality against irrational speech. In Rancière's view, Habermas actually does not transcend the objectifying logic that he wants to overcome – the simple rationality of interest mediation. Refocusing our attention on Aristotle and the distinction between the political human being and the brutish beast, we can say that all there is at stake in the consensual dialogue is two parties or interest groups that announce their needs, their anger and disappointments, or their grievances and sufferings. In this there is no politics. In the consensual dialogue, we do not accomplish the qualitative leap from the useful/harmful to the good and the bad.

Politics, on the contrary, constitutes its own rationality as the rationality inherent in a particular form of communication that is neither an activity between pre-configured parties, nor the brute yelling of beasts. The rationality of *disagreement* is the rationality of the political game about *who* will be the actual parties of the political dialogue. Politics is thus about "giving sound to a speech where one perceived only noise."[28] This notion of 'noise' is very important in Rancière's work. It is of course his participation in the events around May '68[29] and his discussion with Althusser that led him to reflect upon this "noise of the revolt."[30] May '68 taught Rancière about the instability of the hierarchical institutional order, and about the link between this instability and the capacity to deliberate about one's own conditions, a capacity that belonged to the students because it belongs to everyone.

For instance, politics in a factory strike could have a rational argumentative structure that goes something like this: The factory owners could say: "This factory is private property. We do in fact recognize that

28. Jacques Rancière, *Aux Bords du Politique*, Paris, La Fabrique-Éditions, 1998, 120.
29. I owe great thanks to Stephane Douailler for enlightening me about the more practical political part of Rancière's life (personal correspondence).
30. *LA*, 142.

workers are speaking beings, but this fact is of no relevance here." Hence, they perceive the expression of the workers as nothing but noise, and the only thing to do is to wait until it goes away, or call the authorities and *make it* go away. However, there is a second element in the discursive structure, as the workers respond: "We are right to argue for our rights and thus to posit the existence of a common world of argument. And we are right to do so precisely because those who ought to recognize it do not, acting as though they were ignorant of the existence of this common world."[31]

This important example shows us two things: First, a strike is not in itself political. It is only political if it constitutes a litigious community, if it reconfigures a place in such a way that a political subject that did not exist before is now included as an interlocutor in the discussions about the conditions in this place. Before the political strike there were only workers, now there is the name of a new political subject, i.e., the proletariat. Second, this reveals Rancière's critique of the notion of class struggle.[32] The problem with the class struggle is that it presupposes what is to be constructed in the political manifestation of the demos, namely, the antagonism. Politics actually makes us see that the city is only divided into rich and poor. Class struggle is not the secret motor of history; rather, politics is actually constructed by class struggle; hence, politics defines its proper sphere. This is not simply a violent war between two entities (Rancière is not Carl Schmitt). Politics is not the well established dialogue or negotiation between preconfigured parties. Politics is not the market, nor a question of procedural law or ethics. Politics has its own rationality, which is the symbolic struggle about who is to be recognized as political actors.

---

31. *LM*, 82.
32. Cf. Rancière, *LM*, 31, 33, 109–10, 121, and 128.

Global Politics

There is a global police and it can sometimes achieve some good. But there is no global politics.[33]

Why this pessimism regarding global politics? Rancière has three objections to such a notion. First, there is the predominance of the "reign of the 'humanitarian,'"[34] which is Human Rights deprived of all political capacity. (As argued above, human rights do have a political capacity). In this reign there is only the individual suffering a wrong; there are only victims of 'crimes against humanity.' In this way politics is turned into ethics, or proceedings in international courts (i.e., para-politics). Second, there are the wars fought in the name of democracy; there should be no need to argue that these have nothing to do with Rancière's notion of democracy. Third, there is the "utopia of the government of the planet by the auto-regulation of Capital."[35] In other words, there is the global 'police.'

But since 'the battle in Seattle,' have we not witnessed a global re-sistance against this 'empire'? Have Michael Hardt and Antonio Negri not shown us the way towards global politics?[36] Rancière has three main arguments against the authors of *Empire:* First, the concept of the *multitude* "substantializes the egalitarian presupposition."[37] The theory of the multitude is founded on an ontology. This means that politics is founded on a common principle for every human being. In this way, politics becomes ethics: You should be multitudinous! But according to Rancière, *nothing* founds politics, and certainly politics is not ethics. Second, the theory of creativity inherent in the multitude – the equivalent

33. *LM*, 188.
34. *LM*, 172.
35. Rancière quoted in Renaud Pasquier, "Police, politique, monde," *Labyrinthe*, 17 (Winter 2004), 23. Translated by the author.
36. Michael Hardt and Antonio Negri, *Empire*, Cambridge/London, Harvard University Press, 2000.
37. Jacques Rancière, "Peuple ou multitudes?" interview in *Multitudes*, no. 9 (May–June 2002), http://multitudes.samizdat.net/article.php3?id_article=39. Translated by the author.

to the forces of production immanent in *Empire* – implies an immanent teleology, i.e., it is the hazardous turned into necessity. In *Empire* it is only a question of time and place before the creative forces will unleash themselves, and this is the hidden purpose of politics. Rancière would never accept such a teleology; there is no general purpose of politics and no way to predict its historical trajectory. Only time will tell of any future political subjectivizations. Third, the much praised 'nomadism' in *Empire* is no more than the result of ever more repressive or failed states. There are many more states and many more instances of 'the police' than fifty years ago. In short, for there to be politics, according to Rancière, the multitude must give way to the manifestation of the people. There must be a point where the contradiction between global capitalism and the national juridical systems is the occasion for a political manifestation of a group claiming the share for the share-less (the illegal immigrants are needed in the global production, but not accepted according to national law and nationalist tendencies in most countries).[38]

But we can interpret the alter-globalist movement and the manifestation of '*les sans-papiers*' in the church St. Bernhard in Paris in the following way: These manifestations can be understood as groups of people using the principles of democracy – which are, if not inscribed in a global constitution, at least generally praised in the discourse of our international 'leaders' – to construct a global democratic scene where those who are normally not counted as legitimate parties in the discussion of global affairs try to introduce a new political subject. This could be interpreted as the subjectivization of a global people instead of the subjectivization of merely national citizens (in the alter-globalization movement), or of workers without papers instead of just 'illegal immigrants' (in the case of '*les sans-papiers*'). Alternatively, like Hardt and Negri one could interpret these cases as a realization of the unconscious teleological will of the multiple Being. This latter possibility is of course rejected by Rancière. The former is hinted at in the interview *Peuple ou multitudes?*, but in the end it remains an empirical question of symbolic efficacy: does the global

38. Hardt and Negri, *Empire*, 393–411.

'police' (including important parts of the alter-globalization movement itself) succeed in reducing these movements to the *noise* of suffering animals, or are we witnessing the birth of global democratic politics?

I shall conclude my reflections by leaving open the question about these global issues. However, to conclude my thoughts on the nature of political subjectivization, I shall quote Rancière himself. Who could say it better?

> Politics exists wherever *the count* of the shares and the parts of society is disturbed by the inscription of a *share of the share-less*. It begins when *the equality of anyone and everyone* is inscribed in *the liberty of the people*. This liberty of the people is *an empty property*, an improper property through which those who are nothing purport that their group is identical to the whole of the community. Politics exists as long as singular forms of *subjectivization* repeat the forms of the original inscription of the identity between the whole of the community and the nothing that separates it from itself – in other words, the sole count of its parts.[39]

Indeed, genuine political thinking is found precisely where these political subjectivizations change the social-institutional order.

---

39. *LM*, 169, italics added.

Foucault, Relativism, and Political Action

Mogens Chrom Jacobsen

Although Michel Foucault engaged in several political causes, in particular his "Groupe d'Information sur les Prisons" (GIP), one wonders whether this engagement had any foundation in his philosophy. Indeed, he did write a book about prisons (*Discipline and Punish*), but despite the apparent connection between his philosophical thought and his own life, and the fact that this book was, at least to some extent, inspired by the experience in the GIP, one could legitimately ask whether his philosophical assumptions and his analyses are capable of supporting and buttressing such political involvement and engagement. This seems not to be the case.

In this article, I shall argue that there are two elements in Foucault's method, each of which has a different critical potential. On the one hand, he uses strictly empirical description to demonstrate the relativity of the different transcendental or essentialist claims to truth; on the other hand, he employs a series of alternative interpretations that serve to challenge his readers to live without binding themselves to myths. I have divided my argument into two parts. First, I shall argue that empirical description and method cannot quite do without the kind of reason about which he is so sceptical, because, at a more fundamental level, Foucault's relativism must be defended against alternative positions. Foucault must be able to make a minimal claim to objectivity; otherwise his theory will lose its critical potential. This will allow for a minimal conception of reason valid across different perspectives, but this conception would not be sufficient to allow us to understand and interpret the world. Collective political action, however, demands a common understanding of what should be done in a particular situation and hence a more substantial interpretation of the world. For this reason, positions proposing substantial interpretations of the world would have an advantage here. Second, I shall argue that Foucault is not capable of providing us with a normative basis for collective political action, because Foucault's ideal is about free and creative thinking that has been liberated from the hegemony of social, economic, and cultural forms of thinking. This liberation can only be achieved through a better understanding of how the regimes of truth work, but this project seems at the same time to leave us without any normative basis for collective political action.

Foucault and Historical Truth

A careful historical scholar, Foucault responds to other historians and considers their hypotheses and methodological assumptions. In *Madness and Civilization*, for example, he does not hesitate to question whether a group of historians really deserves this distinction. In his view, they fail to provide arguments to support their own theses, and if that were not enough, they also believe madness to be some essential entity, that is just waiting to be discovered a thesis Foucault disproves.[1] In *The Birth of the Clinic*, he criticizes the view that pathological anatomy was not accepted because of religious interdictions that only disappeared in the Enlightenment, but according to Foucault this reconstruction is historically false. Doctors had no problem dissecting dead bodies, and the development of pathological anatomy was not due to the establishment of the clinical schools that were finally able to avoid religious interdictions. This would be careless chronology, since the clinical schools represented an alternative conception of the medical science, which was actually hindering the development of pathological anatomy, a discipline already defined at an earlier date.[2] In *Discipline and Punish*, he wonders how the prison sentence became

1. Michel Foucault, *Histoire de la folie à l'âge classique*, Paris, Gallimard, 1972, 110–11 (*HF*).
2. Michel Foucault, *Naissance de la clinique*, Paris, PUF, 1963, 125–27 (*NC*).

nearly the only form of punishment in such a short time after the French Revolution, when the opinions of philosophers, reformers, and traditional lawyers in the time prior to the French Revolution did not support this practice at all. The usual explanation is that the classical period saw the emergence of some models for punishment by imprisonment, the influence of which was so much more important as they emerged in England and North America. They were influential, Foucault admits, but they do not explain the problem; rather, they are the problem that has to be explained. Foucault's explanation is that disciplinary mechanisms have developed in the military, the school system, factories, etc., which in the end spread to the legal system.[3] In *The Will to Knowledge*, he considers the so-called 'repression hypothesis' according to which the seventeenth century should have been the beginning of the repression of sexuality in terms of interdictions and taboos. However, Foucault objects, proposing the contrary thesis that we have seen a veritable explosion in discourses on 'the sexual' since the seventeenth century. In this context the repression hypothesis seems inadequate. Power works negatively through prohibitions, but it also works positively through the multiplication of discourses, inscribed as they are in the demands of power; hence, according to Foucault, the positive modus of power is the most important.[4]

It is hard to imagine that Foucault would not attempt to lay claim to any sort of truth or objectivity in his investigations. However, in a 1980 interview, he addresses this problem:

The problem concerning the truth of what I say is a very difficult problem for me, and even the central problem. It is the question that until now I have not answered. I use at once the most classic methods: I use historical demonstration or in any case proof; I refer to texts, to references, authorities, and to ideas and facts that are related to each other; I propose some frames of understanding, types of explanations. In

---

3. Michel Foucault, *Surveiller et punir. Naissance de la prison*, Paris, Gallimard, 1975, 135–36, 142, and 297 (*SP*).
4. Michel Foucault, *Histoire de la sexualité I. La volonté de savoir*, Paris, Gallimard, 1976, 25, 71, and 96–97 (*VS*).

this there is nothing original. From this point of view, the things I say in my books can be verified or disproved like any other book about history. In spite of this, the persons who read me, and in particular those who appreciate my approach, often say with a grin: 'After all, you know very well that the things you say are only fictions.' I always answer 'Of course, it is out of the question that it should be anything but fiction.'[5]

In another interview from 1980, Foucault says that in the true sense of the word he is not a historian; rather, he does a kind of historical fiction. A historian could very well object that what Foucault has written is not the truth, for his work is not complete from a historical point of view; it is partial and exaggerated. He may even have ignored some elements that contradicted his own theses. Foucault attempts to create interference between our reality and what we think we know about our history. He wishes his writings to have an effect on contemporary life so that they will have a truth in that life.[6]

The issue concerning the historical veracity of Foucault's analyses was posed a bit differently in an interview from 1967, where he states that it should be possible to define the theoretical model to which his own and similar books belong. This model would make it possible to deal with history in the way he and kindred spirits do. This model belongs to our age, and it is our age and it alone that makes it possible to deal with history in this specific way. He says that his book (*The Order of Things*) is pure fiction; it is a novel, but he is not the inventor; rather, the book is a product of the relation between our age and its epistemological configurations on the one side and the whole mass of actual historical utterances on the other side. Even though a subject is present in the work, it is the anonymous 'one'[7] who is speaking.[8] The point seems to

---

5. Daniel Defert and François Ewald (editors), *Foucault: Dits et écrits 1954–1988, vol. II 1976–1988*, Paris, Gallimard, 2001, 863; text no. 281 (translated by the author, as are all further quotations from this source). Hereafter, *DE-II*.

6. *DE–II*, 859; text no. 280.

7. In the sense of 'what is one to do?'

8. Daniel Defert and François Ewald (editors), *Michel Foucault: Dits et écrits 1954–1988, vol. I 1954–1975*, Paris: Gallimard, 2001, 619; text no. 48. Hereafter, *DE-I*.

be that Foucault speaks within a particular discourse, but probably also within a scientific historical discourse. The form of proof and explanation he uses is valid within this discourse, and here it is objective, or it has some sort of truth. But where does the fiction enter? Here we have to consult Nietzsche for an explanation.

Nietzsche and Perspectivism

We cannot overestimate the importance of Nietzsche for Foucault; indeed, Foucault returns to this enigmatic thinker again and again in numerous interviews. According to himself, it is difficult to estimate Nietzsche's actual influence on his own work. Foucault began reading Nietzsche in 1953,[9] and according to himself, this reading was a revelation.[10] Ideologically, Foucault was a 'historicist' and Hegelian until reading Nietzsche,[11] and reading Nietzsche made Foucault interested in doing research for the first time.[12] Although Foucault commenced his theoretical studies with Hegel, Marx, and then Heidegger, who also became very important to him, Nietzsche came to dominate his thinking.[13] His archaeological method, for example, is more indebted to the Nietzschean conception of genealogy than to structuralism, properly speaking.[14] Foucault even goes so far as to say that he is simply a Nietzschean, and that he tries to see just how far it is possible to proceed with certain points and in certain areas of research with the help of Nietzsche's texts. As he admits, Foucault is particularly indebted to texts from the 1880s,[15] and elsewhere he mentions in particular *The Birth of Tragedy* (1871–72/1886) and *On the Genealogy of Morals* from 1887.[16] At the same time, he also points out that when he uses some theses that would appear to be anti-Nietzschean,

---

9. *DE-II*, 1255; text no. 330.
10. *DE-II*, 1599; text no. 362.
11. *DE-I*, 641; text no. 50.
12. *DE-II*, 1348; text no. 336.
13. *DE-II*, 1522; text no. 354; also see 867; text no. 281.
14. *DE-I*, 627; text no. 48.
15. *DE-II*, 1263; text no. 330.
16. *DE-I*, 1240; text no. 109.

they somehow turn out to be Nietzschean after all.[17]

At least since Nietzsche's time, philosophy no longer seeks to determine a truth that is valid for all times and for everyone; instead, the task of philosophy has become 'diagnostic.'[18] Nietzsche discovered that the particular activity of the philosopher consisted in making diagnoses, like: Who are we? What is this 'today' in which we live? Such diagnostic activity involves a work of 'excavation,' in order to establish how a certain universe of thoughts, discourses, and culture – which is also the universe of the excavator – came into being.[19] We are talking about a diagnosis of the present that attempts to discover the unconscious presuppositions, i.e., the laws and rules of scientific thought, within the areas of the history of science, experience, and human knowledge.[20]

Thus, according to Foucault's interpretation of Nietzsche, 'knowledge' is neither a collection of facts waiting to be discovered, nor does it originate in human nature; rather, knowledge is something invented, which came into being at a particular moment.[21] His interpretation of Nietzsche's conception of knowledge, however, rests on a partial selection of texts, and Foucault does not pretend that this is Nietzsche's own view; rather, he proposes to show that Nietzsche's thought can provide a model for historical analysis. According to Foucault, Nietzsche wants to say that knowledge has neither a nature nor an essence; there are no universal conditions for knowledge; rather, knowledge is, everywhere and at all times, a historical and momentaneous result of conditions that do not themselves belong to the level of knowledge. The texts where Nietzsche claims that knowledge is perspectival can be understood in light of this. Knowledge is not conditioned by factors originating in human nature, in the human body, or in the very structure of knowledge itself; knowledge only exists as separate acts that differ from one another, with no common essence. Through these acts human beings take possession of things by

17. *DE-II*, 1523; text no. 354.
18. *DE-I*, 634; text no. 50.
19. *DE-I*, 640–41; text no. 50.
20. *DE-I*, 693–94; text no. 55.
21. *DE-I*, 1412–13; text no. 139.

force, react to particular situations, and impose certain power relations. Knowledge is always a particular strategic relation, in which humans are entangled. This relation defines the effect of knowledge, and for this reason it will inevitably be partial, biased, and express a particular perspective. Nonetheless, the perspectival character of knowledge is not due to human nature, but stems from the polemical and strategic character of knowledge itself. The determination of reality as knowledge is inherent in the struggle between men, where some parties get the upper hand, at least partly, by imposing their description of the world.[22]

For this reason it is not sufficient to write 'the history of rationality'; instead, one should write the history of truth itself. The question is not whether a particular science approaches the truth or has any access to it; rather, according to Foucault, we should consider truth as a specific relationship between discourse and knowledge (*savoir*). He also asks whether this relationship is in itself a history, or whether it has a history. Certain types of rationality (science, practice, discourse) are not measured according to the truths they are able to procure; rather, truth forms part of the history of such a discourse or practice, like an internal effect of this discourse or practice. If the scientific practice constitutes both the ideal subject of the sciences and their object of knowledge, we should then be able to find the historical roots of the sciences in the mutual genesis of subject and object. Hence, we must ask: to what kind of truth will this lead? Foucault answers this question himself, saying that there is no truth. However, this does not mean that this history is irrational, nor that this science is illusory, but *confirms*, on the contrary, the existence of a history that is real and comprehensible. Indeed, a history is a series of collective rational experiences that abide by precise and identifiable rules, in virtue of which both the knowing subject and the known object are construed.[23] Hence, Foucault can claim, somewhat paradoxically, that those who maintain that there is no truth are, in his opinion, a bit simpleminded.[24] This means that truth as such is produced within a discourse; thus, while

22. *DE-I*, 1418–19; text no. 139.
23. *DE-II*, 873–74; text no. 281.
24. *DE-II*, 1488; text no. 350.

Foucault denies the existence of transcendent or essential truth, truth exists as a product.

For Foucault, then, genealogy should write the history of truth, and, as he explains, this is a 'grey' activity consisting of meticulous and patient documentation. Genealogy according to Foucault maps the particularity of events without recourse to any teleology; it seeks its subjects where one would least expect to find them in sentiments, affections, consciences, and instincts; it maps the recurrence of events without recourse to any theory of development, and provides simple descriptions of the various scenarios, in which they played diverse roles; it even depicts those that never took place, such as Plato's never becoming a Mohammed in Syracuse.[25] Genealogy should not change anything in the particular dispersion of events. Coincidences and small deviations must be mapped along with complete upheavals; one should map mistakes, misjudgements, and miscalculations that have brought about existing things, and matters that are most valuable for us.

We must realize that there is no truth or being at the *root* of what we know and what we are, but only the exteriority of coincidence.[26] On the other hand, genealogy should reconstruct the various systems that tie events and things to a particular teleology, binding them to the arbitrary play of various sorts of domination.[27] If by 'interpretation' we understand the violent appropriation of such systems of rules, which in and of themselves have no essential meaning, in order to endow them with some direction and to subject them to some new will, then the genesis of the human kind is a series of interpretations, and genealogy should be the history about these interpretations.[28] According to Foucault, this was also what Nietzsche called 'real history' (*wirkliche Historie*) in contradistinction to traditional history.[29]

---

25. *DE-I*, 1004; text no. 84.
26. *DE-I*, 1009; text no. 84.
27. *DE-I*, 1011; text no. 84.
28. *DE-I*, 1014; text no. 84.
29. *DE-I*, 1017; text no. 84.

The Theory of Discourse

Foucault was attracted by Nietzsche's attempt to cast doubt on the fundamental notions of knowledge, morality, and metaphysics by means of a particular kind of historical analysis with positivistic leanings and without resorting to any notion of the origin or primacy of the subject.[30] It is precisely this kind of project that Foucault proposes in the *Archaeology of Knowledge*, where we find the same opposition between a new type of investigation and the traditional analyses in the history of ideas and the history of the sciences. The latter looks for continuity, cohesion, and meaning, while the former seeks out discontinuity (thresholds, ruptures, interruptions, changes, and transformations). The traditional analyses seek the origin of all becoming and practice in human consciousness, while the new approach liberates itself from anthropological terminology, seeking the conditions for becoming and practice *outside* the subject. Notions such as tradition, influence, development, mentality, or *Zeitgeist* presuppose that we always speak about the same in the same way or that there is some underlying teleology the progress of knowledge, the self-realization of the Spirit, etc. Likewise concepts such as 'philosophy' or 'biology' are considered to be eternal entities, while notions such as 'book' and 'work' (*oeuvre*) also presuppose a unity, since they are ascribed to a particular author. All these forms of continuity cannot be dismissed out of hand, but cannot be accepted as self-evident.[31]

Foucault's methodological project must be considered as an attempt to work out the Nietzschean genealogical analysis in detail. Such an analysis, however, can only start from the given, which, for Foucault, is the *utterance*, and it is between utterances that relations, correlations, etc. must be established. Utterances, however, are only constituted as positivities as parts of a discourse, since they, considered as practice, are linked to certain conditions, subject to certain rules, and undergo certain transformations.[32] Now, if projecting their description makes one a posi-

---

30. *DE-I*, 1240; text no. 109.
31. Michel Foucault, *L'archéologie du savoir*, Paris, Gallimard, 9–28 (*AS*).
32. *DE-I*, 721; text no. 58.

tivist, Foucault admits to being a happy positivist.[33]

Thus, we must distinguish between two types of investigations: one emerging from the established sciences and traditional systems of thought, and the other, the genealogical or archaeological analysis that Foucault borrows from Nietzsche. The sciences or the traditional systems of thought, which establish both the knowing subjects and the known objects within a given discourse, contain their own conditions and requirements for the production of truth. These discourses are also depicted by Foucault as 'truth games.'[34] The truth, as defined within a particular discourse, exists as such, and it can be the object of an investigation, since it must be possible to establish the truth conditions of the utterances within a given discourse. Foucault alludes to this point when he speaks about the history of truth to be uncovered by the genealogical analysis. The essential difference between the two kinds of investigation consists in the fact that the sciences and the traditional systems of thought try to go beyond what is immediately given, and interpret events such that they fit into a teleological framework, or conform to the primacy of the subject. According to Foucault, however, such interpretations actually violate the events, since a meaning is imputed to them, a meaning determined by certain interests or power relations. The archaeological analysis does not interpret *events*, since it does not assert anything about any transcendent reality, neither about causal motives nor about assumed mental states or intentions. Its only assertions concern *utterances*, and through them, expressed opinions and their dependency on the given discursive context.[35] The archaeological analysis is Foucault's strict implementation of the Nietzschean project. When Foucault in his studies advances alternative explanations for certain events, he engages in interpretation, as we have argued above. Hence, we must understand Foucault as saying that these interpretations are only fictions, that the truth he wishes for them must lie in the future and that these truths should shake up ideas and detach us from habitual conceptions.

---

33. *AS*, 164–65.
34. *DE-II*, 1451–54; text no. 345.
35. *DE-I*, 734; text no. 59.

Foucault's method has two different aspects. On the one hand, the strict analysis of the discourses that uncovers the dependency of interpretations on power relations; on the other, those alternative explanations that shake up established ideas. But what kind of status does the strict analysis have? Would it be perspectival, or would it be the basis for uncovering the other conceptions as various perspectives? This will be the theme of the next section.

The Question of Relativism

As already indicated, to Foucault, analysis in the precise sense means strict descriptions of utterances.[36] Foucault compares his own project to the natural sciences, which also have had to abandon the projection of causal relations onto the phenomena and devote their activities to pure description.[37] These descriptions seem to him objective and positive.[38] Elsewhere he refers to an 'accurate theoretical analysis.'[39] He also talks about how, through empirical studies, one can isolate the level of discursive practices.[40] Much later, he claims that his role is to show people that the opinions they consider true and evident have been produced at a determinate moment in history and that their alleged truths and evidence can be criticized and destroyed. Furthermore, all his analyses oppose the idea of universal necessities in human life, emphasizing the contingent nature of institutions.[41] This type of analysis does not claim to establish any transcendental truth since it describes something immediately given, something positive – nevertheless, it appears to lay claim to objectivity or correctness; it expresses a form of rationality. How can this be the case? Before we take up this subject we must consider a difficulty. In an interview from 1967 Foucault argues that if his type of analysis is acceptable it must be possible to define the theoretical model to which

36. *DE-I*, 618; text no. 48.
37. *DE-I*, 617; text no. 48, 635; text no. 50.
38. *DE-I*, 638; text no. 50.
39. *DE-I*, 683; text no. 54.
40. *DE-I*, 1109; text no. 101.
41. *DE-II*, 1597–98; text no. 362.

it belongs, and that this model makes it possible to treat history as a series of actually expressed utterances. The same model also allows us to consider language as an object of description and as a totality of relations in connection with the discourse and the utterances that are interpreted. In *The Archaeology of Knowledge* from 1969, however, he seems to say exactly the opposite:

> ... it is not possible for us to describe our own archive, since it is from within these rules that we speak, since it is that which gives to what we can say – and to itself, the object of our discourse – its modes of appearance, its forms of existence and coexistence, its system of accumulation, historicity and disappearance. The archive cannot be described in its totality; ... The description of the archive deploys its possibilities (and the mastery of its possibilities) on the basis of the very discourses that have just ceased to be ours; ...[42]

It is not quite clear whether Foucault has changed his mind, or whether there is some subtle difference between defining the theoretical model and describing the archive. I will assume that there *is* such a difference, and consider the quotation as the more general and decisive opinion. Foucault's own analysis, then, is situated within a discourse. But why is it impossible to describe? The reason could be that Foucault seems to think that this would require a certain quantity of utterances as a material basis for the analysis, but insofar as we are about to produce these utterances, we need to wait until the material exists before we can begin to analyze them. But even though we cannot describe our own 'archive,' there must be some kind of discursive practice at work expressing a kind of rationality that unfolds itself in the genealogical, archaeological, or diagnostic method. This practice cannot be situated at the same level as the object it analyses, for then it applies to itself, and we will end up in the liar paradox. The discursive practice that reveals other discursive practices as partial is partial itself. The difficulty is not

---

42. Michel Foucault, *Archeology of Knowledge*, London, Routledge, 2002, 146–47.

that it would be motivated by interests that in itself is not a problem; rather, the salient point is that the discursive practice dissolves its own objectivity and at the same time its own critical potential. If it merely presents itself as one perspective among others, why would one choose this particular perspective rather than some other perspective? That which really changes something in people's minds (*changer quelque chose dans l'esprit des gens*)[43] is the claim that it is possible to show objectively that the other points of view are only perspectives. What makes people think differently and change perspectives, and in the end abandon the belief in any specific perspective, is the objective demonstration that power and interests govern all these perspectives. Foucault knows the liar paradox very well and would certainly not commit this error; the liar paradox can easily be avoided by distinguishing between 'object language' and 'meta-language.'[44] Objective demonstration must then proceed from a more fundamental discourse. This fundamental discourse cannot proceed from some even more fundamental discourse without ending up in an infinite regress; in any case, there has to be a fundamental discourse. Could this fundamental discourse include the categories of logic, and would Foucault accept these categories as part of a trans-historical perspective? Foucault discusses these categories, which he considers as very general, even universal, but unfit to explain in any satisfying manner the way people actually think.[45] Thus, Foucault holds that the universal categories of logic only explain a very limited part of people's thinking, and he is probably right about this, but the role he would further reserve for the universal categories of logic is not clear. He seems, however, to open the door for a trans-historical perspective.

It is characteristic for relativism that not everything can be relativized without self-contradiction. If one claims that everything is relative, then this claim would also be relative. However, one can very well say that all propositions about the world or about morality are relative to some specific thing. We can discuss whether this proposition is relative or not to this or

---

43. *DE-II*, 159798; text no. 362.
44. *DE-I*, 546; text no. 38.
45. *DE-II*, 1597; text no. 362.

that, but we still have to discuss it from 'something' that is not itself a part of this relativity. The same point is valid for Foucault when he describes how our claim to tell the truth is relative to some discursive practice having its foundation in interests and power relations. The categories of description that human beings use to describe the world stem from these discursive practices; thus, they cannot be eternal standards. Our knowledge about the world, then, is relative to the specific discursive practice in which it is expressed. The assertion of relativism, however, is not relative to this discourse; rather, it belongs to a more fundamental discourse that determines the different interpretive perspectives, for the thesis of relativism does not claim anything about the world, but only something about our putative knowledge about the world.

Harvey Siegel defines relativism in this way:

> For any knowledge-claim p, p can be evaluated (assessed, established, etc.) only according to (with reference to) one or another set of background principles and standards of evaluation S(1),...S(n); and, given a different set (or sets) of background principles and standards S(1)',...S(n)', there is no neutral (that is, neutral with respect to the two [or more] alternative sets of principles and standards) way of choosing between the two (or more) alternative sets in evaluating p with respect to truth or rational justification. P's truth and rational justifiability are relative to the standards used in evaluating p.[46]

In short, two conditions have to be fulfilled, namely that different standards may give rise to incompatible propositions, and that there is no neutral or objective criteria for preferring the one rather than the other. It is presupposed both that the standards belong to linguistic communities and that incompatibility consists in a classical logical assertion of the type 'p and non-p.'[47] If the standards just mentioned neither use the same concepts nor relate to the same things, then the assertions in question

46. Harvey Siegel, *Relativism Refuted*, Dordrecht, Reidel, 1987, 6.
47. Nils Holtug, "Er erkendelsesteoretisk relativisme kohærent?," *Filosofiske Studier* 1 (1993), 725.

could never be incompatible, and the notion of relativism does not apply. Would the same not be valid for Foucault's theory of discourse? Foucault maintains that the discourse cannot tell us who spoke the truth, who reasoned most cogently, who lived up to his own postulates to the highest degree, but it can tell us to which extent they spoke about 'the same thing,' were at 'the same level,' were unfolding 'the same conceptual field,' met each other on 'the same battlefield.'[48] It is far from always the case that they speak about the same things. The discourse constitutes the knowing subject and the object of knowledge, that is why the discourses will often concern totally different things, and for that reason they cannot give rise to incompatible assertions. Such disagreements can, however, arise within a discourse in which one is speaking about the same object, but the discourse would probably also contain the standards that make it possible to decide the disagreement, and in that case there cannot be a question of relativism either. It is only in a very abstract sense that we can speak about relativism, viz. when perspectives claim to assert something about a transcendent reality populated by objects and subjects. These kind of perspectives must be mutually incompatible (for example an organically based mental sickness in opposition to unreason's menacing relativization of reason), and, I think, Foucault's point is precisely that we cannot make a choice between them, because they are both illusions.

This does not mean that the more fundamental discourse would have to proceed from some transcendental or essentialist notion of reason; it can very well have its own history and its origin in some particular point in time. But if this more fundamental discourse has its own history, would we not to some extent be obliged to suppose that this discourse is continuous? Although Foucault does not reject continuity as such, he would probably be sceptical about such a notion.[49] First of all, if Foucault wants to influence his contemporaries, he only has to claim that this discourse is common to us; however, if he wants to influence the coming generations, there has to be a commonality between our discourse and

48. *AS*, 166, see also 202–04.
49. Michel Foucault, "Vérité et pouvoir," in *L'Arc. Cahiers méditerranéens* 70 (1977), 16–26, 18. Hereafter, *VP*.

theirs, and then we are not far from claiming that it is also common between previous generations and our time. In the end this cannot be decided by means of transcendental or rationalistic arguments; it can only be decided empirically. So could we then have a meaningful 'discussion' with Aristotle? Would we have, at least, some suppositions and standards in common? I am not certain that Foucault would agree, even though he is in dialogue with Nietzsche and seems to think that Nietzsche was right about some matters. Is reason, which he criticizes so violently in the guise of the primacy of the subject, wholly dispensable? It should be possible to write the history of reason, but this history could very well be much more continuous than Foucault probably would admit.

Political Action

Given our examination of Foucault's philosophical thought, what does this mean for the possibility of political action? Foucault says that he knows very well that he is situated in a context. The problem for us is to know how we can become conscious of this context, and how we integrate it and let it influence our own discourse – the one we are about to utter.[50] Real history is not afraid of being perspectival. Although traditional historians seek to blot out anything that could betray their standpoint and partiality, the historical sense is, according to Nietzsche, aware that it is perspectival, and does not reject the system of its own injustice. The historical sense enables its own genealogy in the very movement of its knowledge.[51] Here we have the second aspect of Foucault's method, where he himself is about to interpret the world, knowing full well that his interpretations are necessarily as unjust, partial, and fictitious as all other interpretations. He wants them to have an impact, and be recognized as having a truth, in his own time. They should change something in people's minds; whether he has ignored some elements or contradicted his own theses is not important. Generally speaking, Foucault is strict and thorough in his analyses, but despite every effort he ignores certain elements; hence, we should not be too hard on Foucault on this account. The argument itself, however, appears

50. *DE–I*, 639; text no. 50.
51. *DE–I*, 1018; text no. 84.

somewhat problematic, for what is it that changes something in people's minds? While it is possible to advance the most disjointed and rambling interpretations, will this have any effect if there is no reason to accept them in favour of some *other* interpretation? Is it not the persuasive capacity of accurate and meticulous analyses that make them effective? But if so, what makes this analysis persuasive? Are we not obliged to suppose that some interpretations are more correct, adequate, or suitable than others?

Furthermore, what is the purpose of these alternative interpretations? Since the 'ideal' of Foucault is purely negative, one might think that it would be sufficient to undermine other interpretations; for he dreams about an intellectual destroying both things that are taken for granted and the so-called universal truths;[52] indeed, he conceives of himself as a sceptical thinker who uses philosophy to *limit* the field of knowledge.[53] Perhaps the role of the philosopher today is to demonstrate that we must begin to realize that humanity can live without myths.[54] The philosopher must critique his or her own time on the basis of retrospective analyses.[55] Ideally, the philosopher's role must be to show people that they are much freer than they believe themselves to be; indeed, the philosopher must demonstrate that the opinions we assume to be true and self-evident have been produced at a certain point in history, and that this alleged self-evidence can be criticized and destroyed; the world can be otherwise. The role of the intellectual, then, is to change something in people's minds;[56] however, not in the sense of changing the content of their minds and replacing it with something more correct or just, but in the sense of changing the political, economic, and institutional *regime for truth-production*. Since truth itself is power, truth cannot be separated from the system of power, but the power of truth can be liberated from certain hegemonic forms, i.e., social, economic, and cultural forms. Hence, to raise the question of political action is to raise the question of truth; it

---

52. *DE-II*, 268; text no. 200.
53. *DE-II*, 1526; text no. 354.
54. *DE-I*, 648; text no. 50.
55. *DE-I*, 1051; text no. 89.
56. *DE-II*, 1597–98; text no. 362.

is not a question of error, illusion, alienated consciousness, or ideology.[57] What this means precisely is not quite clear, but the general idea of what Foucault calls "a new politics of truth" is a new attitude toward truth that liberates truth-production through the disclosure of the function of truth within hegemonic forms. The difficulty, according to Foucault, is not in ascertaining what is true; the real problem is to see, historically, how the effects of truth occur within discourses that are neither true nor false.[58] For all his analyses converge towards the denunciation of the idea of 'something universally necessary' in human life. To be sure, Foucault emphasizes the contingent character of institutions and shows us the range of human freedom that we still have at our disposal. Because of this freedom it is still possible to make changes.[59]

When he is accused for saying that change is impossible; he denies this, because he has always linked the analysed phenomena to political action.[60] Foucault is right, since there is no reason to believe that change should be impossible. But why change anything at all? What should be changed? And to what should it be changed? Of course we can learn to think differently, and we can liberate ourselves from habitual conceptions, but *why* should we do this? The only normative guideline Foucault can offer here is, as far as I can see, Nietzsche's ideal of the *Übermensch* who has no need for illusions and interpretations, for scientific and moral dogmas. The problem, however, is that this is a very individualistic ideal, and it is difficult to see how it can lead to collective political action.

This problem certainly worried Foucault. In 1968 he chose to address this particular problem from a number of questions posed to him by the readers of the journal *Esprit*. One of the readers asked him the following question: "Would a way of thinking that introduces systemic compulsion and discontinuity into the history of the Spirit not make any progressive political intervention impossible? Will it not stand before the following dilemma: – either to accept the system, or turn to a fierce event, an ex-

57. *VP*, 26.
58. *VP*, 21.
59. *DE-II*, 1597–98; text no. 362.
60. *DE-II*, 1600; text no. 362.

ternal outbreak of violence, which alone will be able to overturn the system?"[61] Foucault answers by correcting the reader's perception of his position and by clarifying his position; however, when it comes to the actual problem, he does neither more nor less than identify a progressive political stand with his own methods of analysis.[62] There is not the slightest indication of any constructive political action. In another text, he criticizes humanism, which he, at least on the political level, considers to be any attitude that regards the production of happiness as the goal of politics. He does not believe that this happiness exists; in reality it expresses a teleological stance, asserting that humans have a final purpose. But human beings, Foucault argues, do not have a final purpose; humans just function; they control their own function and are always attempting to justify it, and humanism is simply one of these justifications.[63] It is possible, he claims, to define an optimal social function consisting in a certain relation among the elements of the function, e.g. demographic increase, consumption, individual liberty, and the possibility for pleasure, without appealing to the *idea* of human being. A functional optimum can be defined without being able to say 'for whom' it is beneficial.[64] A purely structural criterion! It is difficult, however, to see how Foucault can appeal to this conception of a functional optimum without presupposing norms: which elements will be part of the definition of this optimum and how will they be weighted? How, for example, do we define individual liberty and pleasure? Clearly we do not have recourse to teleology since we can only describe an optimal relation among some given phenomena; indeed, this is compatible with Foucault's normative requirement that we should liberate ourselves from the tyranny of perspectives. But how could this optimal relation emerge from this normative requirement? Could it conceivably help us define this relation? Foucault has to smuggle some other norms into this process, for which he must account, and it seems difficult to do this without referring to somebody's interest.

---

61. *DE-I*, 701; text no. 58.
62. *DE-I*, 721; text no. 58.
63. *DE-I*, 646–47; text no. 50.
64. *DE-I*, 645; text no. 50.

So far, Foucault's attempt to define a foundation for political action appears to fail, and no others seem to be in sight. It is in fact difficult to see how Foucault could possibly indicate any foundation for political action on the basis of his point of view, and this is due to his individualistic and purely negative normative ideal. Foucault's incapacity to think in terms of collective political action is linked to his rejection of any substantial interpretation of the world. Coordinated action in view of some common goal presupposes some common perception of the world and, of course, a common conception of the goal. This implies an interpretation of how the world works and what we – as members of tribes, as citizens, or as human beings – have in common. This interpretation, however, does not imply any transcendent or essentialist stance; still, it may be tainted by power-relations and maybe this is always the case but this is a question open to discussion which, of course, would be impossible without interpretation.

'Learning' and Signification in Neoliberal Governance

Ingerid S. Straume

When socio-political transformations take place, the field of education offers a particularly revealing vantage point from which to study those changes.[1] Not only is education the institutional locus for conscious – and non-conscious – social reproduction, at times education is also set to accomplish socio-historical change, by attempting to model a *new social type*, as in the many versions of the European fascist or the socialist.[2] Educational issues are often deeply political, always already situated within political, institutional, and moral struggles over what counts as worthwhile societal objectives, i.e., which socio-historical tendencies should be strengthened and which should be downplayed. The academic

---

1. Classical studies are Émile Durkheim, *Professional Ethics and Civic Morals*, London/New York, Routledge 2001 [1957/1904]; John Dewey, *Democracy and Education*, New York, Simon and Shuster 1997 [1916] (*DE*); and more generally, the works of Pierre Bourdieu.

2. From a Lacanian perspective, Dany-Robert Dufour claims that the educational system of late capitalism is set at producing yet a new social type, a subject that is "non-critical," "near-psychotic," replacing the older forms of the "Kantian critical subject" which was paired up with the "Freudian neurotic subject" (Dany-Robert Dufour, *The Art of Shrinking Heads*, Cambridge, Polity, 2008). From a post-structuralist perspective, Simons and Masschelein talk of the "entrepreneurial self" that is promoted in contemporary policy discourse (Maarten Simons and Jan Masschelein, "The Governmentalization of Learning and the Assemblage of a Learning Apparatus," *Educational Theory*, Vol.58, no 4, 2008. Hereafter, *GL*).

discipline of pedagogy also has historical ideals of its own, such as the ancient Greek ideal, *paideia,* and *Bildung* from the German tradition, neither of which have any real correlates in the English language.[3] In contemporary discourse, the leading terms are education, schooling, teaching, and above all: *learning.* Now, if one wants to capture the essence of education or pedagogy, some concepts appear as more indispensable than others; today, 'learning' seems to be that concept, since if there is no learning, there can be no education. Against this (logical) background, it seems somewhat odd that learning was *not* a central concept in the *Bildung* tradition, or in classical Greece, where morality and good conduct were seen as much more important than learning. This historical shift in focus from 'education in a wide sense' (Dewey) to 'learning' is significant in more than technical terms – it also represents an important change in the theoretical foundations, where cognitive psychology and biology have superseded moral philosophy and the humanities.

Today, 'learning' is not only the dominant term in educational settings and theories, it is also widely used in policy discourses on (un-) employment and qualifications, e.g., in the European Union's programs for lifelong learning, in theories of leadership and management, and in organizational reform policies. In many of these spheres, 'learning' has become such a 'natural' and 'inherent' element that the need to provide reasons, justifications, etc. is suspended. Such words, as we know, often play specific roles in the reproduction, preservation, and solidification of existing power structures. Accordingly, the role of 'learning' in Western societies today has been examined by several scholars and elaborated in their diagnoses of *learning society.*[4]

---

3. In the English language 'education' is used to cover more differentiated concepts such as *paideia, Erziehung* and *Bildung.* See for instance Dewey, *DE,* where a point is made to distinguish between education in a 'wide' and a 'limited' sense, and where the former includes moral ideals. To express these notions directly, one must go to the German or Greek terms. Furthermore, the term 'pedagogy' (German: *Pädagogik,* French: *pédagogie*) does not work very well in English.
4. See Simons and Masschelein, *GL*; Jan Masschelein and Maarten Simons, "An Adequate Education in a Globalized World? A Note on Immunisation against Being-Together," *Journal of Philosophy of Education,* Vol.36, no.4 (2002), 565–84 (hereafter,

Within the context of pedagogy, the predominance of *learning* over other concepts gives rise to certain concerns. At the theoretical level, 'learning' tends to displace other pedagogical concepts, such as *Bildung* and 'education in a wide sense,'[5] while at the practical level it often operates in a reductive form. Taken together, as I intend to show, these tendencies limit the political and moral scope of education and pedagogy. From the basis of this insight, several theoretical paths are possible. One is to omit 'learning' in favor of other concepts such as *Bildung*.[6] This would be both legitimate and manageable – and is indeed often done in the philosophy of education, especially within language domains where notions connected to *Bildung* has been developed. The other path, followed in this article, is to explore and possibly broaden the 'discourse of learning' itself. The point to be elucidated here is, in short, that learning must be seen as learning *something*, because everything that exists in the world of humans exists *as something*. Therefore, discussions about learning must be connected to the 'contents' of learning in an intimate way – in terms of meaning and significations – and to the goals of education as such. Having said that, this article will not attempt a substantive discussion of the goals of education; rather, I shall discuss the pedagogical-philosophical *framework* for such discussions, drawing especially on the philosophical work of Cornelius Castoriadis.[7]

The discussion starts from what I see as a reductionist concept of learning. In the first part of the text, I outline contemporary educational policy reforms in Europe, where *learning* appears to be self-evident, natural and unquestionable, along with scholarly criticisms of what has been termed 'learning society.' I then discuss some of the theoretical limitations of this policy discourse, arguing that learning must always

AEGW); Gert J. J. Biesta, *Beyond Learning. Democratic Education for a Human Future.* Boulder, Co., Paradigm Publishers, 2006; and Gert J. J. Biesta, "Against Learning. Reclaiming a Language for Education in an Age of Learning," *Nordisk Pedagogik 25*, no.1, 54–66 (hereafter, *AL*).

5. Dewey, *DE*.
6. Cf. the (somewhat polemic) title of Biesta's article, "Against Learning."
7. Cornelius Castoriadis, *The Imaginary Institution of Society*, translated by Kathleen Blamey, Cambridge, MIT Press, 1987. Hereafter, *IIS*.

be seen as learning *something* and, indeed, as learning by someone. This argument draws on philosophical arguments, especially Cornelius Castoriadis's notion of social imaginary significations and Charles Taylor's ideas of what it means to be a subject. These ideas are discussed in relation to the so-called 'socio-cultural perspective on learning,' which holds an ambivalent position in the discourse of 'learning society'. Finally, I discuss the political and normative questions that are at stake in this investigation, where a restricted view of education and pedagogy serve as an instance of the general tendency of depoliticization in Western civilization.

The Dominance of 'Learning'

First, let us consider the notion of 'lifelong learning' as understood by such transnational policy programs as the European Higher Education Area (regulated by the Bologna Process), the Lisbon Strategy of the EU, and the Program for International Student Assessment (PISA) of the Organization for Economic Co-operation and Development (OECD). In the following, I shall explore the features common to these policies rather than their differences, in order to outline the ideological background against which contemporary discussions of 'learning' unfold in educational institutions like colleges, universities, schools, and preschools.[8]

The Lifelong Learning Programme is the umbrella under which the European Commission began integrating its various educational and training initiatives in 2007. The Commission's homepage states that: "The programme enables individuals at all stages of their lives to pursue stimulating learning opportunities across Europe."[9] The Bologna Process aims to establish *one* coordinated and coherent educational system in European higher education, under the motto *lifelong learning*.[10] Now, in order to coordinate educational standards and infrastructure in different

8. Even though this section is based on European policy programs, the tendencies are not unique, but can be found in, e.g., the USA.

9. http://ec.europa.eu/education/lifelong-learning-programme/doc78_en.htm

10. In 2010, 47 nations had joined the Bologna Process, according to the official website.

countries, it is imperative to measure, that is, to *quantify*. Examples of quantifiable factors are workload, academic level, learning outcomes such as skills and competences, and above all, *credits*.[11] The Bologna Process is meant to promote mobility and control – but not *too* much control; the idea is that mobility, utility, and competition will be combined with academic freedom and institutional autonomy:

> Building on our rich and diverse European cultural heritage, we are developing a [European Higher Education Area] based on institutional autonomy, academic freedom, equal opportunities and democratic principles that will facilitate mobility, increase employability and strengthen Europe's attractiveness and competitiveness.[12]

In the process of assigning and comparing credits, formerly coherent educational programs are disaggregated and broken down into modules. In Norway, for example, 'the credit transfer model' is accommodated through a new grading system in higher education, student exchange programs, and a national system of measuring performance at educational institutions.[13] But even though the London communiqué, quoted above, emphasize the importance of institutions maintaining their freedom and uniqueness in the process, it seems clear that *too* much uniqueness would hinder mobility, employability, and competitiveness, as pointed out by education policy researcher Berit Karseth:

> [T]he Bologna Process represent[s] a curricular standardisation, whereby the management of credit transfer and accumulation becomes the salient task. The aim is to develop a highly reliable space of higher education

11. Measured by the European Credit Transfer and Accumulation System (ECTS).
12. *London Communiqué*, May 2007, http:www.cicic.ca/docs/bologna/2007London Communique.en.pdf
13. Berit Karseth, "Curriculum Restructuring in Higher Education after the Bologna Process: A New Pedagogic Regime?,"*Revista Española de Educación Comparada*, no. 12 (2006), 255–84 (*CRHE*). The Norwegian Government White Paper nr 31 (2007–2008), *Kvalitet i skolen* [*Quality in the School*], promotes a range of indicators for measuring learning outcomes in primary education, including detailed instructions for the management of the educational sector.

which is manageable and predictable; [hence,] the flexibility has to be regulated.[14]

As already mentioned, several policy processes can be read into a greater policy picture. For example, the structure of the EU's Lisbon Strategy resembles that of the Bologna process; both see harmonization and streamlining (i.e., rationalization) as means to accomplish greater mobility and competition. In May 2009, the EU Council endorsed a Strategic Framework for European Cooperation in Education and Training. The aim is for the European Union to become the "the most competitive and dynamic knowledge-based economy in the world".[15] To follow up the efforts set out in the mentioned policy documents, measurement and constant monitoring is needed:

> The periodic monitoring of progress towards a set objective provides an essential contribution towards evidence-based policy making. The strategic objectives outlined above should accordingly be accompanied during the period 2010–2020 by indicators and by reference levels for European average performance ('European benchmarks').[16]

The educational objectives set out by the EU can be summarized very accurately as "key competences and learning outcomes".[17] Once again, measurability is the prevailing principle.

A central concept of the Bologna process is *employability*, which has a double meaning by pointing towards the utility of the education itself,

---

14. *CRHE*, 274.
15. Council Conclusions of May 12 2009 on a strategic ramework for European cooperation in education and training ('ET 2020'). *Official Journal of the European Union*, http://eur-lex.europa.eu/LexUriServ/LexUriServ.do?uri=OJ:C:2009:119:000 2:0010:EN:PDF , 2.
16. Council conclusions, 3.
17. The European Framework for Key Competences for Lifelong Learning defines eight key competences "necessary for personal fulfillment, active citizenship, social inclusion and employability in a knowledge society."

and towards the individual who is supposed to become employable. By means of education, students will become qualified for employment; while utility is the goal to which all other factors must conform. In these processes 'learning' is conceived not only as the actual learning that takes place, but just as often in terms of the *willingness, readiness to learn.* In 1995, the EU Commission put forth a vision of the society of the future, a "learning society." "It is clear," the Commission wrote, "that the new opportunities offered to people require an effort from each one to adapt, particularly in assembling one's own qualifications on the basis of 'building blocks' of knowledge acquired at different times and in various situations."[18] In the Commission's "society of the future,"

> [e]ducation and training will increasingly become the main vehicles for selfawareness, belonging, advancement and self-fulfillment. Education and training […] is the key for everyone to controlling their future and their personal development.[19]

Indeed, the person who does not wish to learn, nor improve his or her skills, forsakes a great deal. The demands on the individual also affect interpersonal relationships, where

> [t]he individual's place in relation to their fellow citizens will increasingly be determined by their capacity to learn and master fundamental knowledge. The position of *everyone in relation to their fellow citizens in the context of knowledge and skills* […] will be decisive. This relative position which could be called the *'learning relationship'* will become an increasingly dominant feature in the structure of our societies.[20]

As noted by Simons and Masschelein, these documents call upon a type

---

18. European Union's White Paper on Education and Training, "Teaching and Learning – Towards the Learning Society," Brussels, Commission of the European Societies, 1995.
19. White Paper, 2.
20. White Paper, 2, emphasis in the original.

of subject who is responsible for his or her own well-being, as well as that of the country or region in global competition, through the subject's willingness to learn, adapt, and manage human capital such as skills, competencies, and knowledge. The implications of this 'subject position' – "the entrepreneurial citizen"[21] – will be discussed below.

There is, however, little reason to believe that the intentions of transnational policy reforms merely trickle down to ground level where they are implemented accordingly. 'International competition' is hardly an ethos fit for primary schools – although this, of course, could vary from nation to nation. In a social democratic context, for instance, this kind of strategic rhetoric challenges the traditional self-understanding that has guided teachers and educators in their work, where solidarity, *Bildung*, and the fostering of a critical attitude have been central. It is therefore all the more troubling to observe the rapidity and depth of the changes affecting the educational sector in many of these countries. Most strikingly, a new language is adopted for describing – and justifying – educational practices, the key term of which is learning in the form of 'learning outcomes,' connected to assessment, accountability, etc. More subtly, the systems erected for control and assessment have evoked a pervasive atmosphere of stress and pressure throughout the sector, where institutions and employees face a 'permanent tribunal' whose standards one can never be sure can be met.[22]

In terms of assessment, a policy with apparent impact on Western school systems over the past 10–15 years is the PISA evaluation system, initiated and conducted by the OECD. The PISA tests are designed to rank participating nations' educational sectors relative to the input/output vis-à-vis the goal of the OECD: *competitiveness*. The tests measure 15-year-old students' competencies in reading, natural science, and math.

---

21. Simons and Masschelein, *GL.*
22. The term 'permanent tribunal' stems from Foucault and is used by Simons and Masschelein, *GL.* Also see Mark Fisher, who, in similar cases, makes vivid comparisons to Kafka and the impossibility of acquittal; only postponement is possible. Mark Fisher, *Capitalist Realism*, Winchester, UK/Washington D.C., Zero books, 2009 (*CRe*).

To be comparable, the competencies measured must be independent of national curricula, culture, and other contextual factors. In order to measure 'pure skills,' the material to be interpreted by the students is provided by the tests themselves. The only background knowledge needed is specific skills and competence in the relevant subject matter. Typically, the test is about understanding a given text, where understanding requires insight into the basic structure of the subject matter itself.

The vocabulary and logic of the PISA tests, which also permeate the European Union's Lifelong Learning policy, enter national school systems via the national curricula, white papers, large and small reforms, and the national media that typically have paid significant attention to the results of the PISA rankings. Measures are taken in local school development programs as well as national and regional research programs, generating a massive interest in evaluation and assessment throughout the sector. In setting the agenda and transforming the vocabulary by which schools – and, much more reluctantly, universities – describe themselves, these transnational policy processes have been extremely successful. Indeed, skepticism about these trends seems to imply a certain backwardness; for what is wrong with children learning basic reasoning skills, reading, writing, digital literacy, and math?[23]

The rhetoric in support of testing is often rights-based, the rationale being that children can always learn more, and better – and since they are obliged to spend a lot of time at school, this time should not be wasted, which it would be if pupils did *not* have 'learning outcomes.' This is substantiated by reports showing that many children leave school without proper reading and writing skills. It seems impossible to oppose these aspirations without seeming unreasonable. After all, education is a human right. Still, I want to argue that the turn towards basic skills is part of a deeper current, whose gravest impact concerns the meaning of education itself. The term 'learning outcome' provides an important clue. In 2007, the OECD noted the progress of certain nations under

23. The five basic skills in the newest Norwegian national curriculum are: to be able to read, write, express oneself orally, do math and digital skills (*Kunnskapsløftet*, 2006). The EU uses eight.

the PISA system (which started in 2000), in terms of *increased learning outcomes*. The criterion of success was to achieve a reasonable balance between the money invested in education (expenditure) and revenue – in terms of learning outcomes – as reported on the OECD's homepage: "However, across the OECD area as a whole learning outcomes have generally remained flat, while expenditure on education in OECD countries rose by an average of 39% between 1995 and 2004."[24]

The formula underlying this argument is derived from classical business management. National education policies are assessed by the OECD in terms of economic criteria and international competitiveness – economic competitiveness – and not rivalry in *qualitative, educational* terms, such as which country has the most stimulating thinking, the most intriguing literature, the most vital public sphere, the wisest population, the leading art scene, or the most humane politics. In a contemporary context, these *qualitative* terms seem strangely outmoded. Nor is competitiveness geared towards increasing pupils' skills at questioning the existing power structures, organizing political resistance, creating new institutions, and so forth. Qualitative and (especially) political concepts clearly belong to a different discursive repertoire – of a more humanist bent, if you like – whereas today's transnational policy reforms treat knowledge (learning outcomes) as neither normative nor contextual. Value-laden terms, such as beauty, significance, or any kind of socio-political critique, hardly count as relevant descriptions of knowledge in this context. And perhaps rightly so: it would certainly be equally wrong of the OECD to describe and measure knowledge in qualitative terms; nor should the European Union standardize 'the meaning of education.' When the aim is to compare different nations on the relationship between investment and output in education, quantitative measures are required; and this invariably leads to an empty and sterile concept of learning.

Today, terms like 'learning outcome,' 'learning product,' etc., saturate the educational systems of most Western countries. They are found in teacher education, educational research, national policy plans, locally in-stigated school development programs, and in face-to-face conversations

24. OECD's homepage.

between teachers and pupils or students. But something goes awry when national agendas are set according to these empty criteria. For instance, where is the space for critique, and creativity? Indeed, in a regime where benchmarking, auditing, and measurement constitute a 'reality' that is not open to discussion, the system could only include such notions by objectifying and quantifying them. However, according to Mark Fisher, systems ostensibly designed to assess performance and activities that are, by their very nature, unquantifiable do not really measure performance and output at all; rather they measure their bureaucratically produced *representations*. "Inevitably, a short-circuiting occurs, and work becomes geared towards generation and massaging of representations rather than to the official goals of work itself."[25] Representations and symbols of benchmarking become the 'real' goals, while the institutional ethos of former days are put on ice, and eventually forgotten.

Only That Which Can Be Counted, Counts

Another important term, around which the entire reform discourse is organized, is *accountability* – a key term in the Lisbon Strategy. Like so many other terms in this sector, accountability has a double meaning:[26] first, it assigns *responsibility* to the partners involved in an enterprise, and second, it signifies an obligation to *keep accounts* (in the sense of keeping records).[27] Accounting in the educational sector specifies the partners' obligations to honor a 'learning contract' where objectives, time frames,

---

25. *CRe*, 42. Fisher goes on to claim that the cherishing of symbols of achievement over actual achievement is an element that late capitalism "repeats" from Stalinism, in a "fusion of PR and bureaucracy," *CRe*, 42–43, 50.

26. The double meanings facilitate implementation of control mechanisms, partly through co-optation and partly by obscurity and new-speak. There is a permanent uncertainty as to what terms 'really mean' which enables agents in power positions to switch meaning contents when facing critical interrogation, thereby keeping others in (perpetual) uncertainty as to whether one has understood 'properly.'

27. Cf. the large apparatus of 'benchmarks' launched by the EU; see, for instance, EU Commission Staff Working Document, "Progress towards the Lisbon Objective in Education and Training, Indicators and Benchmarks," http://ec.europa.eu/education/policies/2010/doc/progress06/report_en.pdf

responsibilities to act on assessments, self-assessments, etc., have been established. In schools, teachers, pupils, and parents enter into agreements that specify the objectives – learning outcomes – that the pupil can be expected to achieve within the timeframe specified by the 'learning contract,' with lesson plans and assignments distributed every one or two weeks. In short, reporting and keeping accounts has become one of the most important tasks for teachers. Naturally, the school management and public administration are among the most accountable.[28]

Accordingly, *assessment* has become a main activity for the whole educational sector, and this is reflected in educational research and school development programs. Better assessments, where students are involved in the planning and monitoring of their own learning processes, are seen as central to improve the efficiency of learning. To complete the picture, a final trend worth mentioning is 'evidence based research' in education; an approach meant to ensure that investments are not spent on policy measures that *do not work*.

All the notions mentioned above – learning outcomes, basic skills, competences, accountability, assessment, evidence based research, etc. – may be included in a certain meta-discourse where these elements become *factors*, that is, they become computable, mathematically expressible, and thus are incorporated in a '*meta-account of education*.' Theories of learning also have a part to play in this account, since 'learning' is one of the few concepts in pedagogy that can be operationalized into quantifiable data such as 'learning outcomes.' Now, if this account should become the real account of education, i.e., the only 'realistic' account, the idea of *education* could be in danger. This concern is voiced by philosopher of education Gert Biesta in a formidable critique of learning programs and the 'new language of learning,' which to him imply the notion of buying and selling. While 'learning' has gained its current, strategic position, 'education' has been pushed to the periphery and this is also true of 'teaching', as pointed out by Biesta: "Teaching has, for example, become redefined as supporting or facilitating learning, just as education is now

---

28. In these matters, the USA is far ahead of Europe.

often described as the provision of learning opportunities or learning experiences."[29]

When education becomes a quest for learning outcomes, it is turned into a commodity, i.e., a good to be purchased and paid for either directly by the consumer or indirectly by the taxpayer. If the product does not meet the consumer's expectations of utility – *employability* – he or she should be able to complain; hence, the importance of *accountability*.

> 'Value for money' has become the main principle in many of the transactions between the state and its taxpayers. This way of thinking lies at the basis of the emergence of a culture of accountability in education and other public services, which has brought about ever-tighter systems of inspection and control, and ever-more prescriptive educational protocols.[30]

The logic of the system posits the recipient of education as a certain kind of customer, called the learner – a term that is now replacing the child, pupil, student, etc., in educational institutions. In the new language of learning, states Biesta, education is adaptable to the customer. Educational institutions and teachers become providers; hence, they must adapt to the market – the market of learning – and 'education' is reduced to technical concerns like efficiency, effect, provision, learning environment, etc. More profound and more fundamental questions concerning the aim or meaning of education can hardly be raised in this framework. The heart of the matter, Biesta argues, is not only a restriction on the professional judgment of the teacher, but more importantly, a weakening of democracy.

A similar concern can be found in the works of Simons and Masschelein, especially in their critique of the governmentality of 'learning society.'[31] In 'learning society,' the foremost asset of subjects or citizens is their

---

29. *AL*, 71.

30. *AL*, 73.

31. *GL*, 391. The term governmentality (French: *gouvernmentalité*) comes from Michel Foucault.

ability – and willingness – to learn, that is, to take responsibility for their lives and "do something about it."[32] This willingness and individual responsibility defines a certain sociological type that Simons and Masschelein call the 'entrepreneurial citizen,' or the 'entrepreneur of the self,' pointing out another key element in the new language of learning. The term *entrepreneurship*, which figures increasingly in educational policy documents, is about "using resources and producing a commodity that meets needs and offers an income."[33] But entrepreneurship is not only a technical matter, it involves certain attitudes: "… an 'element of alertness' – that is, a speculative, creative, or innovative attitude to see opportunities in a competitive environment."[34] As Simons and Masschelein note,

> the entrepreneur of the self is aware that the self is the result of a calculated investment and that the 'success' of the self is not guaranteed as such but depends on whether it meets needs. These could be the needs of a particular environment (a calculated investment in human capital through education or self-organized and self-directed learning) or the needs of oneself as a consumer (a calculated investment in human capital to meet the need of self-realization).[35]

Following Foucault *pace* theorists of modernity like Jürgen Habermas, Simons and Masschelein claim that, in the *entrepreneurial regime*, there is no 'colonization' of the social sphere (life world) by the economic sphere (system) because there is no purely economic sphere: *all is management.* Accordingly, education is no longer set within a "social regime of government" whose rationale is socialization and social norms, or a welfare state where the economic sphere is conceived apart from, or *against* the social sphere. In entrepreneurial regime, the governmental rationality is characterized by "the economization of the social," where problems of governance are conceived in terms of "investment in human capital

32. *GL.*
33. *GL*, 406.
34. *GL.*
35. *GL*, 407.

and the presence of a 'will to learn'," that is, the "presence or absence of entrepreneurship."[36] The "strategic components" of 'learning society' are 'inclusion,' 'capital,' and 'learning.'[37] The ongoing transformation from the social regime of modernity to entrepreneurial governance and 'learning society' also resonates with Zygmunt Bauman's diagnosis of the 'society of consumers,' where

> no one can become a subject without first turning into a commodity, and no one can keep his or her subjectness secure without perpetually resuscitating, resurrecting and replenishing the capacities expected and required of a sellable commodity.[38]

While the regime of entrepreneurship denotes commoditization and economization, it is first and foremost a type of *total management*, where control permeates all socially instituted practices. In the entrepreneurial regime, this control is effectively carried out by the subjects themselves, who, according to Simons and Masschelein, are put before a 'permanent economic tribunal,' where – in the name of 'personal freedom' and 'self-realization'– they are submitted to governmental technologies which operate through the notion of 'freedom.'[39]

> The entrepreneurial self experiences learning as the force to guarantee a momentary emancipation in environments through delivering useful competencies. Learning, therefore, is experienced as a force to deal with the 'mancipium' or the hold of the environment (such as limited resources or needs). Hence, for the entrepreneurial self, learning and living become indistinguishable.[40]

---

36. *GL*, 408.
37. *GL*, 406.
38. Zygmunt Bauman, *Consuming Life*, Cambridge, Polity 2007, 12.
39. *GL*. The influence of Foucault's works on governmentality and biopolitics is clear. The authors also make good use of other studies in the same tradition.
40. *GL*, 409.

The regime of learning is lifelong – like an "indefinite postponement," as noted by Mark Fisher:

> Education as a lifelong process ... Training that persists for as long as your working life continues ... Work you take home with you ... Working from home, homing from work. [...] The carceral regime of discipline is being eroded by the technologies of control, with their systems of perpetual consumption and continuous development.[41]

Since there is no way of knowing whether one may ever be able to fulfill its standards, the 'tribunal of learning' is permanent. To Fisher, the difference between the old/heavy and new/light inspection systems correspond to Kafka's distinction between ostensible acquittal and indefinite postponement, where "[i]ndefinite postponement [...] keeps your case at the lowest level of the court, but at the cost of an anxiety that never ends".[42] The standards are unclear, and often the criteria need to be worked out by the subjects themselves. In European educational systems, this self-auditing now starts at a very early age.

As already mentioned, the proliferation of 'learning' is not limited to the sphere of organized education, it is also used to denote and address various problems like unemployment, poor health / mental health, social exclusion, etc, which in the entrepreneurial regime are conceived as the inadequate management of learning resources, that is, the subject's (deficient) willingness to adapt and learn. Similarly, at the political level, problems concerning social unrest are recast as the need for 'citizenship education,' consisting in 'democratic knowledge, skills, and competencies'; or more generally, as the need for 'organizational learning.' Facilitated by the 'new language of learning,' a great ideological displacement from 'education in a wide sense' to accountability and computation can be witnessed in European welfare policies. The depoliticizing effects of these reconfigurations are massive, as management and self-management replaces the need for politics.

41. Fisher, *CRe*, 22–23.
42. *CRe*, 51.

Learning in Terms of 'Something'

While I endorse the critical points voiced by Biesta and Simon and Masschelein presented above, I also want to develop the discussion somewhat further by widening the analysis to include the 'meaning' of learning. In much of the literature on learning, the learning content, subject matter, knowledge content, etc., are often treated as matters set apart from the learning process itself. This perspective separates 'learning' from its content, and from the social practices in which learning takes place. Here, I want to argue that we cannot understand a particular learning experience unless we look at what the learned content *is learned as*. The twentieth century's classical theorists of learning, Piaget and Vygotsky, both knew this. For instance, Vygotsky strongly emphasizes the notion of culture in his psychology of human learning, and in his descriptions of children's development through play, he insists on the importance of the notion of *meaning*.[43] Piaget, for his part, had a well-developed stage theory concerning children's developmental ability to learn different concepts, such as object permanence or reversibility. Even so, in discussions about learning, the 'meaning aspect' of the 'learning content' is often poorly developed, as learning is portrayed as *form divorced from content*. For instance, when the 'social group,' the community etc. are treated as factors that *enhance* learning – offering 'learning environments' – the cultural meaning *itself* remains unthematized in the background.

Of course, there are scholars who do not follow this script. One is the Norwegian cultural psychologist Karsten Hundeide, who uses anthropological field studies actively in his 'socio-cultural' perspective on children's development. Using his own studies in Jakarta and other anthropological studies, Hundeide has developed a conceptual framework for understanding children's development in terms of 'structures of possibility' and 'socio-ecological tracks of development.'[44] Central

43. Lev S. Vygotsky, *Mind in Society. The Development of Higher Psychological Processes*, Harvard University Press, 1978; Lev Vygotskij, *Tenkning og tale*, Oslo, Gyldendal, 2001.
44. Karsten Hundeide, *Barns livsverden: Sosiokulturelle rammer for barns utvikling*, Oslo, Cappelen, 2003.

to Hundeide is the notion of children's life world as an experienced, hence real, universe of possibilities. He rejects the one-dimensional, linear metaphor of development that has been so central to Western developmental psychology; instead, he pictures children's development as a landscape with several developmental 'tracks,' impregnated with significance and meaning.[45] Hundeide's research cultivates an empirical-phenomenological orientation within the social sciences that promises a richer notion of what it means to develop and learn.

To go further, it would be interesting to discuss the meaning-dimension of 'learning' in more depth. A path to follow is found in Castoriadis's notion of 'social imaginary significations.' When this concept is introduced into a discussion of learning, it becomes clear that everything that can be experienced, learned, realized is experienced/learned/realized *as something* – and therefore that the central aspect of a learning experience is its *signification*, or, at a deeper level, its *meaning* (French: *sens*). This claim, however, will need some elaboration. By way of an introduction, let us first consider Castoriadis' concepts.

By 'social imaginary significations' Castoriadis wants to elucidate that in the always-instituted world of humans – society, history, and culture – all phenomena appear, stand out, and exist *as* something, namely as themselves. Everything we understand and perceive, we understand and perceive as something – and this something, in the simplest terms, is a signification:

> For a society, to say that a term *is* means that it signifies (is a signification, is posited as a signification, is tied to a signification). Once it *is*, it *always* has meaning [...], that is it can always enter into a syntax or can constitute a syntax in which to enter. The institution of society is the institution of a world of significations – which is obviously a creation as such, and a specific one in each case.[46]

Social imaginary significations are socially instituted, that is, they are

45. Hundeide, *Barns livsverden*, 28.
46. *IIS*, 235.

instituted in and by society, and not constructed by the individual. The clearest example of such a social institution is language. Since everything that exists for a society, exists as signification, nothing is insignificant; that is, nothing cannot *not* mean anything to us – not even the signification of 'nothing,' which also means something. Furthermore, a society also consists of significations that have no referents in the real (what Castoriadis calls 'the first natural stratum'), such as gods, spirits, or ideas; and each society also institutes in its repertoire of significations of things that do not exist; that is, they exist as non-real, non-existent:

> [T]he being of non-being, or non-being as such, always exists for society; into its universe of discourse enter entities whose being is or has to be negated, positions that must be asserted by means of explicit negations or that are presented only to be negated. The possibility of 'this does not exist' or of 'it is not like that' is always explicitly posed in the institution of society.[47]

Even the outside of society, that which is absurd and meaningless, is instituted precisely as that.

> Each society, like each living being or species, establishes, creates its own world, within which, of course, it includes 'itself.' […I]t is the proper 'organization' (significations and institution) of society that posits and defines, for example, what is for that society 'information,' what is 'noise,' and what is nothing at all; or the 'weight,' 'relevance,' 'value,' and 'meaning' of the 'information' […] and so on. In brief, it is the institution of society that determines what is 'real' and what is not, what is 'meaningful' and what is meaningless.[48]

---

47. *IIS*, 234.
48. Cornelius Castoriadis, "The Imaginary: Creation in the Social-Historical Domain," id., *World in Fragments. Writings on Politics, Society, Psychoanalysis and the Imagination*, edited and translated by David Ames Curtis, Stanford, Stanford University Press, 1997 (*WIF*), 3–18, 9.

The principle that everything is conceived as something is called *representation*, indicating not so much that things stand for or appear as something else – although this can also be the case – but more fundamentally that things take part in the social institution of significations, where things appear as themselves. To Castoriadis, the implication is that every analysis of human activity must take its point of departure in the social-historical. I shall return to this point below.

Now, let us see what he has to say about learning. To Castoriadis, 'learning' is a biological category, a capacity shared by all animals, but since the human animal is distinct from other animals, human learning needs to be distinguished as such. What, then, distinguishes the human animal? The decisive difference, according to Castoriadis, concerns the radical imagination (*l'imagination radicale*) which other animals to not possess. The radical imagination of the human being enables us to produce representations, significations, and ideas – with or without reference to the reality we share with other animals – which are the essence of the genuinely human world.

Even if learning is a biological category, human learning is special. The key, again, is the notion of social imaginary signification. To Castoriadis, 'true' human learning – or rather, *pedagogy* – means to invest emotions in significations, in the teacher's person, in knowledge itself, and, in some cases, in the very idea of education.[49] To make this point, Castoriadis draws on the psychoanalytic notion of sublimation, which involves emotional investment (*kathexis*) as well as recognition of the cognitive contents of the issue at stake, that is, *legitimacy*, in a broad sense.

> There is no pedagogy if the pupil does not have any investment, in the strongest sense of the term, both in what she learns and in the learning process; and she can only make that investment – that is a fact, human beings are that way – provided she invests a concrete person, through a platonic Eros.[50]

49. Cornelius Castoriadis, "Psyche and Education," id., *Figures of the Thinkable*, translated by Helen Arnold, Stanford, Stanford University Press, 2008, 165–87, (*FT*).
50. *FT*, 178.

The person of the teacher is a kind of emotional catalyst: "If teachers are incapable of inspiring love in children, love both for what they are learning and for the very fact of learning, they are not teachers."[51] The basic idea is that the learning subject becomes emotionally attached to the contents, that is, to the social imaginary significations, in such a way that these significations become part of the subject's proper world (*Eigenwelt*). In other words, the learned and experienced contents become the learning subject's own world. And as previously mentioned, the human world is an instituted world of imaginary significations and meanings. This becomes very clear when we try to understand what a society is. To Castoriadis, a society consists of, and exists by, significations, significations embodied in institutions:

> The being-society of society is the institutions and the social imaginary significations that these institutions embody and make exist in effective social actuality [*effectivité sociale*]. These are the significations that give a meaning – imaginary meaning, in the profound sense of the term, that is, spontaneous and unmotivated creation of humanity – to life, to activity, to choices, to the death of humans as well as to the world that they create and in which humans must live and die.[52]

Examples of social imaginary significations are manifold, from the more obvious cases: God, spirits, virtue, sin, freedom, and justice – to the less obvious ones like nation, citizens, state, market, interest rates, capital, and human rights – and the terrible ones: Gulag, fascism and so on.[53] Everything that exists to human beings exists first and foremost as significations: complex, irreducible phenomena that have no other 'ground' than themselves. Imaginary significations are created by the human imagination, and human beings attribute meaning to everything in their world. But, at the same time, it is important to realize that the social imaginary significations are

---

51. *FT*, 179.
52. Cornelius Castoriadis, "Democracy as Procedure and Democracy as Regime," *Constellations* Vol. 4 (1, 1997), 1–18, 2.
53. See *WIF*, 7.

operative on the collective plane, i.e., society – they are not made or created by individual human beings. All this, to Castoriadis, indicates that society first and foremost must be understood as socially instituted imaginary significations. Everything that can be learned is woven into a background or framework – a society and a culture – that is kept together by its core significations by the 'infra-power' of (imbued) meaning. My contention is that these ideas should somehow be mirrored in theories of human learning – not in order to say anything definitive about what we learn, experience, and so forth, nor to dictate what we *should* learn in each specific case, but, rather, to elucidate that what we learn and experience is always learned and experienced *as something*. The social, historical and cultural dimensions of that which is learned should, in other words, be seen as something more than a context and environment for learning. For instance, the specific 'learning' in a capitalist context should be seen as exactly that, not as 'pure' learning, learning *in abstracto*. From this perspective, learning theories without additional dimensions are apolitical. This important insight should be elaborated much further than can be done here.

The implications reach beyond a traditional critique of positivism – that there can be no neutral, objective, value-less knowledge – in pointing out that the very ideas of neutrality, objectivity, and value-lessness are in themselves social imaginary significations. Still, the fact that such notions have no ground or foundation outside the human world of significations makes them no less real. For all their 'neutrality,' these notions are strongly invested with meaning, as Castoriadis notes:

> … everyone knows today, or everyone thinks they know, that the alleged neutrality, the alleged instrumentality of technique and even of scientific knowledge are illusions. In truth, even this expression is inadequate, and it masks the essential aspect of the question. The presentation of science and of technique as neutral means or as instruments pure and simple is not a mere 'illusion': it is an integral part of the contemporary institution of society – that is, it partakes of the dominant social imaginary of our age.[54]

---

54. Cornelius Castoriadis, "From Ecology to Autonomy," id., *The Castoriadis Reader,*

In modernity, neutrality, value-lessness, and objectivity have been set as *standards* to characterize technique and science – yardsticks by which other phenomena and significations can be measured. This may explain the current obsession with auditing and benchmarking at the expense of meaning and signification. Furthermore, as Charles Taylor argues, representations of objectivity, neutrality, etc. support the notion of a 'disengaged' individual subject possessing freedom, dignity, and power.[55] These significations mark a very specific – modern, allegedly free and independent – subject Taylor's notion of what it means to be a subject can also be connected to our discussion of the concept of learning. To Taylor, being a subject means to 'interpret' oneself *as someone*. This does not necessarily mean to be someone specific, or some determinate 'thing,' but rather, that to exist, for a human being, means to exist *as someone* – and this someone *is something*. As in the case of representation, the idea of our existing 'as someone' does not point to something *else*, something outside of our selves, but rather to the fact that everything – here, subjectivity – is 'tied to a signification.' To be a self, then, means to be part of certain social practices imbued with humanly created meaning.

Taylor also attaches a *moral* dimension to this, since to become a 'moral subject,' to Taylor, means to reflect consciously upon the values (i.e., the significations) to which one is committed, and also to ask oneself whether we want to endorse these values, i.e., whether they are worth our endorsement. This comes close to Castoriadis's ideal of *autonomy*, where autonomy means to reflect consciously upon one's values – which are normally collectively instituted – and ask oneself whether these values are valid, not only *de facto*, but also *de jure*.[56] In Castoriadis's case, it is

---

translated and edited by David Ames Curtis, Oxford, Blackwell, 1997, 239–52, 240. Hereafter, *CR*. Still, according to Mark Fisher (drawing on Žižek), as long as we confess to know this to be an illusion, we can go on practicing as before (*CRe*).

55. Charles Taylor, *Philosophical Papers, Volume I, Human Agency and Language*, Cambridge, Cambridge University Press, 1985, 6. See Ingerid S. Straume, "The Political Imaginary of Global Capitalism," in this volume, where I cite and discuss Taylor's position on these issues more extensively.

56. *CR*, 384–98.

a democratic society that asks itself whether its laws are valid *de jure* – valid in principle – and the same question is posed by the individual subject in Taylor's case. Now, if we leave the notion of neutral and value-free knowledge, the question of 'learning' also becomes a moral question, since everything we learn will – or *should*, if we follow Taylor – enter into the self-reflective processes of the subject's becoming a self. Or, if this is too strong, at least we can say that learning something, no matter what, *does something* to us as subjects – and therefore, that, as learning subjects, we would do well to judge whether a certain education makes us better or worse persons. This, of course, is a paradox, since we can hardly know the answer in advance – for to become capable of passing judgment over one's own education is, in essence, connected to the paradox of becoming an autonomous subject through a temporary submission to someone else's judgment and authority.[57]

If, at this point, one asks how these thoughts relate to the discourse of 'learning society,' outlined in the first part of this essay, the differences in discourse appear overwhelming. Without going into a detailed analysis, my contention is that the underlying logic of the two sets of thinking is radically different. 'Learning outcomes,' 'accountability,' etc. make use of the logic of *computability*, where means and results can become measurable factors, and – in principle at least – compared. 'Education in a wide sense' draws on a discursive repertoire of reflection, meaning, critique, problematization, trust, paradoxes, and creativity – processes that seem completely beyond the logic that quantifies and measures.

The Socio-Cultural Perspective on Learning – Politicized

I have argued that, in the current Western educational policy regime, the dominant concept of learning stands in a rather problematic relationship to notions such as significance and meaning. As already mentioned, the socio-cultural perspective on learning, inspired by Lev Vygotsky, *could* be a way out, as a theory that takes context, culture, and meaning seriously. A major point in the reception of Vygotsky's thought in educational

---

57. See e.g. Alexander von Oettingen, *Det pædagogiske paradoks*, Århus, Klim, 2001.

studies is that the 'locus' of learning is the social sphere, whose meaning is internalized, as described here by Ivar Bråten:

> Higher psychological processes are formed by the culture developed through history, coming to expression through a series of signs and symbolic systems of varying complexity. And these systems of signs and symbols are transferred to the mind of the individual where they become psychological tools of thought, because they permeate the interaction between the individual and the social context.[58]

The processes of internalization consists of a series of transformations, Vygotsky states, where

> [e]very function in the child's cultural development appears twice: first, on the social level, and later, on the individual level; first, between people (interpsychological), and then inside the child (intrapsychological). [...] The internalization of socially rooted and historically developed activities is the distinguishing feature of human psychology, the basis of the qualitative leap from animal to human psychology.[59]

Vygotsky's interest in the social aspects of the developmental process is evident, and he frequently uses terms like meaning, history, culture, etc. It is therefore all the more striking that the 'socio-cultural perspective on learning' has become dominant in teacher education, the literature and the universities *during the same period* in which the 'new language of learning' and the discourses of 'entrepreneurial society' have become dominant at the level of policy. Somehow, the two currents are increasingly merged at various (practical) levels, based on the notion that *knowledge is something actively constructed by individuals engaged in practices within a socio-cultural*

---

58. Ivar Bråten, "Om Vygotskys liv og lære" in *Vygotsky i pedagogikken*, edited by Ivar Bråten, Oslo, Cappelen, 1996, 23, author's translation.
59. Lev. S. Vygotsky, *Mind in Society. The Development of Higher Psychological Processes*, edited by Michael Cole, Vera John-Steiner, Sylvia Scribner, and Ellen Souberman, Cambridge, Mass / London, Harvard University press, 1978, 57.

environment. Hence the importance on creating an *environment for learning*, where, in Biesta's words:

> ... the activity of the teacher is no longer orientated towards the transfer of knowledge but geared towards the provision of environments that facilitate and stimulate [...] autonomous and self-directed learning. [60]

In order for the two perspectives to merge successfully, a certain short-circuiting is required, a main element of which is the reductionism from 'meaning' to 'learning.' Instead of pursuing this discussion, however, I want to argue that Vygotsky's insights could be elaborated further by drawing on Castoriadis's notions of social imaginary significations, discussed above, and *politicized* by drawing on his distinction between the 'instituting' and 'instituted society.[61] Unfortunately, there is only room for a brief outline of how this might proceed.

Vygotsky and Castoriadis agree that symbolic systems, significations, and meaning are not the products of individuals, but social in origin, and both are interested in language as a case in point. Language and culture are, to Vygotsky, constitutive for the individuals' thinking – 'thinking tools' – not vice versa:

> Verbal thought is not an innate, natural form of behavior but is determined by a historical-cultural process and has specific properties and laws that cannot be found in the natural forms of thought and speech.[62]

This is clearly in line with Castoriadis's view, that language is the foremost example of a social *institution*, and that the social-historical has primacy over the (always-already socialized) individual. When Vygotsky says that

60. In Masschelein and Simons, *AEGW,* 568.
61 For a presentation of these concepts, see Ingerid S. Straume, "The Political Imaginary of Global Capitalism," in this volume.
62. Lev S. Vygotsky, "The Genetic Roots of Thought and Speech," in *Thought and Language*. Edited and translated by Eugenia Hanfmann and Gertrude Vakar. Boston, Mass, MIT press, 1962 [1934].

thought development is determined by language, i.e., by the linguistic tools of thought and the socio-cultural experience of the child, one could easily identify socio-cultural experiences with the notion of social imaginary significations, such as religion, rationality, democracy, capitalism, etc.[63] Now, to be socialized, employing Castoriadis's terminology, means to embody the social order of significations, and insofar as we endorse and find pleasure in these significations, the socialization process is successful.[64] The social imaginary significations become standards by which individuals interpret their experiences; making communication and thinking possible. The distinction between the 'instituting' and 'instituted society' – where the instituting society is the creative dimension, 'that which' creates a society[65] – further highlights the *creative* aspect of the institution of society, setting a task for education, among other things, to enhance the (individual and collective) ability to create new meanings and institutions.[66]

Today, scholars who adopt the socio-cultural perspective tend to focus on the *tools* and *processes* of learning such as information and communication technology and the media – where 'culture' is being studied (if at all) in terms of 'cultural artifacts' – and informal *learning arenas*, social *groups* and *networks*; but steer clear of properly political discussions about the significance and meaning of learning and education in a specific culture. This is of course legitimate, since culture,

---

63. In fact, in "The socialist alteration of man" (*The Vygotsky Reader*, edited by René van der Veer and Jaan Valsiner, Oxford, Blackwell), Vygotsky talks about the socialist 'type of individual' in much the same way as Castoriadis talks about various social types in different social-historical regimes; see, e.g., Castoriadis, *IIS*, 318.
64. *IIS*, 315.
65. "Society is self-creation. 'That which' creates society and history is the instituting society, as opposed to the instituted society. The instituting society is the social imaginary in the radical sense." Cornelius Castoriadis, *Philosophy, Politics, Autonomy. Essays in Political Philosophy*, edited and translated by David Ames Curtis, New York, Oxford University Press, 1991, 84.
66. "An autonomous society, as a self-instituting and self-governing collectivity, presupposes the development of the capacity of all its members to participate in its reflective and deliberative activities." Castoriadis, *WIF*, 132.

language, community, etc. can *either* be talked of as context, tools, and prerequisites for something, e.g., learning, *or* as *specific* significations and meaning, with political aspects. Choosing the former, however, involves a reductionism that has implications for the notion of learning and for the theory itself. In my view – following Castoriadis in particular – the term 'culture' can hardly be understood in the sense of 'pure context.' Culture is the framework from which everything else begets meaning, including the terms we use to describe these issues (this is why the discourses of 'learning society' and the 'entrepreneurial subject' are of such great cultural importance). And, according to Castoriadis, meaning keeps a society together; meaning ensures that a given society is perceived as *one* society, a functional unity, even though it consists of different and particular institutions:

> [T]his unity is in the last resort the unity and internal cohesion of the immensely complex web of meanings that permeate, orient, and direct the whole life of the society considered, as well as the concrete individuals that bodily constitute society. This web of meanings is what I call the 'magma' of social imaginary significations that are carried by and embodied in the institutions of the given society and that, so to speak, animate it.[67]

If Castoriadis is right in saying that human beings maintain their insti-tutions in so far as they offer meaning, then meaning becomes the most important dimension of any culture; and this implies that our notion of 'learning' should be more attuned to 'meaning' than it currently is. If we take the socio-cultural perspective on learning *seriously*, we must also *question* the contents and meaning of education in specific social-historical cases. This is not just a theoretical project; it is also a political one, as I shall argue in the last part of this text. But first, let me draw the preceding parts more closely together.

I have argued that 'learning' should be seen as specific learning; learning of *something* and, following Taylor, learning *as someone*. To talk

67. *WIF*, 7.

of learning as 'pure process,' 'elements,' or 'modules,' are just some of the many reductionisms in the field of education. The Bologna process has followed this path by breaking up formerly coherent educational courses into modules that can be compared and evaluated against each other.[68] 'Education' is conceptualized as choices between schools that offer various learning outcomes. In this scenario, notions representing *cultural meaning* are absent, while education and schools/universities become pure, transparent 'context.' In this scenario, the significance and meaning of that which is learned is inaccessible to, or not worthy of, any deeper reflection. The principle of sublimation of the learned 'contents'– so central to practices of teaching and learning – has become theoretically extinct. Sublimation means that individuals adopt society's significations and make them their own. Through sublimation, we are socialized as members of a culture, into our professional roles, etc. Learning, in *this* connection, implies more or less conscious choices of *who we want to be*. Henceforth, the processes involved in learning market economics and the discography of a musician I really like are only superficially similar. Learning involves intent as well as sublimation, where emotions are – sometimes deeply – involved.

The Problem

What is the problem with a concept of learning that does not include the socio-political dimensions outlined above, such as meaning, signification, and specific cultural reflections? In and of itself the concept may not pose any serious threat; some may even claim that my concerns represent an elitist critique, with little regard for practical realities and political necessities. In my view, however, there are good, *political* reasons to worry when collective notions of education and its *raison d'être* are impoverished, as my examples have shown. European educational policy is dominated by a general reductionism and, more specifically, an instrumentalism where interest in the *means* of education replaces discussions about educational objectives, i.e., meaning. In many settings, learning is talked of as pure

---

68. Karseth, *CRHE*, 267.

process; learning becomes the only objective of education; but learning of what, learning by whom? The general response is: 'Basic skills' and 'competencies' – 'goals' against which no sensible person can be opposed. In this instrumentalist framework, the only yardstick of education is efficiency, i.e., what 'works' and 'how well does it work'; orientated around categories like outcomes, evidence, accountability, etc. Again, these are categories that seem harmless enough in themselves; for what is wrong in knowing whether public money is well spent, according to the intentions? And who would want a public education where pupils do not learn, i.e., with methods that do not work? It would seem that those who are critical of these statements are also critical of *quality in education* itself.

An interesting detail, though, is that quality assessment regimes never seem to employ qualitative language. As I have shown, substantial, phenomenological, and normative issues are non-existent in this discourse; indeed, the regime of quality assessment *avoids* qualitative issues. So where is there room for discussing normative issues, e.g., the justifications and legitimacy of educational policy practices? As far as I can see, matters of efficiency in effect *trump* legitimacy and justifications by *totalizing* the discursive field. The most important thing is to find out whether something works: 'if it doesn't, the discussion ends, and if it does, we should be able to measure it.' Tragically, the time to ask questions of significance, importance, and justification never seems to enter into today's educational policy discourses.

In the region from which my examples are derived, mainly the Nordic social democracies, national developments seem to be increasingly dependent on international policy processes aimed at the standardization of educational policies in a large geographical area (the European Union). These processes conceal the fact that decisions over schools and the education of new generations are profoundly political matters – they are *everybody's* concern, since schools, colleges, and universities affect the larger society and its future by way of social reproduction, and possibly, by facilitating breaks with the dominant social imaginary from which new social forms may arise. In the end, the overarching question is what and who we want to be, as a society. If discussions about education are not framed so as to engage in moral-political discussions of this kind, this is a democratic problem. Furthermore, an impoverished notion of education obscures the various possibilities in human life; opportunities to live a life as someone, a life imbued with meaning and significations, making for a richer social and personal reality, and on a deeper level, for socio-political creativity.

If we would start speaking of learning in terms of significations and meanings, new opportunities to reclaim the language of *education* may arise. As I have argued, discussions about schools and education should make use of words that make these activities *meaningful*, allowing us to ask: What is the political, moral, and global significance of *this* education? We would need to look for words that allow us to express and see the *importance* of our activities, as individuals and collectives. This will allow for strong evaluations[69] of the educational systems, but also, strong critiques and new creations. In short, it should be possible to raise questions of *why* we have schools; questions that can hardly be raised under the current regime, where 'learning' is seen to be self-sufficient, yet curiously empty.[70] Most importantly, when contents, significations, and meanings are included in discussions of the educational systems, these discussions become a part of society's reflection upon its own norms and institutions. And finally, this enables us to talk of an education that aims at autonomy and political agency.

---

69. Charles Taylor, *Sources of the self*, Cambridge, Cambridge University press, 1989.
70. Dufour (*The Art*) and Fisher (*CRE*) both argue that in neoliberal capitalist societies, there is a fear of, or refusal of, education.

Deterioration of Trust: The Political Warning in Kubrick's "Eyes Wide Shut"

Håvard Friis Nilsen

A legendary director behind classics like *Dr. Strangelove, 2001, A Clockwork Orange,* and *The Shining,* Stanley Kubrick (1928–1999) died merely a few days after finishing his final film: *Eyes Wide Shut.* Kubrick said he thought it was his best film.[1] Few critics agreed with his assessment; reviews were mixed, and viewers seemed confused: What was this film about? The story of sexual frustrations of a married couple, with Freudian undercurrents, seemed remarkably old hat. Lack of any clear theme or message was a recurrent point in the many negative reviews, along with accusations of aesthetic superficiality. The film was described as a "decorous gavotte ... more studied than a fashion shoot";[2] "portentous" and "bizarrely devoid of life."[3] Some reviewers specifically criticized Kubrick for lacking a social or political perspective; a case in point is Stuart Klawans' review in the leftist weekly, *The Nation,* which concludes that *Eyes Wide Shut* is "the work of an artist who long ago stopped paying attention to the world around him."[4] Contrary to these reviews, I will invite the reader to view this film as one of Kubrick's most political films, with a perceptive eye for the many structural similarities between the

1. Geoffrey Cocks, *The Wolf at the Door. Stanley Kubrick, History and the Holocaust,* New York, Peter Lang, 2004, 139 (*WD*).
2. James Hoberman, "I Wake up Dreaming," *Village Voice,* July 1999.
3. David Denby, "Last Waltz," *New Yorker,* July 26, 1999, 84–86.
4. Stuart Klawans, "Old Masters," *The Nation,* August 9, 1999.

period when the story was written and our present times of financial instability and crisis. Rather than merely exploring the individual erotic tensions and desires between the main characters, I believe Kubrick in his final film put across a *political* message: a warning against a society where the social fabric of *trust* deteriorates into a hermeneutics of suspicion, paving the way to an increasingly authoritarian political climate.

Kubrick, Schnitzler, and Freud

Stanley Kubrick's birth and death coincide historically with two moments of financial turbulence. He was born in 1928, shortly before the financial crisis of 1929, and died in 1999, at a time when the international financial markets again showed major signs of fragility. Kubrick's father was American and his mother Austrian; his final film was based on a story by one of Austria's greatest writers, written and published four years before Kubrick's own birth. Through the adaptation of Arthur Schnitzler's (1862–1931) *Traumnovelle* from 1925, Kubrick's final film was a sort of homecoming. This was also expressed in the fact that *Eyes Wide Shut* was the first film since his early production *Killer's Kiss* to take place in his hometown of New York City. Kubrick had planned doing a film on this story for a long time, and had secured the film rights already in 1971, nearly three decades before its completion. Apart from changing the context of the story from "roaring twenties" Austria to 1990s USA, from post-WWI Vienna to post-Cold War New York, Kubrick remains remarkably faithful to Schnitzler's novella. While *Traumnovelle* was written after the collapse and demise of the Habsburg Empire, *Eyes Wide Shut* takes place after the collapse and demise of the Soviet Empire, a point Kubrick hints at in the musical opening: the hypnotically suggestive *Jazz Suite* by Soviet composer Dmitri Shostakovich, written in 1938, is like a sombre Viennese Waltz. It was composed at the time of Hitler's annexation of Austria, the *Anschluss* of 1938, as well as during the political terror of the Moscow Trials. Kubrick never selected music for his films arbitrarily, and this work by Shostakovich reflects an authoritarian political climate.

It is common to read *Traumnovelle* as a literary tribute to Sigmund

Freud.[5] Trained as a medical doctor and neurologist, Arthur Schnitzler wrote in Vienna during a period of prolonged social tension, just before the end of the Habsburg era to the beginning of fascism; and died shortly before Hitler's rise to power in Germany. Much of Schnitzler's work deals with erotic and psychological themes, and he had been a medical assistant for one of Freud's teachers, Theodor Meynert. Schnitzler had a masterful skill of hypnosis, like his own father, who was also a medical doctor.[6] There was not a lot of private contact between Schnitzler and Freud, but both were aware of their commonalities as medical doctors with literary and psychological interests. Schnitzler admired Freud, and sent him a telegram at his 50th birthday in 1906, where he acknowledged the inspiration from Freud. Freud for his part, acknowledged Schnitzler as one of his equals, and wrote that he felt they agreed fundamentally on "many psychological and erotic problems."[7] Freud had expressed this feeling of convergence the year before, in his paper "Bruchstück einer Hysterie-Analyse" from 1905 [*Fragments of an Analysis of a Case of Hysteria*]. Despite this exchange of letters, they did not meet privately on this occasion. Many years later, in 1923, Freud wrote to Schnitzler on his 60th birthday, and stated that he had *avoided* him, out of fear of "a *double*" [*Doppelgänger*]: "Your sense of the reality of the unconscious and the human drives, your dissolution of the cultural-conventional securities, and the way your thoughts dwell on the polarity of love and death; all this seems uncannily familiar to me."[8] They met for the first time a month after this letter, and then sporadically until a last meeting in 1926, the year after the release of *Traumnovelle*.

---

5. Arthur Schnitzler, *Traumnovelle*, id., *Gesammelte Werke in Einzelausgaben. Das Erzählerische werk*, bd. 6, Frankfurt am Main, Fischer Taschenbuch Verlag, [1925] 1981.
6. Cf. Carl Schorske, "Politics and the Psyche: Schnitzler and Hofmannsthal," id., *Fin-de-siecle Vienna. Politics and Culture*, New York, Vintage Books, 1981.
7. Sigmund Freud in a letter to Arthur Schnitzler, May 8, 1906. Translated by the author.
8. Sigmund Freud in a letter to Arthur Schnitzler, May 14, 1923. Translated by the author.

Kubrick's film may have been no less of an intended tribute to Freud than Schnitzler's story: As Geoffrey Cocks points out, Kubrick was an "early and messianic" reader of Freud who pressed *A General Introduction to Psychoanalysis* on all his friends.[9] Schnitzler's story was written merely four years before the market collapse of 1929, in a period of turbulent financial capitalism. The nation of Austria had emerged after the downfall of Emperor Franz Joseph's kingdom, and from having been at the centre of an empire, Vienna was suddenly a capital in a small republic with a population of 6–7 million. Governed by social democrats, the city of Vienna was emblematic to progressive politicians throughout Europe; and the later Scandinavian welfare states modelled a lot of their systems on the Austrian health care system in 'Rote Wien,' 'Red Vienna,' as it was called at the time.[10] The popular support of the welfare model was solid, but it was also hated by the economic elites, and the forces unleashed by the collapse of the financial markets tightened the political sphere of opportunities.

Like the married couple in the story, which will be presented shortly, Austria as a whole suffered from a deterioration of trust: Public faith in the economic and political institutions eroded, and the support of parliamentary democracy was fragile. The subtext seems to be precisely what Freud wrote to Schnitzler shortly before the latter wrote the story: "the dissolution of the cultural-conventional securities,"[11] where the stark symbolism of crude power and authority could appear abruptly from underneath the thin protective coating of bourgeois culture.

Authority and Desire

The story is about a married couple gradually entering a marital crisis. William and Alice Harford (played by the real-life couple, Tom Cruise and Nicole Kidman), leave their home for a party at Victor Ziegler's (Sydney Pollack), a patient of Dr. Harford's who is obviously extremely

9. *WD*, 4.
10. Cf. the Norwegian postwar Prime Minister Einar Gerhardsen's memoirs, *Minner og meninger*, Tiden norsk forlag, Oslo, 1974.
11. Sigmund Freud in a letter to Arthur Schnitzler, May 14, 1923.

rich, perhaps a captain of industry or a successful financial broker.

Bill and Alice Harford both have flirtatious encounters with others at the party. Harford is, not unwillingly, led aside by two beautiful women. But he is soon summoned by one of the servants, and asked to come immediately to Ziegler. He is shown into Ziegler's bedroom, where a naked woman lies lifeless on the bed. Ziegler is getting dressed, and explains matter-of-factly that the woman has taken an overdose. He hopes Harford can resuscitate her.

Ziegler apparently puts a great deal of trust in Harford. To involve Harford in his relations with a drug-addicted prostitute shortly after he and his own wife welcomed the Harford couple to the party shows that he counts on Harford's discretion. At the same time, this is a trust without mutuality or reciprocity, the power relations are clear: almost like a caricature of capital-labour-relations, this scene shows the handsome, affluent doctor for a moment reduced to the obedient wageworker, who must carry out the dirty work and otherwise keep mum. Harford succeeds in reviving the girl: "Mandy, look at me." She awakens and looks him in the eyes. Significantly, this moment of shut eyes opening is the moment when the woman on the bed realizes she owes her life to Harford; he saved her. Ziegler escorts Harford out of the room: "I trust this is between the two of us."[12]

The next morning, Alice is jealous. She wonders where Bill went with the two beautiful women, and we sense a breach in the marital trust. He evades the issue, but during the talk, which develops into a discussion on sexual morality, she gets her revenge: she describes an encounter during one of their trips abroad, in the early days of their marriage. Her eyes met the gaze of an officer who awakened her desire. She could not get him off her mind, and had wild sexual fantasies about him. While making love to Bill and making plans for the future and their daughter, her thoughts were with the officer: "That afternoon you and I made love and talked about our future, and our child. Later we were sitting on the balcony

---

12. Stanley Kubrick and Frederick Raphael, *The Screenplay of Eyes Wide Shut*, 1996 (*EWS*).

and he passed below us without looking up. Just the sight of him stirred me deeply and I thought if he wanted me, I could not have resisted. I thought I was ready to give up you, the child, my whole future."[13]

This story hits Harford, who enters a jealous rage. The precious memory of an intimate and happy vacation is suddenly changed into a gnawing nightmare: he broods over ceaseless tormenting images of Alice and the officer in a sexual embrace. From this moment on, he drifts with the flow of events and loses his self-control. The breach in his trust in Alice makes him *want* to lose it; it has awakened an urge to become instinct-driven without any restraining obligations, responsibilities, or loyalties. His lack of restraint is a thirst for revenge after Alice castrated him, as it were, by directing her desire towards a different object than him, towards a man in an officer's uniform.

Later on, Harford meets his friend, the pianist Nick Nightingale (Nachtingall in Schnitzler's story) in a bar. Nightingale tells Harford about a job he will have later that night in a private party, a mask ball involving a ritual sex orgy. This is now exactly what Harford wants. He forces Nightingale to reveal the password to the entrance: "Nick, you can trust me. I won't say a word about this to anyone." A moment later, he repeats: "Trust me." Nick reveals the password, *fidelio,* obtains a costume, and heads off to the party.

Fidelio — Loyalty and Trust

'Fidelio' means faithful. Faithfulness, loyalty, and trust are preconditions for friendship, marriage, convictions, alliances, and power structures. Thought, love, and power all require assurances of mutual trust. The material symbols of assurance, like the wedding ring, the identity card, or the graduation diploma, are all present in *Eyes Wide Shut*. In Kubrick's film, we witness a society where trust deteriorates, with increasing measures of surveillance and security; a society of suspicion. Everyone needs to legitimize himself constantly, since the general trust is low. Locks, key cards, alarms, cameras the whole gamut of security check points in an increasingly militarized public space: Kubrick has taken

13. *EWS.*

great care in showing all the security measures we hardly even notice anymore. Two years after the release of Kubrick's film, the terrorist attacks on September 11, 2001 accelerated this development towards risk elimination and disintegration of trust. It is as if Kubrick sensed and anticipated the coming political climate.

One of the oldest security measures of all is *the password*, the secret signal that determines exclusion or inclusion. Seemingly an ironic password, *Fidelio* opens the gates to a party where all relations are external and no one is supposed to show their true identity. Like an inversion of the happy Viennese masquerade ball in Johann Strauss II's operetta *The Bat*, this is a sexual celebration of patriarchy, solemnly arranged with a chanting priest in the background.

Harford believes himself to be safely hidden behind his mask, but he has unwittingly dropped clues giving away the fact that he is an intruder: the guests came in limousines, he appeared in a taxi. He handed over his winter coat to a servant, and his name is on the collar. A naked, masked woman approaches him, whispering: "You don't belong here. There is still a chance for you to get away." Is it a real warning, or just a teasing, playful way of increasing the sexual tension? Harford stays on. "You must leave at once," she repeats. "It can cost your life and mine."[14]

Harford procrastinates, and is suddenly led to a room where the music has stopped (the blindfolded Nightingale is led away from the piano by two men), and where the guests now may witness a trial – *his* trial. He is asked for the password, and also for a new password, "the password of the house," which he does not know. "I must have forgotten it." "That is unfortunate. Because here it does not matter whether you have forgotten it or whether you never knew it." Exposed as an intruder, Harford is requested to remove his mask. The scene depicts how subjectivity and freedom may be restricted and objectivized through the *gaze*, in this instance through the enforced removal of the mask. The mask is an old part of the repertoire of power, always involving an element of secrecy and objectification of the other – the one who *sees* has power as the

---

14. *EWS.*

perceiving subject, the one who *is seen* is the vulnerable object. As an additional humiliation (which is not included in Schnitzler's story) the priest commands Harford to undress.

At that point, the woman who warned Harford steps forward, and says she is willing to redeem him. This causes astonishment among the guests, and it is clear that it is a serious matter. Harford is now said to be free to go, provided he never speaks of this evening again to anyone, or makes any inquiries. Harford asks what will happen to the woman, and says he cannot allow anything to happen to her. He is informed that there is nothing he can do. *"When a promise is given here, there is no turning back!"* The promiscuous nature of the party seems to require absolute loyalty, discretion, and trust, while its logic of desire and lust is persistently borders on violence.

The Dream

When Harford returns from the party and enters the bedroom at night, Alice awakens from a nightmare:

> ... something terrible had happened — our clothes were gone. I was terrified as I had never been before, and felt such a burning shame that it almost consumed me. At the same time I was furious with you because I thought it was your fault. And this sensation of terror, shame and fury was more intense than any emotion I had ever felt before. You felt guilty and rushed away naked, to go and get clothes for us.[15]

The structure of the dream is reminiscent of the Book of Genesis. The paradise of the Garden of Eden contains a prohibition: Adam and Eve are not allowed to partake in God's power as symbolized by the fruit of Knowledge. This is the original source of their temptation and desire: the object is to become part of God's power and knowledge. Their transgression leads to their nakedness and shame. And nakedness and shame are central elements in Alice's dream. Additionally, there is further

---

15. *EWS.*

a structural similarity between Alice's desire for power as expressed by the officer in his uniform, and Bill's wish to be included in the closed circles of the power elite. They are both sexually drawn to power symbols, which become a way for both of them to overcome their feelings of hurt. Harford feels castrated and needs to restore his honor and dignity as well as his masculinity. Alice feels scorned by Harford, and has the same needs, a need to restore her sense of dignity and getting even, partly by incorporating power (having sex with the officer) and partly by humiliating him as he has humiliated her. The relation between sexuality and power lies embedded in language. Etymologically, potency and power are synonyms, meaning possibility, ability and force. The ruler is the potentate. From German soldier helmets in WWII to the erected steel-and-glass skyscrapers on Wall Street, power is expressed as potency, in a patriarchal symbolism. Harford's wish to participate in a sexual orgy is a dream of a *quick fix*, a restoration of his sense of agency after being humiliated by Alice's dream. And as it so happens, Alice's attraction to power and authority in the dream also refers to a sexual orgy, caught up in the dialectic of shame and desire, power and lust:

> I was lying in a lush garden, stretched out naked in the sunlight, and I was far more beautiful than I ever was in reality. And while I lay there, a young man walked out of the woods. He was the young Naval officer I told you about from the hotel. He looked at me ... and slowly took me in his arms ... and we began making love. I seemed to live through countless days and nights – there was neither time nor space. And the more we made love, the more our hunger for each other increased. And just as that earlier feeling of terror and shame went beyond anything I had ever felt, so nothing can be compared with the freedom and happiness and the ... *desire* that I now felt. Then I realized there were other couples around us hundreds of them, and they too were making love. Then I was making love to the other men, and as soon as my longing was satisfied with one, I wanted another. I can't say how many I was with. And yet I didn't for one moment forget you.[16]

16. *EWS.*

She blames Harford for her feelings of shame, and when she later sees him bound to a pole to be crucified and tortured, she laughs out loudly to show that she feels no compassion.

To be seen as an object, to be an object under the Other's gaze, this is the root of many instances of shame. If one is 'caught in the act,' 'with one's trouser's down,' shame comes flushing in, as one cannot transcend the situation, and is reduced to a mere object.[17] This is the situation Harford finds himself in when exposed and humiliated in front of all the mask-clad guests. The closed circles of the elite may symbolically be compared to a paradise lost; Harford's wish to become part of the spheres of power and authority, his dream of entering the 'right circles,' underscores his sense of vulnerability and limited social prestige compared to the upper-class life of his patient Victor Ziegler: it is experienced as a lack. While Harford is caught as an illegitimate intruder and shamefully expelled from the sexual orgy, Alice feels shame as he has left, she feels scorned, and therefore joins the orgy as revenge, in her dream. At the very moment trust deteriorates between them, the Harford couple both react by anxiously being drawn to spheres of power as a safe haven.

The significance of trust is an important element in any concept of power, and may bring out the differences between Max Weber and Hannah Arendt's notions of power. The patriarchal notion of power is expressed in Max Weber's definition: "the chance of a man or of a number of men to realize their own will in a communal action even against the resistance of others, who are participating in the same action."[18] Hannah Arendt criticized this concept, and claimed that this was not a definition of power, but of *violence*.[19] According to Arendt, power is the ability to achieve something *in common*. To Weber, power is the ability to do something in spite of lacking trust; to Arendt, mutual trust is a precondition for legitimate power. A democratic concept of power must be grounded in participation and mutual trust. When the

17. Cf. Jean-Paul Sartre, *L'être et le néant,* Tel, Gallimard, Paris, [1943] 1998.
18. Max Weber, *From Max Weber: Essays in Sociology*, translated and edited by H. H. Gerth and C. Wright Mills, New York, Oxford University Press, 1946, 180.
19. Hannah Arendt, *On Revolution*, London, Penguin, [1963/65] 1990

common ground of trust evaporates between them, the Harfords are attracted to a ruthless sphere of sex, humiliation, revenge, and desire; in a sense, moving in the Weberian direction.

The Invention of Victor Ziegler

The lack of trust and the general climate of social disintegration apparent in Kubrick's film are prevalent also in Schnitzler's story, where the anti-Semitism of the Viennese elites has a pronounced presence, contributing to the claustrophobic situation of Fridolin, the main protagonist. As Geoffrey Cocks convincingly argues in his extraordinarily rich analysis of Kubrick's films, the Holocaust is an underlying theme throughout Kubrick's career.[20] Cocks also points out, however, that despite the centrality of this theme, Kubrick often chose to downplay Jewish elements in his films, and *Eyes Wide Shut* is an example in point. While Fridolin in Schnitzler's story is a Jew, Harford is not.

One of the very few direct references to anti-Semitism in Kubrick's films appears in the opening scene of *Lolita*, where Clare Quilty (played by Peter Sellers), dressed in a Roman toga, says to Humbert Humbert (James Mason): "You are either an Australian or a German refugee. This is a gentile's home. You better run along." Otherwise, anti-Semitism is expressed in more subtle ways, or not at all, and Kubrick has been criticized for conforming to Hollywood stereotypes by avoiding Jewish references: In *Eyes Wide Shut* it is clear that he minimized the element of anti-Semitism compared to Schnitzler's *Traumnovelle*. Whereas Fridolin is the object of anti-Semitic aggression, Harford is the victim of homophobia, attacked by some street thugs who, provoked by his suave appearance, call him a faggot. More than downplaying the Jewish element of social marginalization, however, *Eyes Wide Shut* takes a different direction than Schnitzler's novel. With the character of Victor Ziegler, Kubrick has created a variation of a patriarchal figure, the theme of which he consistently explored in his films, but this time incorporating a modern mix of authority and power put across in a boyish, open and friendly style. Ziegler is not a character in Schnitzler's story; he is Kubrick's own invention.

20. *WD*.

When Ziegler summons Harford the day after the party, Harford arrives in an agitated mood, as he has revealed that the woman who redeemed him at the party has been found dead of an overdose. Ziegler opens with a light and courteous tone, offers Harford brandy, and promises to send him a crate of the distinguished brand. The informal atmosphere is, however, glossing over a hard upholding of differences in power relations. Ziegler reveals that he was at the party the day before. He says he realized that it was Nightingale who had led Harford to the party, and he is furious with him: "I recommended him to these people and he betrayed my trust." This is the final time the word 'trust' appears in Kubrick's screenplay.

Approaching the character of Ziegler in the film, we might begin by asking what kind of a name 'Victor Ziegler' is, and what *associations* does it have? First and foremost, he represents power and authority. The connotations of 'Victor' range from its imperial origins in ancient Rome to the 'V'-sign Winston Churchill and the allied forces used during WWII. 'Ziegler,' on the other hand, which means 'brick-layer' in German, hardly gives us any associations to allied forces or the winning side of WWII. If we look for tacit references to Nazi or Holocaust history — and, as Geoffrey Cocks has taught us, in Kubrick's films, we often should — the name Ziegler may remind us of Adolf Hitler's favourite painter, *Adolf Ziegler* (1892–1959). Kubrick, who had a lifelong interest in the history of the Holocaust and Nazi period in Germany, and married the daughter of an actor in a Nazi theatre, was surely aware of this man. Adolf Ziegler was the executive enforcer of making the German art world conform to Nazi ideology, and the one responsible for the exclusion of all so-called '*entartete Kunst*' (degenerate art) from galleries and public spaces. A common trait between the two Zieglers — the historical one and the fictitious one — is the role as functioning censors: while Adolf Ziegler was the censor of the Nazi Art world, Victor Ziegler sustains the censorship Harford is under — *do not go further into this*. But whereas Fridolin the Jew was changed into Harford the gentile, for this role, Kubrick *did* select a Jewish actor: his friend Sydney Pollack (1934–2008), born of Russian

Jews. With the invention of Victor Ziegler, Kubrick seems to have replaced the nameless and faceless members of Schnitzler's Viennese Catholic upper strata with a character encompassing a peculiar mix of connotations, ranging from victorious Allied forces and a friendly Jewish New York businessman to a repressive Nazi censor. Ziegler thus comes across as a friendly fascist.

The Ages of Finance Capital

In 1923 and 1928–29 respectively (around the time Schnitzler wrote his story), the finance minister of the Weimar Republic of Germany was the Vienna-born social democrat Rudolf Hilferding (1877–1941). Hilferding's main economic treatise, *Das Finanzkapital*, had been published in 1910. In this major and influential work he shows how the world economy had entered into a phase very different from the age of small-scale industry characteristic of British free-market liberalism. Hilferding interpreted his contemporary economic situation as one of monopolistic finance capitalism. One of his central points – shared by many economists of his day, regardless of political stance – was that finance capital at its worst formed a parasitic function on the real economy, i.e., the production of goods and values. At the beginning of the 20th century, theories of finance capitalism as opposed to productive capitalism were widespread across the political spectrum, ranging from a revolutionary Lenin in Russia to a reactionary Werner Sombart in Germany, or from a conservative Joseph Schumpeter to the social democrat Rudolf Hilferding, both from Vienna. After the Second World War, this theoretical distinction disappeared as neoclassical mathematical models replaced historical analyses in mainstream economy. In the German-speaking world, notions of 'finance capitalism' resonated too strongly with inter-war anti-Semitic rhetoric (Werner Sombart was an example of this), and were thus discarded. In Marxist theory in the 1950s, Lenin and Hilferding's concept of 'finance capital' fared little better: it was specifically challenged and replaced by the notion of 'monopoly capital.'[21] This new concept was meant to

---

21. Paul Sweezy, *Theory of Capitalist Development*, New York, Monthly Review Press, 1942.

bolster a theory of capitalism in a historical period where finance capital was regulated, and one generally believed that the stock market frenzy of the interwar years was a phenomenon of the past. The concept of 'monopoly capital' as well as the neoclassical models both blurred the understanding of different economic periods, and how these periods were regularly haunted by financial crises. Regardless of political views, to Sombart, Schumpeter, Hilferding, or Lenin, periods of unprecedented accumulation and concentration of capital, followed by financial crises, were a matter of course. Such periods of financial turbulence form the backdrop to both Schnitzler's story and Kubrick's film.

The contemporary Venezuelan economist Carlota Perez (1940–) has followed in Hilferding's tracks and developed a model for understanding the interplay between historical periods of finance capitalism and periods of its opposite: *productive capitalism.*[22] Periods of productive capitalism are characterized by *techno-industrial paradigms* as a driving force of the economic growth. In periods of finance capitalism, however, these paradigms have lost their growth potential, and growth is to a large extent driven by speculation in the so-called FIRE-sector of the economy (Finance, Insurance, Real Estate). These periods usually end in financial crises, often accompanied by social unrest and upheavals. The years before 1929 were precisely such a period, and so were the years before the financial instability of the late 1990s and the early 2000s. Periods of financial capitalism are periods with a widening social gap, where conspicuous consumption among powerful elites goes hand in hand with rises in poverty.

22. Wolfgang Drechsler, Rainer Kattel and Erik S. Reinert, *Techno-Economic Paradigms: Essays in Honour of Carlota Perez,* Anthem Press, London, 2009.

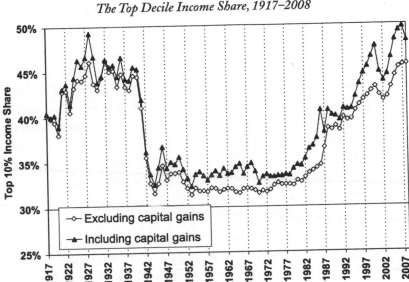

Figure 1
The Top Decile Income Share, 1917–2008

The figure shows the concentration of economic power in social elites from 1917 to 2007.[23] There is a remarkable convergence between the moments when Schnitzler wrote his story and Kubrick made his film. Not since the mid-twenties had the richest 1% in the US had such a large percentage of the total wealth as in the late 1990s and early 2000s. The figure is comparable to European statistics as well. It is an expression of two periods in economic history marked by an unregulated finance economy, where the FIRE-sector of the economy plays a dominant role compared to productive industry. At the moment of a financial crisis, faith and trust in continued growth, in sustained economic development, and in the stock market, simply erodes. This is a very concrete expression of a deterioration of social trust in a central modern institution. Although neither Schnitzler's story nor Kubrick's film is dealing directly

23. Emmanuel Saez and Thomas Piketty, "Income Inequality in the United States, 1913–1998," Quarterly Journal of Economics, 118 (1), 2003, 1–39, updated version, http://www.econ.berkeley.edu/~saez/

with questions of finance, the overarching historical transition from a market economy based on trust and faith in the market to a collapse of this fundamental trust is a significant historical parallel that lies in the background of both works, whether the two artists consciously reflected on this fact or not. As pointed out by the Viennese economist Karl Polanyi, who lived through the transition as the editor of Vienna's foremost financial newspaper, *Der Oesterreichische Volkswirt* (*The Austrian Economist*), the erosion of trust in the market economy was the single most important factor behind the rise of authoritarian fascism.[24] When faith in the economy collapsed, fascism arose as a mechanical response; and not, as Polanyi reminds us, through popular mass mobilization but through the mobilization *of the elites*.

The Meaning of Eyes Wide Shut
As Carl Schorske points out, Freud's texts were written in a context where the social elites felt threatened, and where the general culture was marked by disintegration and enforced morality.[25] Freud describes the censorship and the prohibitions that prevail wherever there is a conflict of interests, and how a typical reaction is to look away or shut our eyes to the dealings of power. Displacement and repression are ways of mastering conflicts. When modern forms of power express themselves through tacit warnings and prohibitions – signs like whispers, indicating what might make doors or windows of opportunity open or close – it usually leads to self-censorship. *Eyes Wide Shut* – the title of the film is contradictory, hinting at a state between wakefulness and sleep, between consciousness and dreaming, but also points to an *active*, voluntary state; one may *choose* to shut one's eyes to what is going on, one may choose not to take a stand, and look the other way. This is a common way of reacting to arbitrary power.

In his essay *Terror and Dream*, the German historian Reinhart Koselleck describes a series of authentic dreams from persons living under the Nazi

24. Karl Polanyi, *The Great Transformation: The Political Origins of Our Time*, Boston, Massachusetts, Beacon Press, [1944] 2001.
25. *Fin-de-siecle Vienna.*

regime.[26] A common recurrent theme in the dreams was a prevalent fear of *coming across as too conscious and alert*. Knowing too much, talking too much, or asking questions was dangerous. A significant feature of authoritarian situations is thus, according to Koselleck, *the necessity of being stupid*. Kubrick shows us a similar situation in the midst of an era of individualization. He warns against a social development where power is concentrated in the hands of a tiny elite, whereas impotence, resignation, and self-imposed ignorance characterize the broad general public. Both Schnitzler's story and Kubrick's film end in ambiguity. There is no apparent heroic resistance against the secret society of the power elite, in other words, no will to 'fight the power.' Neither is it obvious whether husband and wife have restored confidence and trust in their relationship. What we see is an acknowledgment of the futility of control: they can neither control superior powers nor each other; loyalty is never guaranteed; they must be thankful for the moments in which they are *awake*. Just as Freud states, we can never fully control the unconscious, but only hope to enlarge the rational agency of the 'I' as much as possible: *Wo Es war, soll Ich werden*. When Harford returns to his wife, he is the one who has to confess. From the rather hollow phrase "I would never lie to you" in the beginning of the film, one of his last sentences in the film is "I will tell you everything!" Openness is a precondition of restored trust.

In the film's final scene, an apparent mood of resignation is expressed by the married couple realizing that they cannot require, promise, or fulfil complete openness or transparency in their relationship. The trust between them has to be created and recreated in spite of this. Schnitzler's story and Kubrick's film were made respectively in the 1920s and 1990s, two periods marked by finance capitalism and a strong concentration of wealth among the economic elites, and the message of the two works seem similar: they seem to warn against the possible development of authoritarian political measures. When trust evaporates, the desire for power, authority, and *total control* surges forth. Both Schnitzler's story and

---

26. Reinhart Koselleck, *Futures Past. On the semantics of historical time*, MIT Press, London, 1985.

Kubrick's film are located in one of the areas Freud attempted to map: the uncertain, unruly, dark space between promise and desire, between the jealous lover and the beloved, between the dictator and his subjects – a space opening for jealousy or despotism, paranoia, or dictatorship.

About the Authors

Johann P. Arnason is Emeritus Professor of Sociology at La Trobe University, Melbourne, and visiting professor at the Faculty of Human Studies, Charles University, Prague. His main research interests are in social theory and historical sociology, with particular emphasis on the comparative analysis of civilizations. Publications include *Civilizations in Dispute: Historical Questions and Theoretical Traditions*, Leiden, 2003, and *Axial Civilizations and World History* (co-edited with S. N. Eisenstadt and Bjorn Wittrock), Leiden, 2004.

Kåre Blinkenberg has a degree in the history of ideas and social science from the University of Aarhus, Denmark. He has published translations of Alain Badiou (including *Abrégé de métapolitique*), J.-J. Rousseau (*Discours sur l'économie politique*), and various texts on postmodernity and political philosophy, including the work of Alain Badiou and Jacques Rancière.

D. T. Cochrane holds an MA in economics from the University of Ottawa. He has been involved in several social and economic justice organizations. His current research focuses on reconceptualizing the commodity as a conflicted site of both cultural-material creation and capital accumulation.

J. F. Humphrey holds a Ph.D. in philosophy from the Graduate Faculty of the New School for Social Research, New York, and is an Assistant Professor in the Department of Liberal Studies, North Carolina Agricultural and Technical State University. He has published translations (Joan Stambaugh's *Problem of Time in Nietzsche*) and articles on the history of philosophy, ancient philosophy, and the work of Cornelius Castoriadis.

Mogens Chrom Jacobsen holds a Ph.D. in philosophy from Copenhagen University. He has published texts on Jean Bodin, Immanuel Kant, John Rawls, utilitarianism, and human rights.

Anders Lundkvist is educated as a political scientist at Århus Universitet, Denmark. He has written on the political economy of Denmark, Europe, and the USA. His main theoretical work is on capitalism versus democracy: *Hoveder og Høveder. En demokratisk kritik af det private samfund* ('Votes and Money. A Democratic Critique of Private Society'), three volumes, 2004. His latest work is "Den danske kapitalisme og demokratiets forfald" ("Danish Capitalism and the Degradation of Democracy"), in *Dansk Nyliberalisme*, edited by Anders Lundkvist, 2009.

Håvard Friis Nilsen is a historian and social scientist educated at Universities of Strasbourg and Oslo. He was Research Fellow and University Lecturer at the Department of History, University of Oslo 1999–2005, and Visiting Scholar at Department of History and Philosophy of Science, University of Cambridge 2000–01. He is presently Director of the Norwegian think tank and publishing house Res Publica.

Ingerid S. Straume holds a Ph.D. in the philosophy of education from the University of Oslo. She has published texts on environmental politics, political thought, moral philosophy, political *Bildung*, and the work of Cornelius Castoriadis.